ECK ROBERTSON
AT THE CROSSROADS OF AMERICAN FIDDLING

American Made Music Series

ADVISORY BOARD

David Evans, General Editor
Barry Jean Ancelet
Edward A. Berlin
Joyce J. Bolden
Rob Bowman
Curtis Ellison
William Ferris
John Edward Hasse
Kip Lornell
Bill Malone
Eddie S. Meadows
Manuel H. Peña
Wayne D. Shirley
Robert Walser

ECK ROBERTSON AT THE CROSSROADS OF AMERICAN FIDDLING

CHRIS GOERTZEN

University Press of Mississippi / Jackson

The University Press of Mississippi is the scholarly publishing agency of the Mississippi Institutions of Higher Learning: Alcorn State University, Delta State University, Jackson State University, Mississippi State University, Mississippi University for Women, Mississippi Valley State University, University of Mississippi, and University of Southern Mississippi.

www.upress.state.ms.us

The University Press of Mississippi is a member of the Association of University Presses.

Copyright © 2025 by University Press of Mississippi
All rights reserved
Manufactured in the United States of America

∞

Publisher: University Press of Mississippi, Jackson, USA
Authorised GPSR Safety Representative: Easy Access System Europe - Mustamäe tee 50, 10621 Tallinn, Estonia, gpsr.requests@easproject.com

Library of Congress Cataloging-in-Publication Data

Names: Goertzen, Chris, author.
Title: Eck Robertson at the crossroads of American fiddling / Chris Goertzen.
Other titles: American made music series.
Description: Jackson : University Press of Mississippi, 2025. | Series: American made music series | Includes bibliographical references and index.
Identifiers: LCCN 2025003888 (print) | LCCN 2025003889 (ebook) | ISBN 9781496857132 (hardback) | ISBN 9781496857149 (trade paperback) | ISBN 9781496857156 (epub) | ISBN 9781496857163 (epub) | ISBN 9781496857170 (pdf) | ISBN 9781496857187 (pdf)
Subjects: LCSH: Robertson, Eck, 1887–1975. | Fiddlers—United States—Biography. | Fiddlers—Texas—Biography. | Fiddle tunes—United States—History and criticism. | Fiddle tunes—Texas—History and criticism. | Fiddling—Competitions—Texas—History—20th century.
Classification: LCC ML418.R634 G64 2025 (print) | LCC ML418.R634 (ebook) | DDC 787.2092 [B]—dc23/eng/20250214
LC record available at https://lccn.loc.gov/2025003888
LC ebook record available at https://lccn.loc.gov/2025003889

British Library Cataloging-in-Publication Data available

CONTENTS

ACKNOWLEDGMENTS VII

INTRODUCTION IX

CHAPTER 1. Young Alexander Campbell "Eck" Robertson. 3

CHAPTER 2. Eck Robertson, "World Champion Fiddler" 29

CHAPTER 3. The Robertson Family in Borger, then Eck in Amarillo . . 57

CHAPTER 4. "Arkansas Traveller":
    Eck's Musical Inheritances from Minstrelsy and from Fiddling
    Traditions of the Eastern and Southeastern United States 90

CHAPTER 5. "Sally Goodin" and the Texas Fiddle Revolution 118

CHAPTER 6. "Sally Johnson," "Done Gone," and the Consolidation
    of the Texas Fiddle Repertoire and Style 137

TUNE ANTHOLOGY 160

REFERENCES 243

INDEX 249

ACKNOWLEDGMENTS

This book draws on the previous published research of others more than has any of my earlier work; Eck's life and music are not new topics! And I received further generous amounts of help along the way. When I told indefatigable fiddle researcher Steve Green that I was writing a book about Eck, he turned over a stunning storehouse of newspaper articles and other materials about Eck and early Texas fiddling to me, shortening my efforts by at least a year. Rachel Morris, of the Center for Popular Music at Middle Tennessee State University, gathered up the Center's resources concerning Eck and particularly about the tune "Arkansas Traveller" with a level of efficiency and good cheer which, if broadly applied, could solve many of the world's problems. Paul Wells, founder of the Center, endured countless little requests once again. For other indispensable bits of help, I also thank Kathleen Campbell, librarian at the Country Music Hall of Fame, Preston Cary of the Wilbarger County Historical Museum, Warren Stricker at the Panhandle-Plains Historical Museum, Deborah Reece of the Hutchinson County Historical Museum, and Julie Parker of the Hopkins County Museum and Heritage Park. Special thanks to Harry Bolick for critical help diagnosing and repairing a major misunderstanding during the last stage of readying this book for publication.

My wife, Valerie Goertzen, travelled with me around the Panhandle during the summer of 2020, searching for bits of Eck's history. She also helped with many of the figures. How lucky I am.

INTRODUCTION

It's the fourth weekend in April, so Valerie and I are in Hallettsville, Texas, for the annual Texas State Championship Fiddlers Frolics. We arrive early both Saturday and Sunday, planting our folding chairs in the front row in order to sit with friends who, like us, are recording the event. 2023 sees perennial champion Wes Westmoreland III as co-emcee. The names of influential fiddlers of past generations pepper the stage banter, among them Major Franklin (1904–1981) and especially Benny Thomasson (1909–1984). Just one name from the generation before Thomasson and Franklin is heard, that of Alexander Campbell "Eck" Robertson (1887–1975).

The pivotal moment in Eck's story is familiar: On June 30 and July 1, 1922, he and Henry Gilliland (1845–1924) recorded a handful of fiddle tunes at the Victor Talking Machine Company in New York. The men had known one another for some years. They lived near one another, Robertson and his family in Vernon in the Texas Panhandle (about 175 miles ESE of Amarillo and 165 miles WNW of Fort Worth, on the well-traveled route now called US 287), and Gilliland about thirty-five miles due north of Vernon in Altus, Oklahoma. Gilliland was active gathering fiddlers into formal organizations and fostering fiddle contests, while Robertson would frequently win those events. He worked in the music business, tuning and repairing pianos in and around both Vernon and Altus, but yearned to earn his living fiddling.

Both Robertson and Gilliland were regularly hired to fiddle for dances at Confederate Reunions. In June 1922 both men were at a reunion held in Richmond, Virginia. We are not sure just how they conceived the idea of traveling from there directly to New York to try to record some tunes. Gilliland, a city clerk and justice of the peace in Altus, had mentored a local youngster there decades earlier, a boy who then ended up living in New York as a lawyer who numbered the Victor organization among his clients. I imagine that this connection came up in conversation between Gilliland and his ambitious younger friend Eck, who I expect argued for the trip north.

On June 30, Eck and Gilliland, dressed respectively in colorful cowboy garb and a Confederate uniform, played two tunes for the Victor executives, tunes both fiddlers knew and must have practiced together. The first was "Arkansas Traveller" (also frequently spelled "Arkansas Traveler"). They played some sections of the tune in unison and other parts with Eck at the upper octave, their fiddling tightly coordinated. The other melody was "Turkey in the Straw," arranged similarly but sounding less polished; the fiddlers' plans hadn't had long to coalesce. The RCA executives invited Eck to return the next morning, and he decided to balance those two veteran hit tunes with more modern offerings. "Sally Goodin" (spelled "Sallie Gooden" on this occasion), while old and well-established, was arranged in a revolutionary way, and "Ragtime Annie" was indeed a rag, a member of a young genre that had only recently made its way from pop music into use in oral tradition. Victor issued "Sally Goodin" and "Arkansas Traveller" on the first disc resulting from this pair of sessions, thus coupling one popular, nineteenth-century minstrelsy-flavored piece and one newly transformed one. The second record echoed that pattern, with "Turkey in the Straw" representing the minstrel world, joined with "Ragtime Annie," a young tune. The third record that came out of this session had two venerable pieces on a single side, "Sally Johnson" and "Billy in the Low Grounds," then a recently composed piece on the flip side, "Done Gone." Thus all three discs followed the same formula, an older selection complementing a young one (or young arrangement, in the case of "Sally Goodin").

Eck wasn't in the studio again until 1929. That year, he recorded "Run N----- Run" (issued as "Run Boy Run") and "Great Big Taters in Sandy Land" with older Baptist preacher (and prolix prohibitionist) Dr. J. B. Cranfill (the results sounding like the earlier duets with Gilliland). At about the same time, he also recorded a handful of tunes that Eck played with his family band, his wife Nettie on guitar, his young son Dueron strumming a tenor banjo, and his daughter Daphne on tenor guitar. These included "Texas Wagoner," "There's a Brown-Skin Girl Down the Road," "Brilliancy Medley," his own composition "Amarillo Waltz," "Brown Kelly Waltz" (two sides), and the song "The Island Unknown" (also two sides). This mix of ages and of genres of fiddle tunes fits well with that of the 1922 recordings, though taking advantage of the abilities of the family ensemble to include an unusual ballad. An additional few tunes were played in the studio but not released, including one intriguing number, "My Experience on the Ranch," likely a comic monologue or skit. This selection revisited the cowboy theme introduced by Eck's cowboy outfit in the 1922 sessions. All in all, Eck's small commercially recorded repertoire offers a remarkable variety of sources and of total impressions, reaching beyond the fiddle world's typical meshing of affable, danceable, and nostalgic—Eck also deployed an arsenal of ambitious virtuosity. These recordings don't fill many minutes; they constitute the tip of an imposing iceberg of a personal fiddle repertoire, one inviting exploration.

INTRODUCTION

Today's Texas fiddlers respect Eck's versions of today's Texas fiddle standards, the versions of those tunes that Eck played in those early commercial recording sessions—especially "Sally Goodin"—and they perform stylistically updated versions of those tunes. Many of these modern fiddlers also know that Eck drew on a generous swath of fiddle tunes outside of what would become the Texas standards. This opens a conversation that points in two directions. Concerning that broader repertoire: what were Eck's "non-Texas" tunes and the styles they represent like? Did those melodies and styles have a part in shaping Eck's revolutionary "Sally Goodin"? Thinking in the other direction: What features of Eck's "Sally Goodin" influenced today's Texas standards not just through sheer amount of laudable virtuosity and of delicious elaboration, but in specific techniques of variation?

Fiddle tunes are an old musical galaxy, but still full of surprises and questions. The most basic puzzle is why these short tunes have such enduring appeal. Through most of the eras of fiddle history that are well enough documented to think about in detail—starting in the late eighteenth century—most fiddle tunes are even more compact than they initially seem. Typically, two swiftly passing eight-measure strains contain quite a bit of repetition within those already brief sections. Each tune has binary elements on two levels, an alternation of effect between the two strains, and in performance, a sense of alternating stripes: the first strain twice (one color of stripe), the other twice (the other color stripe), then the first stripe recurring, then the other. This doesn't add up to much musical material!

Why do so many of us still love these absurdly brief bits of melody? How has their typical presentation in performance been modified over time to nourish our affection? This book concerns a crucial time and place of such adjustments, focusing on Eck Robertson and the tunes he played during his youth and early maturity, especially his favorite tune and most enduring hit, "Sally Goodin." Eck was a leader in the filtering and transforming of fiddling in Texas, in the earliest steps in the creation of contemporary contest fiddling. The first three chapters are biographical, about Eck and the personal and cultural factors that led him to identify himself as "Famous Cowboy Fiddler" and "The World's Champion Fiddler." I add considerable detail to previously published sketches of Eck's life, repair some oft-repeated misconceptions about his childhood years, and try to put his activities in historical context. The other three chapters are about his music—his surviving recorded repertoire—tracing how parts of his repertoire were filtered and developed in the direction of contest fiddling, while other parts were not.

The last third of the book is a tune anthology, transcriptions of Eck's commercial recordings from the 1920s and other recordings done during interviews in the 1960s. For some of these pieces, I add earlier versions of the tunes, that is, versions published in nineteenth-century music books or written out in personal tune collections. For a handful of Eck's pieces, I add

INTRODUCTION

transcriptions of contemporary performances. Of course, transcriptions are no substitute for sound recordings. But the recordings are nearly all available on YouTube and, in a majority of cases, also as purchasable artifacts in various formats. Transcriptions of Eck's performances are relatively reliable, since he was a careful arranger and, on occasion, a composer—not an improviser. He was more interested in "getting it right" than in toying with a tune's identity during a performance.

ECK ROBERTSON
AT THE CROSSROADS OF AMERICAN FIDDLING

Figure 1. A versatile dog-trot building illustrating materials and construction techniques likely matching those employed in building the cabins in which Eck Robertson lived as a boy in Hunt County, Texas. This building, now located in the remarkable Hopkins County Museum and Heritage Park, "was built on the Lucille McKay farm at Reilly Springs in 1910" (information offered on the placard in front of the building). The village of Reilly Springs is about thirty-five miles from each of two locations in neighboring Hunt County where I believe the Robertsons lived. Photograph Valerie Goertzen. My thanks to eminent architecture historian (and fine fiddler!) Howard Marshall for helping me better understand the structures pictured in this photograph and in those shown in Figure 5.

— Chapter 1 —

YOUNG ALEXANDER CAMPBELL "ECK" ROBERTSON

Eck Robertson grew up in a family of tenant-level farmers that included many fiddlers. He pushed hard against the difficulties characteristic of his time and place and became an ambitious, skilled, and influential musician who dreamed of stardom and prosperity. He moved through his long life with great energy, intermittent drama, and sparks of fame. He raised himself from his dirt-poor background to a blue-collar job in the music business, to steady work punctuated with weekends traveling to fiddle, often in public view. His fiddling brought him considerable joy and many friends. Although he did not experience nearly as much fame and financial success as he felt he deserved, he achieved a distinguished place in the history of American vernacular music.

The details of Eck Robertson's life come to us from three kinds of sources: surviving public information found in censuses and in newspaper articles, testimony both from Eck (from interviews conducted in the 1960s) and from his relatives; from memorial prose; and, last, from items that he assembled and saved himself, such as advertisements and handwritten repertoire lists. Unkind and arbitrary historical circumstance has unsystematically but energetically edited this complicated ocean of information—a census burned, newspaper issues survive unevenly, and so on. As a biographer working soon after 2020, I have the disadvantage of not being able to talk to Eck or his contemporaries or his children, but the complementary advantage of being able to quote previous published research about Eck, some of which was based on evidence that is no longer available. Also, data searching has gotten easier due to steady advances in the digital indexing of censuses, newspapers, and graveyard records.

The earliest citation of the name Alexander Campbell Robertson that I have seen is in the census of 1900. Earlier writing on Eck (for instance, Wolfe 1997, 15) has his family moving from his birthplace in Arkansas directly to the Texas Panhandle, and remaining there. But more information is available now, and the narrative has become much more detailed.

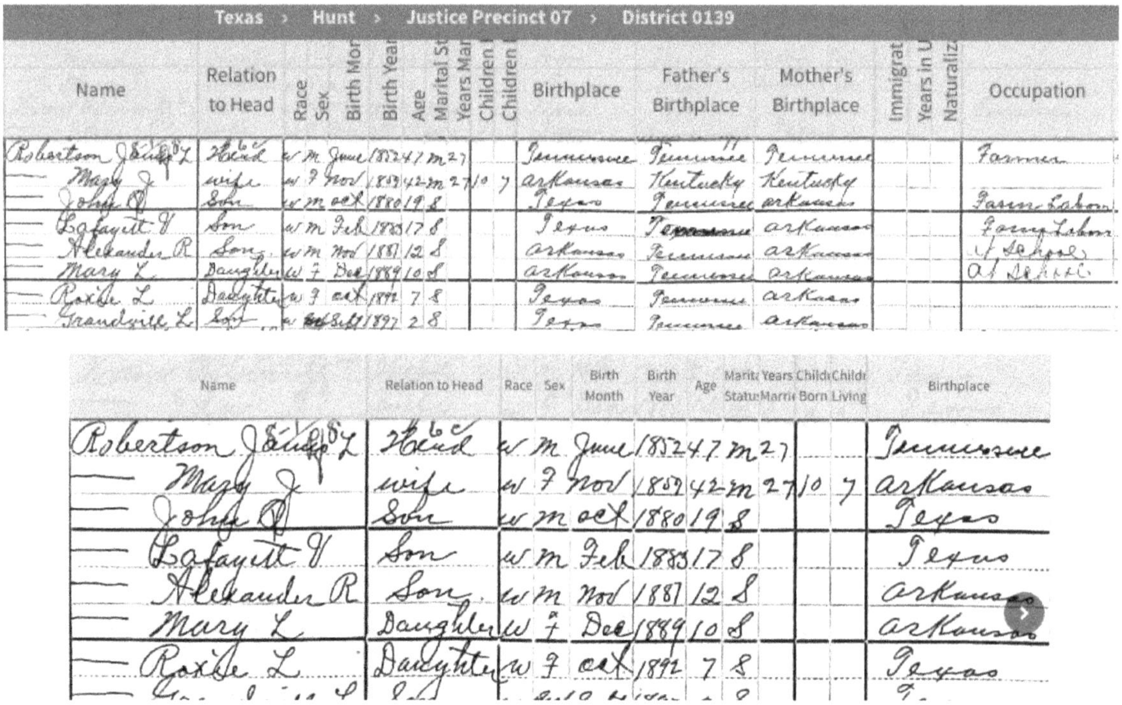

Figure 2. 1900 census entry for James L. Robertson family in Hunt County, Texas, widescreen above closeup.

A slice of the census page listing the James Leander ("J. L.") Robertson family is pictured in figure 2, along with an enlargement of the left-hand side of this family's entry.

This entry contains quite a bit of information, despite the constraints of the census process (and a small mistake: Eck is mistakenly called "Alexander R." in this census). Eck's parents, James Leander Robertson (1852–1935) and Mary Jane Reed Robertson (1857–1939), were renting farmland in rural Hunt County, Texas. Their farm was in a part of that county located some forty-five miles east and about ten miles north of the center of today's Dallas, distant from the Texas Panhandle. County census records show that this area of the state was substantially further along in terms of economic and cultural development than any part of the Panhandle.

We can narrow down where in Hunt County the family lived in 1900. The top of the census page reads: "Texas Hunt Justice Precinct 07 District 0139" (a census enumeration area in the southeast part of the county). Of the four borders of this enumeration area, only one is complicated: The western boundary of the district was an uneven line described in the census records as follows: "Including Quinlan Village, all territory [in Hunt County] east of the following line: beginning at the bridge on Caddo Creek, on the Greenville and Terrell Road, thence south with said road to the Sabine River, thence down said river to the Texas Heartland RR, thence south with said railway to the Precinct line." Thus, the description starts from a point that is still easy to locate, a bridge over Caddo Creek on what is now Highway 34, about three miles north of the small settlement of Quinlan. From that point, the western border of the district meanders south to the county line. To find the northern edge of the "justice district" we start again at that bridge over Caddo Creek; that northern border was a latitude line extending due east from that point. The eastern and southern edges of the census district were the county lines. Some of the geography itself has changed, notably that the headwaters of the Sabine River have been partially diverted, covered in 1960 by a large reservoir built to serve the Dallas area, Lake Tawakoni. Indeed, it is possible that the land that the Robertsons farmed in southeastern Hunt County is now under water.

I will briefly postpone looking more closely at the Robertson residence of 1900, because that year's census shows that that particular farm wasn't the family's first stop in Texas. There was at least one but probably two earlier occasions this family resided in the state. The 1900 census notes that the first two children listed in the Robertson family entry had been born in Texas, then the next two children—including Eck—were born in Arkansas, then the last two in Texas. Where were the family's first Texas homes? We don't know. The 1890 censuses may have contained useful information, but most of those records were consumed in a 1921 fire in the Commerce Building in Washington, DC, including nearly all of the Texas censuses.

In one common pattern of moving west, some families shifted to their new bases gradually. They tried out a new area for a few years, returned to their previous homes, thought things over for a year or two, then committed to the new location (my wife's father's parents did this). Might Eck's family have followed this pattern? I discovered some evidence supporting that speculation. We don't know the location of their very first stay in Texas; Blanton Owen wrote that the family moved from Arkansas to Hamlin (1991, 2), a tiny town about 130 miles ESE of Lubbock, an area more like the Panhandle than like East Texas in geography, vegetation, and stage of development. I don't know the source of Owen's information (actually, Eck would end up in Hamlin briefly as a young adult). However, a map of land ownership in Hunt County that was drawn in June 1894 suggests where the Robertson's second Texas residence may have been. The map includes a section marked "Mary Robertson" (see figure 3). Could that have been James Leander Robertson's wife Mary? I found no evidence either supporting or undermining this possibility. Two other women named Mary Robertson appeared in the census of Hunt County in 1900, but various factors show that neither could have been James's wife. But if the "Mary Robertson" property belonged to our Robertson family, why was her name associated with the land rather than his? Should we be surprised that this farm was located well north of what would become the family's home by 1900?

Let's backtrack a bit and fill in some blanks. Mary Robertson grew up near Delaney, Arkansas. James and Mary married there in 1873, and their

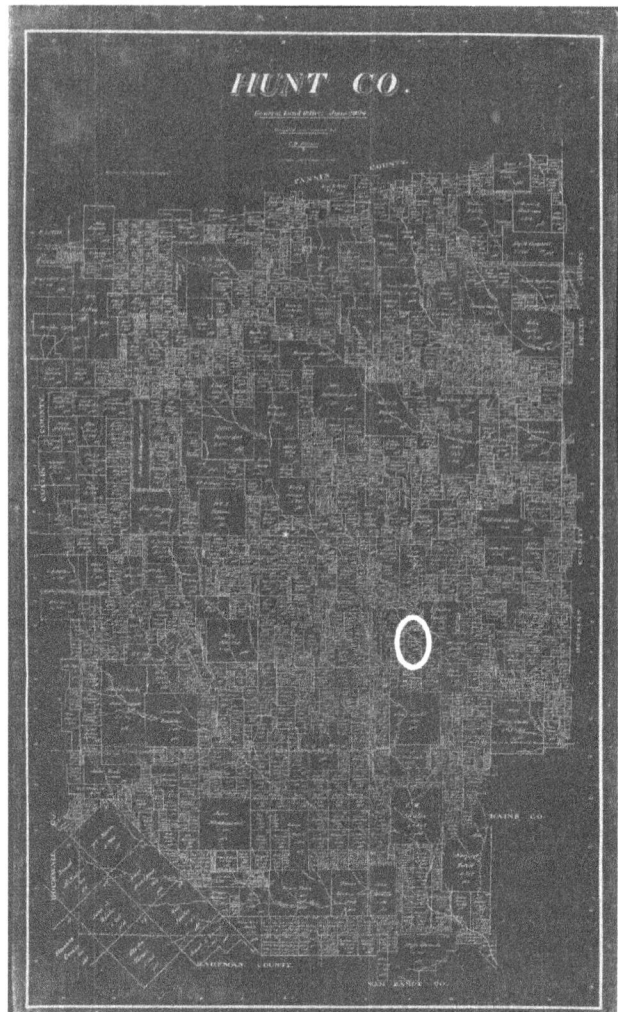

Figure 3. Ownership map of Hunt County, Texas, 1894, with plot labelled "Mary Robertson" circled, countywide and close views (from Pressler [1914]).

first child was born in Delaney in 1875. (That was Joseph Larrimore Robertson [1875–1960]; by 1900 he had married and moved out of his parents' home, and so wasn't listed as part of their household in that year's census.) The Robertsons settled somewhere in Texas. Perhaps that was Hamlin, as Owen specified. The next two children were born in Texas, the census notes (these were the first two children listed in the Robertson household entry in the 1900 census). Perhaps the Robertsons' first attempts to farm in Texas were unsuccessful. Perhaps Mary Robertson just wanted to be near her mother for Eck's birth. The last three sentences all feature the word "perhaps"; I am well out on a limb here. In any case, the family returned to Arkansas, where Eck and his sister Mary L. Robertson were born. In one possible scenario, the elder Mary's parents then paid for the plot of land in Hunt County labeled "Mary Robertson" that is circled in figure

2.3. This map labels plots of land by owner as of 1894. It is a surprise to see a woman's name on such a map; that didn't fit conventions of the day. But Mary's parents may have been a bit wary of James Robertson. He had almost no formal schooling, his first bride had died within a year of their marriage, and he was seized by religious passion the year before he and Mary married (Nichols 1935, 8). He followed the teachings of Alexander Campbell, a Scotch-Irish immigrant to the United States who advocated independent-minded, nondenominational, quite aggressive Protestantism; Campbellite preachers in Hunt County would earn a reputation as "rough, uneducated men . . . intensely dogmatical, egotistical, and intolerant" (Harrison 1976, 185). Might Mary's parents have perceived James as being emotionally volatile or otherwise flawed, a person that trouble followed? Whether or not that was true, Mary's parents might have first owned the property, then given it to her—specifically her—for absolutely any reason.

The county land ownership map was drawn in June 1894. The Robertsons had returned to Texas around 1890 (Eck stated that he was three when they moved to Texas; Seeger interview 1963). They would have their last two children there; these two could have been born on the Mary Robertson land. But this was not where the family was living by 1900. By that time, they were renting land somewhere in one of the rectangles marked at the bottom of figure 7—the evidence for that will be given below—and by 1910 they moved elsewhere, far away. In fact, they relocated many times. This history of frequent upheaval for James Leander Robertson's family, common in this time and place, would be the pattern that Eck's own nuclear family would also follow through the early 1940s.

While we can't locate the Robertsons' 1900 residence very precisely, the earlier homestead can be found, because the land labeled "Mary Robertson" on the 1894 map had streams marked on it. It lay between the current path of US 69 and Caney Creek, in a neighborhood one can now reach from US 69 by driving down Mallard Drive, up Canvasback Drive, then east on a mile-long driveway onto what is now a truly beautiful ranch (definitely not the same homesite where the Robertsons lived in 1900, instead being situated about seven miles north of the census enumeration district in which they would later farm). Valerie (my wife) and I drove to the Mary Robertson plot in the summer of 2021. We stood near a luxurious home at the center of the property, and took pictures in several directions (figure 4). I asked the current owners (who don't wish to be named) if they had noticed any ruins of nineteenth- or early twentieth-century structures on their property; they had not. As we stood in front of their large home, we were just twenty yards from the tallest tree in the area, one likely planted long, long ago, shading a beautifully configured area. It is a perfect home site. The logical place on this property for the Robertson's cabin would have been in precisely the same idyllic spot; several generations of house must have been built there, each erasing visible traces of its predecessor.

Figure 4. Two contemporary views of the land that was labelled "Mary Robertson" in the Hunt County map drawn in 1894. Photographs taken in 2021 by Valerie Goertzen.

Hunt County has plenty of two kinds of soil, sandy and loamy, which specialists divide up into numerous subcategories (see a general map of the county's soil types at https://texashistory.unt.edu/ark:/67531/metapth130296/m1/1/; and see Harrison 1976, 14). Deep loamy soils dominate the southern part of the county, in some locations very gently sloped and in others moderately sloped; the central part of the county including the Mary Robertson plot fits this profile, too. It's good dark soil, holding nutrients well and accepting water well, though prone to erosion and to consequent depletion of nutrients (from both erosion and from intense use).

The Mary Robertson land may have looked much like these contemporary photographs during the 1860s–70s, that is, before a surge in immigration filled much of East Texas with what was essentially sharecropping. The farm some eight miles south, where the Robertsons lived by 1900, probably also resembled these pictures. Before the Civil War, this had been stock-raising country. Railroads arrived in the 1870s, and speculators bought up much of the land. Masses of immigrants from the South arrived—in this part of Hunt County, many from Tennessee and Arkansas. Arrivals like the Robertsons aimed to be at least partly subsistence farmers, but were quickly pushed into a sharecropper status by merciless rental rates. Most of these immigrants raised some corn and vegetables, and kept a few pigs and perhaps cows, but had to devote progressively more of their modest acreages to cotton to keep pace with their rent. Eck's family owned about two dozen pigs, we learn from an anecdote repeated in several interviews—the Robertsons were doing well by local standards, working very hard and managing to scrape by.

ECK LEARNS TO FIDDLE

In an extended interview conducted in 1962 at Eck's home in Amarillo by Szabo Nagy and Pat Riggs (then anthropology students of Roger Abrahams at the University of Texas), Eck talked about learning to fiddle during the years the family lived in their home in south Hunt County. Perhaps the word "interview" doesn't describe the conversation adequately. Eck acted as if he was thoroughly accustomed to talking about his life and beliefs. Many questions addressed to him did not elicit direct replies, but rather stimulated him to tell chunks of his story in the order he chose, to string practiced anecdotes together. Forms of the quotes given below have been printed before, but are worth repeating at length. These paragraphs are from my own transcription of that lengthy 1962 interview. Eck described his first experiences fiddling like this:

> I was already a fiddler before I ever seen a fiddle. . . . I made my first fiddle out of a long-neck gourd, and killed the family tom cat, and tanned his hide myself [somewhat uneasy laughter] in the ash bank, and put it on my gourd fiddle for a top. And I learned to play a few tunes on that gourd fiddle and got to be pretty good playing it. And then my brothers, two or three of them, made them a gourd fiddle, and I can remember before we ever got a [real] fiddle, was sitting in the corner of a residence and playing for a square dance and waltz and so on; we was kids on them gourd fiddles; didn't even have a fiddle. And we . . . played long enough and good enough to play for dances before we ever seen a fiddle. . . .

Getting an actual violin was the next step, one taken surreptitiously by Eck's older brother:

> My brother [John Q., "Quince"] got to where he'd set up late at night, and wouldn't work very much in the field, you know, on the farm. Father called him up to the pigpen one day. He had twenty-two head of hogs, of pigs, shoats, in a pen, and he was feeding his pigs. And that boy was helping carry the feed out there or something, and he told him, he said, "Son," he said, "I don't want to be hard with you, or nothing [of] the kind" he said, "you're gonna have to quit setting up late at night and playing that gourd fiddle," and said, "We've got to have more work done, and you've got to do more work on the farm, and do better work, and so and so." He said "take more interest in the stock, and feeding the hogs and horses, and cattle and so on." He had several head. He said "You're wasting your time, and so on and so on. Why don't you take more interest. I'll tell you what I'll do," he says, "I'll give you the best pig is in that pen if you promise me you'll do that, and take more interest in your work. I'll let you pick the pig out of there, the best one in there if you want it. Take more interest in the stock, feeding the pigs and the stock."

But after a few weeks of ebbing participation in this plan, Quince quietly traded the pig for a violin, "about a three dollar and twenty-five cent Sears, Roebuck fiddle probably." When their father figured this out, he bawled out the boy, but also picked up the fiddle and surprised the boys. This preacher was a fine fiddler.

That Eck had first learned to fiddle on a homemade gourd instrument should not surprise us. Rural citizens in places like Hunt County had negligible disposable income; they had difficulty taking advantage of the blossoming availability of consumer goods through Sears & Roebuck and other mail order companies. Sears' price for a mid-range basic violin outfit (instrument, bow, case, box, and so on) was indeed $3.25 in 1897 (Sears Roebuck & Co. 1897, 498); Eck did not specify that price at random! It's difficult to calculate the evolution of the buying power of the dollar, but a difference by a multiple of twenty to thirty is probably not too far out of line, yielding an adjusted price of such a 1897 Sears fiddle at from $65 to $97.50. That may still sound cheap, but we must keep in mind that a large percentage of the value of a violin was created through patient, meticulous hand work, which was poorly paid by modern standards. Even when materials cost plenty, hourly remuneration for such skilled labor remained modest.

The second most expensive model Sears sold through that catalog was advertised as replicating the work of Austrian luthier Jacob Stainer; Eck would own and treasure one of these violins beginning in the 1920s (cost in 1897: $8.65; Sears Roebuck & Co. 1897, 499). The nature of his first, handmade functional substitute for a violin—the one he described as consisting of animal hide topping a gourd body—takes the violin back to the basics of how stringed instruments are constructed: strings stretched over any flexible top vibrating over any resonating chamber. The resulting sound must have been heavy on rhythmic definition and light on sensuous beauty, a workable sound for accompanying dancing, which was the instrument's primary purpose. House-raisings in frontier areas, certainly including Hunt County, were capped with dances accompanied by fiddlers (Harrison 1976, 256).

That anecdote highlights that fiddling was a favorite activity for many of the Robertsons. His father and at least one of Eck's uncles played—we don't know his name—and he was a major influence on Eck. And several of Eck's brothers fiddled; Eck would praise his older brother Quince especially highly.

> I'd played a few parties and what we called "play parties" . . . near home . . . even for several miles away, and my brother older than me and him and another fellow had played dances right smart. . . . At that time, when I was on the farm there, and a little kid, I played a five-string banjo more than I did the fiddle. . . . [I] got to playing the banjo with the boys older than me. . . . The oldest one of the boys that played the fiddle, he got to playing dances, and him and another feller that was . . . always hung out with us a lot—but he was a fine fiddler. And they'd ride off on their horses to go play for a dance and they'd slip back after I'd [pre]tend to go to bed, you know, and my father and mother sleeping in the north room, and [there was a] hall between it and the other room, and I was sleeping in the south room; they was sleeping in one county, and me in the other, just a hall between us. And they'd [the errant boys] slip back to the back window, and slip me out at the back window, and take me to the dance on the horse behind them, to play the banjo with them, see. Now that's kind of a scheme we had to get away from our parents to play dances. They didn't know anything about me being out. They thought I was asleep in the back room. And they'd [the older boys] bring me back, you know, about, anywhere from midnight to two o'clock in the morning, and they'd be sometimes even three or four o'clock before the family got up, you know . . . slip me in the back window, and I'd go to bed!

This excerpt impinges on several topics. First, we learn much about the Robertson family's cabin. Rural families like theirs built their homes out of lumber from trees they felled themselves. They made single-room log cabins, then later might expand these into dogtrot homes—two rooms separated by a breezeway, with the entire construction under a single roof. Such homes were then the customary solution to the need for shelter in this warm climate (Fehrenbach 2000, 297). Plenty of pictures of dogtrot homes can be found through an internet image search, but those photographs portray beautiful, painstakingly restored examples of the genre. Extra trouble was taken in the construction of these high-end examples.

Figure 5. One multipurpose single-structure building and one dogtrot building—in terms used by specialists in vernacular American log buildings, a "single-crib barn" and a "double-crib barn"—moved from their original locations within Hopkins County, Texas (immediately east of Hunt County). These buildings are now located in the Hopkins County Museum and Heritage Park. The dogtrot building is the same one pictured in Figure 1, but now shown from the front. Photographs Valerie Goertzen.

The lumber was squared off, with each round log shaved so that the new cross section became a rectangle—more refined than in the majority of dogtrot cabins. The photographs in figure 5 are of one single-room cabin and one elementary dogtrot construction. Both buildings were moved from their original locations in Hopkins County (which borders on Hunt County) to the Hopkins County Museum and Heritage Park in the county seat, Sulphur Springs. Both buildings were built from the types of lumber that would have been available to the Robertsons, and built within thirty miles of both the "Mary Robertson" plot of land and the Robertsons' home in 1900. In both cases, the logs were left minimally trimmed, not squared off—the budget option. Neither of the two structures pictured is a perfect dogtrot cabin, but considered together, they can yield a good visual approximation of the house in which Eck was a boy and teenager.

Most families built their own homes. When they arrived on the land, they lived first in a dugout, or simply camped out while constructing a single cabin like the one pictured in figure 5. (Roofs would have been made of slabs of lumber, rather than the sheet metal often doing the job on the preserved structures.) Another single cabin also located in the Hopkins County Museum and Heritage Park grounds that is about the same size as this one was said to have housed a family of eleven. In time, families who could do so would build another room near the first one, and extend a roof across the pair and over the space between them, the "dogtrot." The building pictured in this figure that is in a dogtrot configuration actually functioned as a "corn crib," a building for drying ears of corn (this is the same structure shown from the back in figure 1, at the beginning of this chapter). To transform the appearance of this corncrib in imagination into a closer semblance of the Robertson cabin, revise this dogtrot construction as follows: make it a foot or two taller, chink the gaps between logs with mud and grass, and shrink the windows somewhat, so that a small teenaged boy and his banjo could slip through a window, but not his adult-sized older brother. And pretend there is a door on the center-facing side of each cabin, the side accessed from the "dogtrot" rectangle. This photograph shows some miscellaneous modern equipment stored in the dogtrot, out of the rain; that was one traditional use of the space. Eck described the Robertson home simply, as a "square room box house [with a] hall between the two rooms" (Seeger interview, 1963).

We learn from the Riggs/Nagy interview excerpted above that J. L. and Mary Robertson slept in one room, and the kids in the other (at least the boys), and that the door to the boys' room was locked at night. But they managed to get out to play at local house dances anyway. Eck named one room the north one and the other the south one, and claimed that the rooms were in different counties, suggesting that the Robertson land was near or even right on the southern border of Hunt County, that is, the border with either Kaufman County or with Van Zandt County (which stretches to the southeast). Thus, the J. L. Robertson family lived within one or the other of the rectangles drawn on the map in figure 7. A last hint at the location of their home in 1900 results from J. L. Robertson's ardent avocation. He already operated as a part-time minister in addition to working on the farm during the family's years in Hunt County. A newspaper article from 1897 describes a stunt-infused triple wedding at which he officiated. I reproduce that article in figure 6. Please note that this wedding

> **VERY MUCH MARRIED.**
>
> **Took Three Counties to Hold the Couples and Their Friends.**
>
> Kaufman, Tex., Sept. 8.—(Special.)—A triple alliance was entered into last Sunday afternoon in the extreme northeast part of Kauffman county by six young people that attracted much attention. Rev. J. L. Robertson married with one ceremony Wm. Taylor and Sylvania Moody, R. K. Sells and Rose Pierce and Tom Stone and Pet Parker. The three young men lived in Hunt county and the young women in Kauffman county. The minister who performed the ceremony stood in Hunt county, the young folks were standing in Van Zandt county, and the audience, which consisted of many people, stood in Kauffman county while the nuptial ceremonies were going on.

Figure 6. Article from the September 16, 1897, *Austin Texas Weekly* about a triple wedding conducted by Eck Robertson's father, James Leander Robertson, on September 8.

was staged at the intersection of Hunt, Kaufman, and Van Zandt Counties, with the three couples standing in one county, the minister in another, and all other attendees in the third. I marked that location with a star in figure 7. If in 1897 the Robertson family already lived on what would still be their farm in 1900, that home was located within one of the rectangles in the figure, and not too far from the star. Eck specified that their first farm was about 160 acres in size, and the second, some eight miles south, was larger, 200 acres (Seeger interview, 1963); that second one must have been the one at the county border, near the star on this map.

What did the boys' ensemble sound like? Since young Eck initially played some kind of banjo in what was apparently a string trio, perhaps the kids played in old-time style, in which a five-string banjoist plucks single notes matching much of the fiddle's melody, but devotes every other offbeat to the drone played on the fifth (shorter) string. But maybe he instead strummed either a five-string banjo or a tenor banjo (like the one his son Dueron would play a generation later). In any case, Eck would have heard plenty of fiddling when he was a young boy at the sorts of parties at which he would accompany dancing later. And Robertson family gatherings must have included plenty of fiddlers, since Eck spoke of uncles who played. His father, who wanted to earn his living preaching rather than farming, had also fiddled as a young man, but seems to have temporarily given it up when religion overtook him in his early twenties.

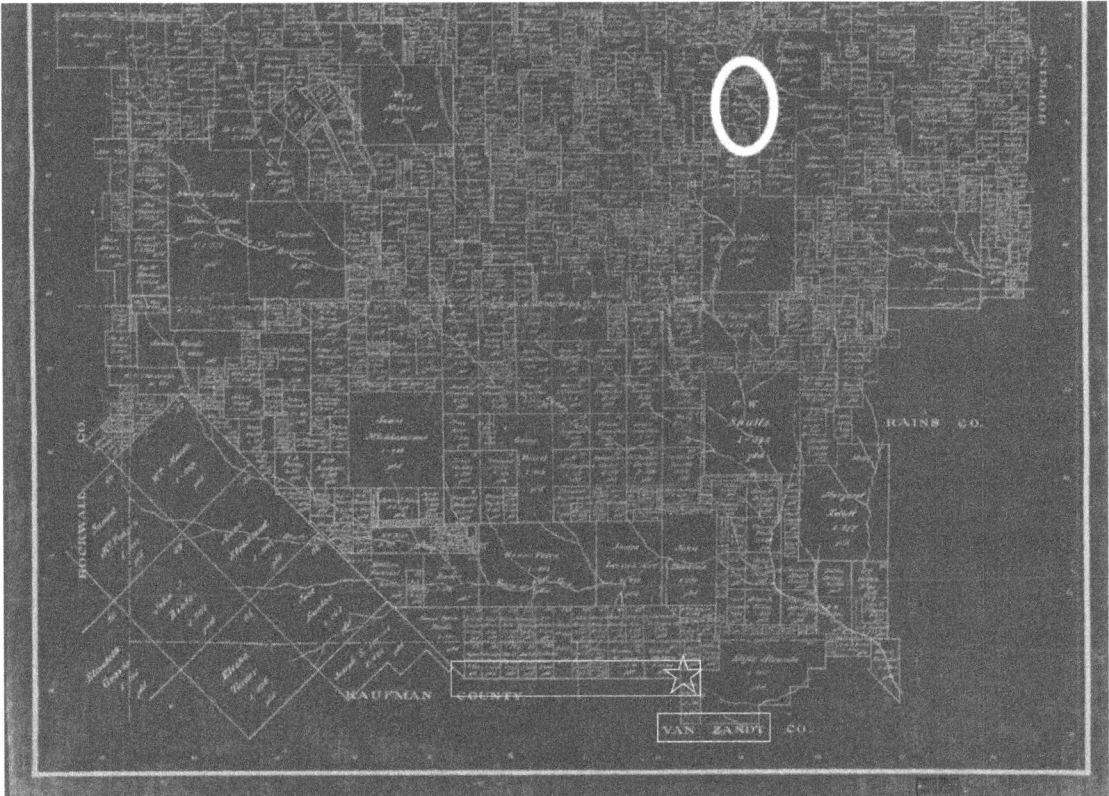

Figure 7. The locations in the southern part of Hunt County, Texas where the Robertson family may have lived in 1894 (within the drawn oval) and more certainly did live in 1900 (within one of the rectangles, likely near the star).

Regardless of how convincing the reader finds my reconstruction of where in Hunt County the Robertsons lived during their early years in Texas, we are sure that the family moved away from this part of east Texas before the 1910 census. The basic predicament for many families in Hunt County was this: the originally good soil capable of producing generous crops had lost its luster, its nutrients swiftly depleted and crop yields halved (Ross 1937, 8–9). And absentee landlords pushed tenants so hard that thousands of the restless and ambitious souls who had brought high hopes to Hunt County in the 1870s–80s moved on. Historian Kyle G. Wilkison discussed this factor in his *Yeomen, Sharecroppers, and Socialists: Plain Folk Protest in Texas, 1870–1914* (2008). Wilkison did much of his work in the archives of Gee Library of Texas A&M University–Commerce; it is a stroke of luck for those of us who are interested in Eck Robertson's life that it was Hunt County that became the epicenter of Wilkison's research. "Between 1870 and 1910 a population explosion and the arrival of the national market via new railroads drove land prices beyond the reach of self-sufficient but land-poor Texas yeomen. Increasingly concentrated land ownership and the rise of the absentee landlord forced the abandonment of diversified production [allowing] self-sufficiency in favor of cotton" (2008, 2). This was neither surprising nor entirely unwelcome, since so many residents came from the Deep South, and were accustomed to cultivating this crop (Ross, 1937, 3). Wilkison further noted that in the early 1900s, most residents of the heavily populated counties of the eastern third of the state—and Hunt County was among the most rapidly growing counties, prime "blackland" for cotton production—were "culturally southern" (2008, 5). I would add that the affluence of the large landowners who exploited legions of impoverished farmers like the Robertsons dated from before the Civil War. An essential ingredient of the landowners' wealthy status was economic behavior predicated on growing cotton, and certainly based on having owned slaves. However, their tenants in Texas, a majority of whom living near the Robertson home in 1900 were whites from Tennessee or Arkansas, were not amenable to being treated like enslaved people had been. They were hard workers trying to better themselves; their adventurous spirits and hopes for upward mobility were demonstrated not just by their moving to a newly developing part of the country, but by how well they supported education. In the column of the 1900 census specifying occupation, "farmer" was in first place, of course, with "teacher" in second position in Hunt County (Harrison 1976, 64), and with "physician" in third position. That Eck and his younger siblings were listed on the 1900 census as being "in school" was just as routine as the fact that his older brothers had transitioned to being "farm laborers."

Reading through the Hunt County census records from 1900 provides a broad context for Eck's childhood in terms of demographics, timing of settlements, and educational ambition. In District 0139, where the Robertsons then lived, there were 1700 residents counted. (Note that this district included a prison. About fifty individuals listed in this census were either prisoners working for the railroad or these convicts' guards; I didn't include this self-contained population in formulating the following generalizations.) The vast majority of heads of household in Hunt County, Hopkins County, and nearby areas were farmers; two physicians and two teachers were listed in the enumeration district in which the Robertsons lived, along with three "woodchoppers" living near the lone saw mill operator in the district. The hamlet of Quinlan was home to a real estate agent, a notary, a blacksmith, and a sewing machine salesman. A majority of the heads of household were born outside of Texas, many coming from the Mid-South—Tennessee, Arkansas, Missouri, and Illinois (probably from the southern part of that state)—with smaller numbers from the Deep South, from Alabama, Mississippi, Georgia, Virginia, and North Carolina. But nearly every child was listed as having been born in Texas. The ages of these children demonstrate that the flood of immigration to East Texas was in the late 1870s through the 1880s, when the arrival of railroads opened up "vast markets for a black land cotton production" (Harrison 1976, 133). We see crowds of immigrants arriving, not knowing that they would encounter rapidly deteriorating soil. These hard-working poor people were ambitious in terms of both education and financial rewards. It's no surprise that so many would move on so quickly, among them the Robertsons.

The Robertson farms in Hunt County doubtless included some land devoted to corn and a variety of vegetables for their own consumption, and hog pens—remember, the pig that Eck's brother Quince traded for a violin was one of nearly two dozen hogs that the Robertsons owned. The family could not have avoided devoting a sizeable portion of the land to growing cotton—rent had to be paid. Indeed, the increasing percentage of land that had to be worked for that specific reason pushed tenants like them toward "slippage to permanent half-cropper status" (Wilkison 2008, 44). Evidence of this grew steadily—for instance, county hog production was gradually cut in half (Wilkison 2008, 17). Overproduction of cotton led to dipping crop prices, and high interest rates and high transportation costs added to growing debt. Land ownership in Hunt County became an increasingly less worthy goal or likely prospect. Wilkison reproduced telling statistics: In 1910, "88% of all 'share tenants' had resided on the present farm for four years or less.... Further, 45% had lived on their present farm one year or less, while only 4% had resided on their present farm for 10 years or more" (2008, 103). The Robertsons did not belong to that stubborn tiny minority. They had moved on.

But have I counted all the places Eck lived before the 1910 census? Maybe not. Guitarist John Fahey enjoyed several extended conversations with Eck. Fahey's favorite anecdote among those that Eck related to him concerned Eck's courtship of Nettie "in the Ozark Mountains" (1995, 33). He added that "After they got married, they decided to move west to West Texas" (1995, 35). Does the phrase "in the Ozark Mountains" place Nettie in Arkansas soon after 1900, with the Robertsons residing there a third time? Yet another possible stop is suggested by Eck's having recorded a tune—one that he likely wrote—entitled "Stumptown Stomp." Where did that title come from? Later in life, he would write an "Amarillo Waltz" reflecting years of residing in Amarillo, and a "Borger Bounce" (or "Borger Wiggle") referring to living years in rough-hewn oil town Borger. Did the James L. Robertsons live for a time in or near a "Stumptown"? The town of Grand Saline is located some twenty-five to thirty miles southeast of where the Robertsons resided in 1900 (assuming that one could then travel easily through the land now submerged in Lake Tawakoni). Grand Saline then included a neighborhood called Stumptown, a nickname referring to an early stage in many a settlement's growth, a time when entrepreneurs in a hurry cut down trees in an area where houses are planned, but do not take the time to uproot and clear the stumps. Elvis Allen, Chairman of the Historical Commission of Van Zandt County, sent me this message about the founding of just such a neighborhood: "Around 1914 a daughter of S. Q. Richardson, Sally Fielder, opened up acreage immediately south of the railroad as the 'Fielder Addition' to Grand Saline. It soon became known as Stump Town because the trees were not removed by her prior to selling the lots. The buyers were tasked with the clearing of their new purchase. Over time it became known as Stump Town only, and the Fielder Addition name has been forgotten by the new generations. More specifically, from Hwy.110 west to 1st. and from the railroad to Hwy. 17 is the Fielder Addition or Stump Town" (email July 22, 2021).

Grand Saline consisted of just a handful of cabins in 1845 (Mills n.d., 59). Extracting salt there systematically dates back to well before the Civil War; the history of the city is essentially a narrative of innovations facilitating obtaining the salt in progressively larger quantities. The Texas and Pacific Railroad reached the town in 1872, and the town was incorporated in 1895. The Fielder Salt Company was organized in 1901 (Mills n.d., 56–57), and the concomitant increase in salt production led to increased employment and the creation of "Stumptown." In the 1900 census, "Grand Saline" is not an official division; but "saltworks" employees and other city-type workers—from blacksmiths to a dentist—are found in Van Zandt County, Justice Precinct 4, District 1031 (between pages 20 and 36). Listings of a half-dozen individuals with the profession "saloon man" reminds us that many of the workers in the salt industry were single men. Two music teachers appear, Alabama native Nonnie P. Simpson, aged eighteen, living with her father (a bartender; page 29), and Tennessee native Mary A. Walters, aged thirty-eight, who boarded in the home of a cotton buyer . . . right next to Lou E. Spasko, a "saloon man" from Georgia.

Grand Saline is about twenty-eight miles southeast of where I believe the Robertsons lived in 1900, while Greenville, county seat of Hunt County, is about twenty-five miles to the north of their farm. Either could have been the main actual city that young Eck saw now and then. He certainly had visited Grand Saline, and later gave his report on how it had earned its nickname: "You could walk all over town on stumps, and never touch the ground" (Seeger interview, 1963). Greenville, a railroad hub, certainly had more of the trappings of turn-of-the-twentieth-century progress than Eck got to experience in his daily life, and Grand Saline was soon similarly advanced. Elvis Allen of that city shared the photograph given in figure 8 with me; he believes it was taken in about 1910. Another nearby settlement on the way from southern Hunt County to Grand Saline, but closer to the Robertson family farm, was Wills Point. A good reference point for that farm might be the address of 11784 on FM 751, near the boundary between Hunt County and Van Zandt County, and on the most direct route between Quinlan in Hunt County and both Wills Point and Grand Saline. From that address on FM 751, it's 23.9 miles to Greenville, and, in the other direction, ten miles to Wills Point and twenty-eight miles to Grand Saline.

During Eck's early teenage years—this was shortly before the Ford Model T made travel easier for both car owners and hitchhikers—the difference

Figure 8. Photograph of Grand Saline, Van Zandt County, Texas. Grand Saline resident and historian Elvis Allen, who sent me this picture, speculated that it was probably taken in about 1910.

between the over twenty miles to the substantial towns of Greenville or Grand Saline and the ten miles to smaller Wills Point mattered in terms of practicality. The longer trips would have required overnight stays; the shorter one was more manageable. It happens that there were more music teachers living in Wills Point—six or seven—than in the two bigger cities combined. Perhaps there was a "female seminary" there; such girls' finishing schools typically employed music teachers, even on faculties totaling just a half dozen instructors. But did Eck ever seek out a music teacher? There's no evidence that he did. He doesn't seem to have ever been attracted by the prospect of learning to read music or, for that matter, book learning in general. He is quoted as saying that "printed notes look like Chinese and make about as much sense" (*Amarillo Globe Times*, August 20, 1976, 27). Yes, the 1900 census has him "at school," and he was literate, but his years of formal education didn't leave enough of an impression for any reminiscences of that ingredient of his childhood to come up in any interview.

Where did Eck perform as a teenager? First and foremost, he played at the dances held routinely in connection with house-raisings held by low-income families much like his own, that is, *most* house raisings in his and nearby counties at that time. At these dances, the music might be furnished by a single fiddler or by a serendipitously constituted string band (perhaps fiddle, some kind of banjo—more often five-string, perhaps an organ; Seeger interview 1963). This was the convivial "house raising" at the end of the building process, the speedy community capstone to the long-term solitary or family gathering and shaping of wood. Authors of county histories regularly mention such neighborhood dances as an indispensable part of the reward for the big group effort. Eck's usual boyhood role in the family-and-friends bands led by his brother Quince was playing a banjo; he must have learned tunes on that instrument before he was a competent fiddler, and certainly before he had a real violin. As a result, he knew many melodies well before he could work on technique. And we must keep in mind that the usual way that melodies were worked out on five-string banjo was shaped by the banjo's typical style, inherited from the musical textures of blackface minstrelsy. A tune played on the solo fiddle could sound like it looked on the page—a fluid lineup of pitches, none needing to be omitted. The fiddler would probably enhance a performance, and increase its volume—by having certain of the basic pitches of a key reinforced through playing the easiest double stops, ones including a fingered or open string melody note plus an added open string note, probably on the tonic or fifth of a scale. The same tune played in a blackface minstrel or vaudeville performance added at least a banjo. The minstrel banjo could play melody, but had an additional nonmelodic responsibility, adding a drone by sounding the short string, a recurring off-the-beat reinforcement of that fifth note in the scale. The result in old-time string band performance—directly descended from blackface minstrel style—starts with a texture we call heterophony, in which at least two versions of a melody are played at once. And, just as the ensemble-performed melody has two identities at once, so does the flavor of the drone additions to the sound contributed by the two different instruments. So accumulate a few clues to the sound of the band with which young Eck played. Of course, if young Eck's instrument was a tenor banjo, he probably was strumming a percussive accompaniment.

FIDDLE CONTESTS

Eck must also have attended fiddle contests from a young age, though we have no direct evidence of his having done so. The best-documented fiddle contests in Texas from ca. 1900 to about 1910 were in East Texas, on or near a line stretching from Dallas to Galveston. In that part of Texas, populations were dense enough to produce enough fiddlers to make up a critical mass for competition and for fun; you could expect that enough musicians lived within a reasonable distance of the contest venue. And some towns hosting contests were big enough to support newspapers in which to advertise the events. A successful contest in one community would have interested fiddlers and sponsors in neighboring communities. But 1) many contests were so small that they were learned about and organized solely by word of mouth, and so were unlikely to enter the historical record, 2) many of the ones that were publicized in papers were then lost to known history because physical examples of those specific issues don't survive, and 3) that the inclination to compete that was served in contests must have spawned plenty of smaller, spontaneous unpublicized meetings of fiddlers that were simultaneously jams, confrontations, and learning sessions. I base my remarks on articles that I saw first because copies of them were sent to me by fiddle scholar Steve Green, articles that I later encountered on my own in the manner that curious readers can emulate, by performing searches through the cost-free Texas Digital Newspaper Program or NewspaperArchive.com (many schools and public libraries subscribe to this paid service).

These events were normally called "Old Fiddlers' Contests," with the world "old" referring both to the nostalgic element emphasized and to the ages of the participants. Some articles specified who the organizers were—for instance, "Camp Sterling Price, United Confederate Veterans" (*El Paso Daily Herald*, March 1, 1900, writing about a Dallas event). Modest admission fees were charged. Profits might support various specific good causes, an "orphans home" (*Houston Daily Post*, April 15, 1900, 18), a school building, a piano for a school, and the like. Or those profits might simply nourish the coffers of the specific group that organized it, a group that supported an evolving roster of laudable causes. In many cases, local merchants donated the prizes in acts of seeming generosity that were also a collective tacit admission that the event would stimulate the local economy. Sizes of donated prizes must have reflected sizes and relative prestige of the participating businesses; at one contest, first prize was a nice watch, but seventh prize merely a cigar (Decatur, Texas, *Wise County Messenger*, April 27, 1900 [page not given]).

Contests substantial enough to be announced in newspapers varied in size, from as few as ten fiddlers (*Houston Daily Post*, December 25, 1902, 7) to "nearly 50" (*Bryan Texas Eagle*, March 22, 1900). The fiddlers might live nearby, from no further away than the host community or "adjoining counties" (Jefferson, Texas *Jimplejute*, October 7, 1905), or might travel a hundred or more miles. Nearly all contestants were local, but some larger contests likely attracted stars from further away, men with high levels of enthusiasm and/or expertise who would anticipate that their travel costs would be offset by prize money (see *Wichita Daily Times*, December 10, 1912). Judges were generally local men, often themselves fiddlers, hopefully impartial (see the *Weekly Herald* of Weatherford, Parker County, March 22, 1906); frequent reassurances that the judges would be fair suggests that this had surfaced as a concern. Classes of competition, which in later decades would be based on age, might be absent altogether, or might instead be detailed in ways meant to be inclusive and/or amusing.

Steve Green gathered up a half-dozen articles from the *Houston Daily Post* that were advertising or, later, reporting on a fiddle contest which was held on February 9, 1900, in Brenham, a small town located a little less than halfway from Houston to Austin. Brenham is the county seat of

Washington County, site of the signing of the Texas declaration of independence. The anniversary of that event was celebrated by a "ball" held in a rural blacksmith on March 2, 1837. "The blacksmith shop was illuminated with sperm candles [burning oil harvested from sperm whales], and the music was supplied by a few stringed instruments, to which the merry company danced the Virginia reel, knocked the back-step, or cut the pigeon wing, just as they saw fit" (Pennington 1915, 102). The town of Brenham would have its first building with glass windows by 1844, three churches by that time, train connections during the 1860s–70s, sidewalks, sewers, and public schools during the 1870s (Pennington 1915, 34–49).

Town leaders created the 1900 fiddle contest "for the benefit of a local charity," which would end up being the town's venerable Episcopal Church. However, I think the primary motivation was to gather a crowd to buy tickets . . . and food, and merchandise. The organizers wrote that they hoped to entice Tennessee Governor Bob Taylor to play—he and his brother Alf were avid fiddlers, and Bob was going to be in the area at the time. He didn't respond, but Judge V. W. Grubbs of Greenville, a prominent member of the state legislature, did register for the contest, saying he would come directly from Austin if possible. That he "telegraphed that he missed the train [by] just three seconds" was lamented in the longest article concerning the contest, printed two days after the event (*Houston Daily Post*, February 11, 1900, 8). In that same article, the reporter gave a list of over a hundred tunes said to have been played, and a separate list of all of the contestants and where they lived. I checked the distances between each contestant's home and Brenham. If we omit the absent Judge Grubbs from the calculations, and do take into account the dozen participants from Brenham itself, the average distance the contestants covered to get to the contest was only 21.4 miles. Whatever the ambitions of the organizers, this was a truly local event, well-populated because fiddlers were thick on the ground. The exception among those expected to come was Judge Grubbs, who lived far away, in Greenville, within a few dozen miles of Eck and his family. Fiddlers must have been equally common there, and they must have gathered in fiddle contests, even if none proved to be as extravagant and well-publicized as the one that took place in Brenham in 1900.

I will look more closely at Eck's specific tunes and performance styles in the second half of this book. But the broad ways that dance, minstrel, and contest venues shaped Eck's learning of his repertoire matter, too. Whether or not the banjo he played was the five-string variety, he probably learned blackface minstrel style first (he heard plenty of music in that style during his late teens, while playing with minstrel groups in Oklahoma). From that experience, he knew melodies not as fixed lineups of one pitch after another—shaped just the same every time from performer to performer and performance to performance—but rather as short but endlessly different expressions. Thus, well before he pioneered his own approaches to systematic variation, he lived in a musical world in which immediate, audible variety was taken for granted. In addition, he grew up in a musical environment in which a fiddler might sometimes have a band to play with, but other times might have to go it alone, be obliged to produce a complete-sounding solo performance, one that was full enough and loud enough to support dancing. A dance accompanist needed to produce versions of tunes that were rhythmically strong, melodically coherent (and sometimes self-sufficient), performances balanced enough to do the job without help. In sum, a fiddler like Eck needed to be able to craft a versatile version of a tune, a version that "worked" as a solo, or in the mix of melodies created by playing with a five-string banjoist, or in the melody-plus-harmony format created when the fiddle was accompanied by guitar or tenor banjo or keyboard, or in the complex textures of a full string band.

When Eck got old enough to seek his fortune outside of the family, when he was ready to spend time away from home, he could have sought out formal training on the violin—he could have moved to a big city like Dallas or to one of the closest sizeable towns, Greenville or Big Saline or at least to Wills Point, with its surprisingly large complement of music teachers. Or he could have sought out an informal apprenticeship with some senior fiddler wherever he lived. But when Eck first set out to travel by himself, he didn't go to any of these nearby cities or to any other relatively modern or cultured destinations, nor did he seek out a specific musical guru. His first trip alone was north into the countryside of Oklahoma, then called "Indian Territory." In the interview with Nagy and Riggs in 1962, Eck described this first extended trip:

> Well, I was about sixteen years old, the first trip I ever made away from home . . . I left home unbeknownst to my folks, and went to Oklahoma. [He got a temporary job hoeing for an Indian farmer whose wife played accordion. They enjoyed his fiddling, and wanted him to stay. But after a few days he moved on.] I walked from there to Madill [midway between Durant and Ardmore; an unlikely walk today, since the extensive modern reservoir called Lake Texoma blocks the old route]. I had a friend that lived there . . . But he didn't have anything that I could do. . . . I just kept going, walking, figured I'd come to a town sometime another. And I finally come up on a high bluff and I looked down in the valley and there was lights of a town, about two miles of me. [It was] after dark, me starving for water and food. I went down there, got in there, and walked in to a drug store; there's one drug store and one restaurant in the town. I walked in there, and there's a man in the drug store—he was a doctor, and I didn't know that, of course. But I just asked him a question: if there's a restaurant in town, and he said "Yeah, right up the street there's the only one there is in the town. But it's right up the street, that next block, a block or two," something like that, is what he said.

It turned out that Eck had happened upon a group of musicians who would appreciate his playing.

> I . . . walked up there to that restaurant and . . . ordered the biggest steak I could get. [I was] setting there eating and I looked around in the corner and saw an old organ, an upright organ . . . and a fiddle in a boxed case . . . I asked the man that was running the restaurant—he's a pretty old feller, . . . I said "Looks like you have a little music in here once in a while; you got fiddle and organ sitting over there." "Yeah," he said . . . "Me and the doctor play some," said "he plays the organ . . . I do, and he plays the fiddle." He said "We have a little music in here every once in a while." And it caused him to suspicion that maybe I was a musician; he spoke up and asked me if I was a musician. I said "Oh yeah, I played a fiddle a little." So he insisted on me playing after I got done eating—playing him a tune. So I charmed him . . . For three days and nights I stayed right there and slept behind that counter on a cot. He wouldn't let me leave. And he had the biggest entertainment that next night after I was there. . . . I expect two hundred people that night that we had the jamboree there at that restaurant. There wasn't even standing room in the place for them. And some of the cowboys come fifty miles to that entertainment.

Blanton Owen was able to draw on interviews with at least one of Eck's daughters for his short article on Eck published in the *Old Time Herald* (fall 1992, 20–25). I will reproduce two paragraphs from that fine article:

> Eck soon found employment in medicine shows that traveled throughout the Indian Territory. He was able to hone his natural showmanship from the various pitchmen, magicians, dancers, comedians and other musicians while traveling with these shows, which were the prime source of entertainment for many rural audiences. Eck traveled on the medicine show circuit intermittently for several years, and it was during this time that he worked hard to master trick fiddling, a feature of this musical showmanship he never abandoned.
>
> In 1906, nineteen-year-old Eck married his fifteen-year-old childhood sweetheart, Jeannette Belle Levy. Within a year of their marriage, Eck and Nettie, who played guitar, piano and mandolin, put together a show of lantern slides depicting local ranches and ranch activities, often with Eck prominently featured. They took their "picture shows" to theaters and "airdromes" (large, open-topped tents) in area towns and performed fiddle and piano music before, during and after the screening. It was a natural step, therefore, for Eck to provide musical entertainment for silent moving pictures. (22)

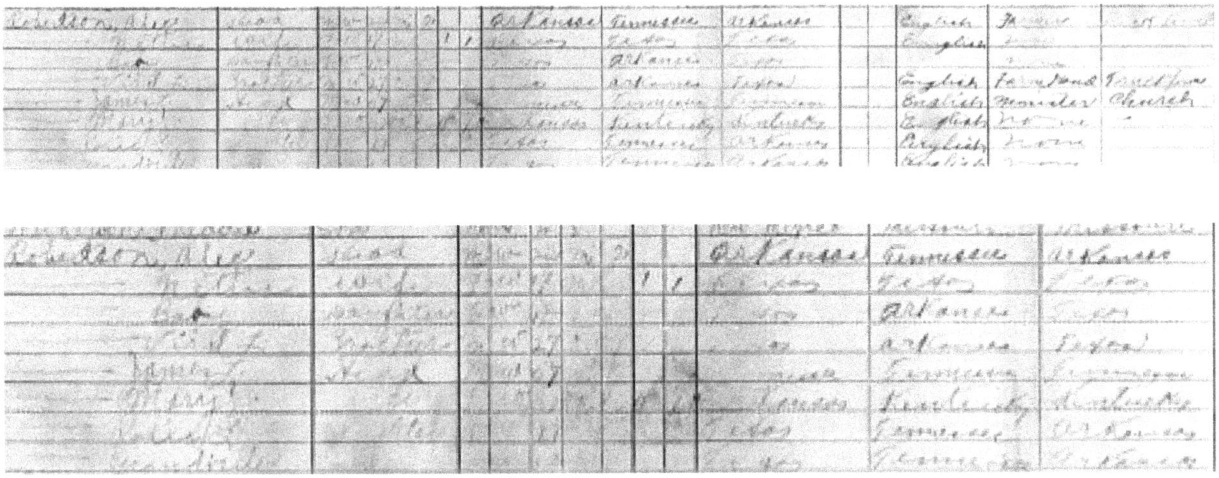

Figure 9. The census of 1910 finds the elder and younger Robertson families living in Lubbock, in the southern edge of the Panhandle; widescreen above closeup (TX>Lubbock>Justice Precinct 2>District 0154). These records are not easy to read.

As a postscript to the extended Robertson family's stay(s) in rural Hunt County, the 1910 census has them living near Lubbock, in the Panhandle, in the general area in which many family members would spend the rest of their lives (see figure 9). Eck's nuclear family had grown. Eck and Nettie, their first daughter—not yet named—and Eck's elder brother "Vird" (Lafayette V.) boarded in one cabin, while James and Mary Robertson and that older couple's two remaining minor children resided in the neighboring separate building. The extended family stayed in this location very briefly—less than three years, I estimate but the census record documents a number of significant developments. Eck, at age twenty-three, is called a head of household, and the simple classification of "farmer" has been refined for this census. He was called a "truck farmer," one concentrating on growing vegetables for sale (his brother Vird was classified as a "farm hand"). His father must have still farmed, but is officially declaring on this census that he is a "minister"; his longtime vocation of preaching had become his profession.

Most farmers relocating from East Texas to the Panhandle were seeking a better opportunity to exercise their professional skills and earn a decent living, to farm independently, out from under the pressure of the cotton business and shedding the status of sharecroppers. Indeed, while cotton was grown in the Panhandle, it never became a staple crop there. But this population's move to the Panhandle was actually a retreat in historical terms, a new, early 1900s land rush parallel to the migration to East Texas two decades previous.

Lubbock, like the Panhandle in general, was at an early stage of development when the Robertsons arrived. The last battles with the main indigenous population the Comanches—the Red River Wars—finished erasing the Indian resistance only in 1874–75. The army forces were the African American "Buffalo Soldiers," likely called that because they wore buffalo-hide coats. Lubbock scholars Carlson, Abbe, and Monroe felt that the half-century ending with those wars had a decisive effect on Texas character: "The long, difficult struggle, roughly 1825 to 1875, of westward pushing Texans to make a living in semiarid and sometimes hardscrabble lands, while simultaneously trying to secure the land from Comanches unwilling to surrender it, accounts in part at least for the strong sense of Texas chauvinism that still marks citizens of the state" (2008, 27). A decade dominated by slaughtering buffalo followed, then large ranches took over most arable land, first for sheep—the 1880 census of the environs of present-day Lubbock found that most of the twenty-five residents were sheepherders. The cattle ranching boom would take place in the early 1880s (Carlson, Abbe, and Monroe 2008, 31–32). Only in the early 1890s did military posts give way decisively to small towns. A shift away from ranching toward farming soon afterward was complicated in both political and practical terms, but the state could earn more money selling small plots of land to farmers than larger acreages to ranchers. That is, a shift in state policy in 1905 made it easier for farmers to outbid the ranchers on specific small parcels of public domain lands, so the balance of farm and ranch shifted toward farming, even though the land was difficult to work. In sum, agriculture in the Panhandle went through several stages very quickly, from open-range cow country and cowboys to hybrid farmer/stockmen to diversified farming to intensified cotton cultivation—at this point, the Plains was reaching the status that Hunt County had reached decades earlier—and finally to a generally more varied economy (Carlson, Abbe, and Monroe 2008, 9). Lubbock itself grew quickly in response to this series of transformations: the census of 1900 found less than 300 citizens, that of 1910 some 1,938 people (including the Robertsons). In 1920, the census found 4,051 residents. That may have proved to be too large a settlement for the comfort of the Robertsons. In any case, they swiftly moved on.

New professions cited in that 1910 census tell an interesting story. The job classification of "farmer" became subdivided. Lubbock was in the midst of the series of agricultural changes summarized above. In the census, we still see a good number of "stock farmers," but they are now vastly outnumbered by "general" farmers. In Justice Precinct 2, District 1054, the only two "truck farmers" listed were Eck (assisted by his older brother Vird) and a John Doyle; that page of the census also includes two dairy farms. Perhaps their neighborhood had better than average access to water. Just a few professionals working outside of agriculture resided in this part of Lubbock and environs: a carpenter, a bricklayer, even a jeweler and a wallpaper salesman, a few builders, and a couple of "house movers." Citizens in the two villages competing to be the county seat had made the sensible decision to consolidate, and the buildings constituting both villages were literally moved to a location between them, even a two-story hotel.

Working-class families like the extended Robertson clan, who moved often, were in greater touch with the world than we might romantically imagine. But most ways that they interacted remained intensely local—much of the detail of their lives was shaped by families, neighbors, and the whims of landowners. Cultural information, including fiddling, tended to be eclectically pan-South, ambitious within limits imposed by poverty. However, information was passed on primarily face to face—one might imagine that process keeping transmission and change at a deliberate pace—but with a regular infusion of new faces and new information and ideas contributed through the mobility of individuals and the instability of their neighborhoods.

In Lubbock, Eck had moved out of the mainstream of farming, but even as a "truck farmer" remained restless. A "general" farmer named William Baggett living very near Eck's Lubbock residence had three enterprising children; though still living at home, their declared professions were respectively operator of a "dry goods store," a "real estate agent," and, for daughter Eula, "music." The census did not specify which avenues within this profession she pursued; gender-channeled patterns of the day suggest that she taught singing and/or keyboard instruments, and, as part of that instruction, how to read music. Eck must have known this family. Eula Baggett's musical activity may or may not have had anything to do with his personal ambitions, but I think that the idea that one could make a living in the profession of music by adding strategically to the chancy income available through performing must have intrigued and encouraged him. What would become his new mix of occupations beckoned.

Figure 10. View north on Main St. (from the intersection of Main and Wilbarger) in Vernon in 1917. The large building on the left is the More Theatre, then the only sizeable auditorium in Vernon. Eck performed there many times. This illustration comes from the image collection of local museum head Preston Cary. It began its life as a snapshot of unknown origin that Mr. Cary acquired. He had the new version blown up, framed, and then reproduced in his book on Vernon (2013, 56); the original was lost. Photograph of manipulated copy of snapshot by Valerie Goertzen.

— Chapter 2 —

ECK ROBERTSON, "WORLD CHAMPION FIDDLER"

Around 1918, the James L. Robertson and Alexander C. Robertson families moved to Vernon, another small but rapidly growing Panhandle town. The 1920 census (figure 11) shows Alexander C. Robertson (Eck) no longer identifying himself as a farmer of any kind, but rather belonging to the professional world of music as a piano salesman. The word "salesman" looks messy on the page—in fact, the census bureau's modern automatic reader misreads the word, identifying Eck instead as a piano "statistician." It is tempting to picture Eck identifying his profession for the census taker, but stumbling over his declaration. In this willfully imagined sequence, Eck tries out several words, none of which referred to how he wished to earn a living—by fiddling. The census taker corrects his entry several times, writing one word over another, finally leaving the Robertson home a bit confused and the record messy. In an alternative scenario, Eck says "fiddler" or "musician" to the census taker, but Nettie is listening, and insists that the recorded profession reflect how he actually earns a living.

I am almost certainly making too much of the physical muddiness of this census entry! However, it is an undeniable and uncomfortable fact that while Eck's ambitions and his best source of joy centered on his fiddling, most of the money he could make in the field of music had to do with pianos. We know that he also did quite a bit of repairing of bowed and plucked stringed instruments later in life, activity begun in a tiny way when he built his own proto-fiddle when he was still a youth in Hunt County. But tuning, repairing, and sometimes selling pianos would remain at the center of his income while he lived in Vernon and in all of his many subsequent homes in the Panhandle.

In 1921 Eck placed an ad in the *Vernon Daily Record* offering his services as a piano tuner and instrument repairman. The wording of this advertisement constitutes a double illustration. It lists the skills Eck could exercise and also illustrates his individual brand of humor. The "ten dollar reward" title of the ad reflects his combination of wit and braggadocio, an aspect of

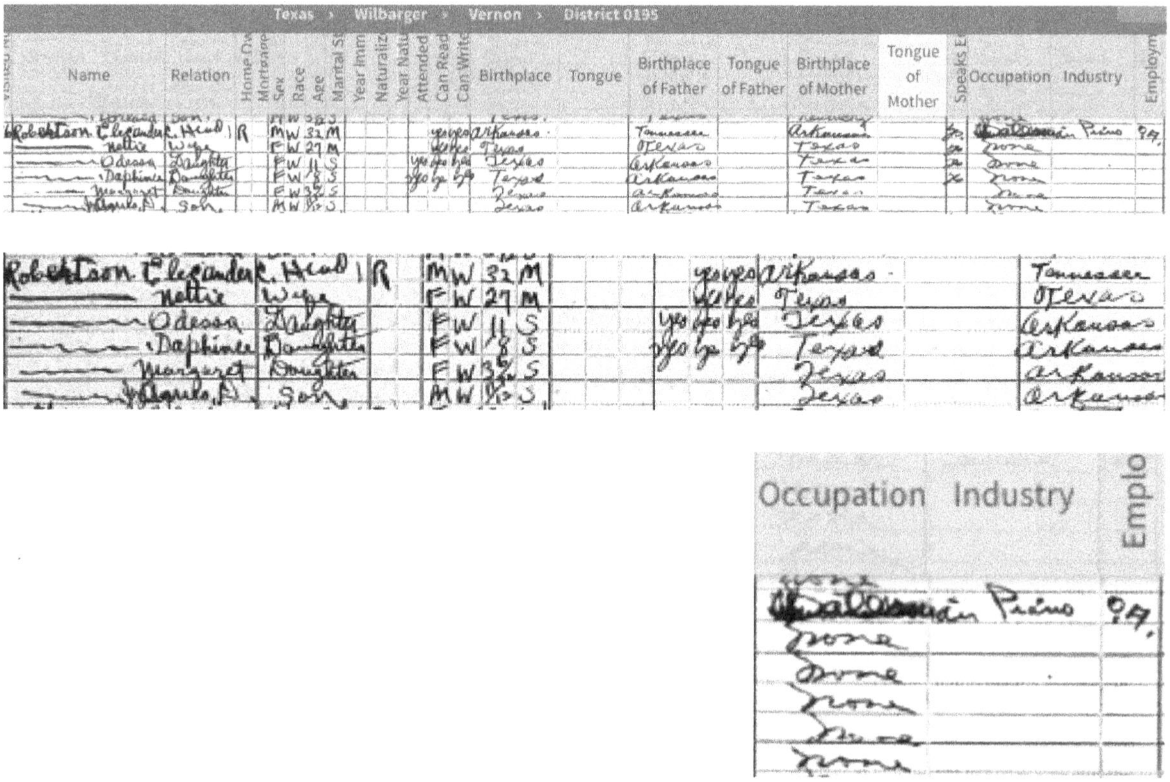

Figure 11. The Eck Robertson family in the 1920 census, when they lived in Vernon, widescreen view above closeups of the left and right ends of the entry.

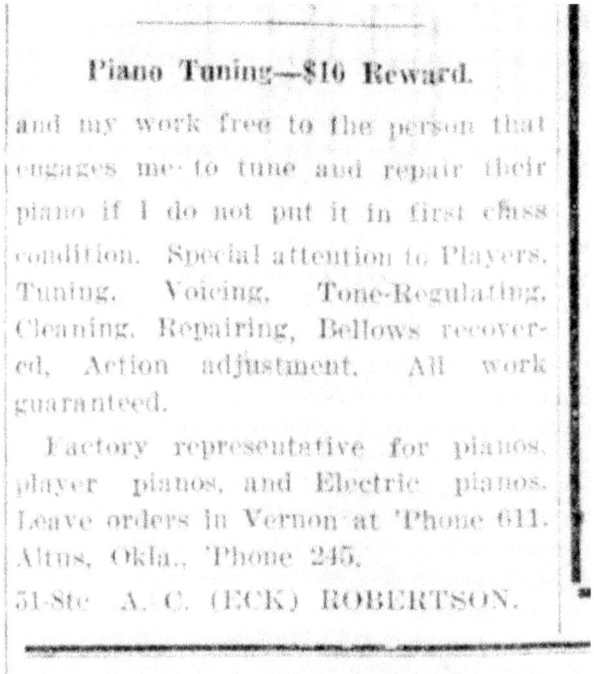

Piano Tuning—$10 Reward.

and my work free to the person that engages me to tune and repair their piano if I do not put it in first class condition. Special attention to Players, Tuning, Voicing, Tone-Regulating, Cleaning, Repairing, Bellows recovered, Action adjustment. All work guaranteed.

Factory representative for pianos, player pianos, and Electric pianos. Leave orders in Vernon at 'Phone 611. Altus, Okla., 'Phone 245.

51-8tc A. C. (ECK) ROBERTSON.

Figure 12. Eck advertised his piano tuning and repair services in the *Vernon Record* several times in July and August 1921; this ad is from July 15.

his self-presentation carried over from his experience on the minstrel and vaudeville stages. In addition, the ad shows how advances in technology had helped him expand his professional geography: the automobile now allowed him to maintain offices both in Vernon and in Altus, Oklahoma (about thirty-six miles north), while the telephone enabled potential customers to reach him in both locations.

Eck later upgraded his wares by developing a working relationship with the Baldwin company. He saved a letter from the Dallas branch of the Baldwin Piano Company dated July 26, 1923 (letter now on deposit at the library of the Country Music Hall of Fame and Museum in Nashville). The letter reads as follows:

Mr. A. C. Robertson
   Vernon, Texas

Dear Sir,
   We find that we failed to return copy of your contract which we are doing today properly accepted by us.
   We are pleased to make this arrangement with you as we believe it means the beginning of a mutually pleasant and profitable arrangement and we feel quite sure that you will sell a number of our goods at a very nice profit to yourself. If we can help you in any way do not hesitate to call on us. We trust that you have arranged to meet Mr. Maxwell in Wichita Falls. He has instructions from us to ship you some goods from Wichita Falls and Burkburnett in order to save you the delay of waiting until they come from the factory.
   Yours very truly,
   THE BALDWIN PIANO COMPANY
   By [initials indecipherable]

We don't know how soon after the census of 1910 the Robertson families had left Lubbock, nor where they went from there, nor precisely when they settled in Vernon. In a parallel mystery, we can't pin down when Eck shifted decisively from agriculture to a patchwork of music-related jobs for his livelihood. A good candidate for a stop between Lubbock and Vernon is the town of Clarendon, on the road from Ft. Worth to Amarillo (now called US 287), about 120 miles northwest of Vernon and sixty miles southeast of Amarillo. Eck once remarked that he and his older brother Vird (Lafayette V.) worked many years together selling pianos and pump organs (Seeger interview, 1963). One of his daughters placed that activity in Clarendon, although she also said that the business failed in the Great Depression, which would place the stay in Clarendon after rather than before the longer stay in Vernon. However, given how readily and frequently Eck and his family moved, there's a good possibility that they resided in Clarendon more than once.

Eck would remain in the Texas Panhandle for most of the rest of his life. In figure 13, asterisks appear at each of the locations where Eck lived, and the dates next to those asterisks note when the evidence is from. Those dates also automatically indicate the type of evidence. 1900, 1910, 1920, 1930, and 1940 mark census records, while most of the other dates come either from newspaper articles that concern fiddle contests and that specify where the contestants live, or from the lengthy interview with Seeger (1963).

Today's US Highway 287 travels from the upper left of the map to the lower center, through Amarillo, Clarendon, and Vernon, then west of Dallas (going through Fort Worth). The "Western Trail," which had been an important cattle trail, passed from south to north, through Vernon and near Altus, Oklahoma. This entire area was financially and culturally "younger" than the parts of East Texas in which Eck grew up; the Panhandle had initially attracted far fewer settlers, and so offered less formal culture but arguably more economic opportunity to the Robertsons than had the East Texas locations of Hunt County and Van Zandt County. With each major shift in where he lived (stays lasting more than a year or two), Eck was pursuing the frontier in relative terms. This characterized his family's overall move from East Texas to the Panhandle, their pause in the relatively young village of Lubbock, and finally his taking his family to a similar settlement in Vernon and then to the brand new town of Borger. Finally, he turned around in this journey back through history; his eventual landing in Amarillo kept him in the physical Panhandle, but no longer seeking out frontier conditions and promising but risky economic opportunities. In that last major move (1940), he shifted to a mature city. It was a relocation precipitated by family tragedy and turmoil. He would settle firmly into a fairly stable job tuning pianos and repairing keyboard and stringed

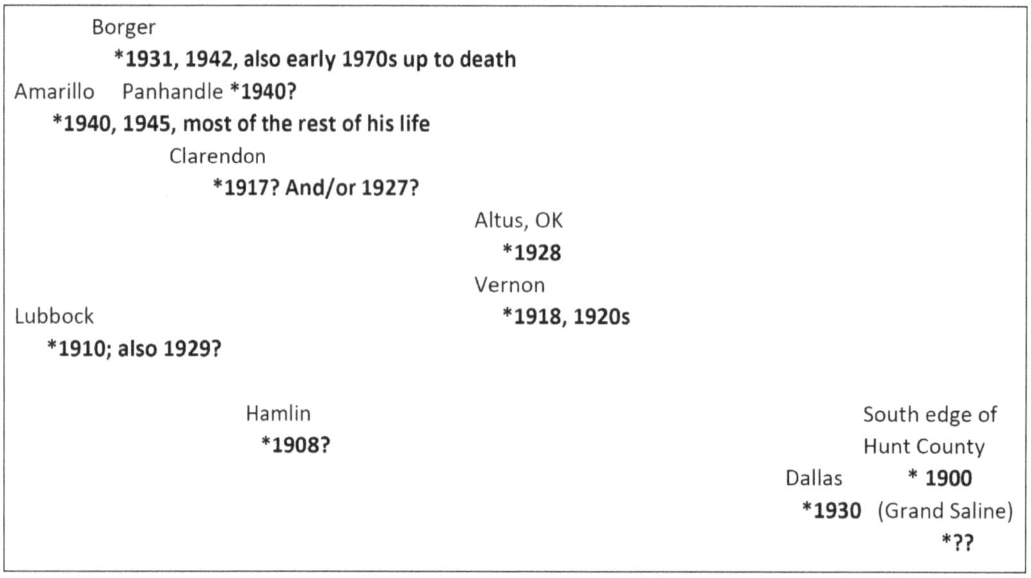

```
       Borger
           *1931, 1942, also early 1970s up to death
Amarillo   Panhandle *1940?
   *1940, 1945, most of the rest of his life
           Clarendon
               *1917? And/or 1927?
                                    Altus, OK
                                      *1928
                                    Vernon
Lubbock                               *1918, 1920s
  *1910; also 1929?

                Hamlin                              South edge of
                 *1908?                              Hunt County
                                           Dallas      * 1900
                                              *1930  (Grand Saline)
                                                      *??
```

Figure 13. Verified locations where Eck lived, starting with the location given in the census of 1900.

instruments, even while he looked back toward earlier times, remembering when fiddle contests and fiddle-accompanied dances were more central to social life, and when he won those fiddle contests almost routinely—the time in his life when he still imagined a career as a performer.

Despite how hard life in the Panhandle was, many people made room in their lives for music. I found a few adjacent newspaper ads compactly illustrating the varied texture of life there (*Amarillo Daily News*, June 8, 1927, 14). The scan of the page was hard to read, so I have retyped the section to try to reproduce the visual flavor:

> FOR SAL.Deering Combine;
> fifteen foot cut, with grain bin, $1000; R. S.
> Pavillard. Box 1040, Amarillo.
> MILK GOAT for sale, $49. 703 Jackson.
> FOR SALE—1871 Fiddle. 617 East 4th.
> TYPEWRITER for sale. "Corona Four."
> Standard key board, portable typewriter. $40.
> Good as new. Phone 381.
> **36. For Sale or Trade**
> FOR EXCHANGE. That wonderful business
> corner at W. 6th and Harrison. 100 feet on
> W. 6th. Will exchange my equity of $18,000
> for clear business or residence property or
> for approved oil royalties. Might consider
> part in high grade oil stock. For personal
> reasons will give a good trade and quick deci-
> sion. Brokers take notice. O. M. Hergerson,
> Owner. 1009 ½ W. 6th St. (No phone.)
> GOOD PIANO to trade for car. Phone 1708-J_

The earliest clear evidence that I have seen of Eck's activity as a money-making performing musician is an advertisement of an elaborate "fiddlers' convention" published in the *Vernon Record* at the beginning of 1918. The ad shows that Eck had become well known as a fiddler, and was already famous for his version of the tune most associated with him today, "Sally Goodin" (I will usually spell the title this way, following modern convention, though reproducing Eck's own spelling—"Sallie Gooden"—in quotations from his time).

More's Theatre, in downtown Vernon, was the town's main entertainment venue. It's the largest building shown in the photograph leading off this chapter, the building to the left of the buggy in the main street. That an "Old Fiddlers' Convention" was staged in that capacious auditorium tells us that fiddling fit comfortably into many people's lives; it was still broad-based entertainment. Indeed, placing this particular event in More's

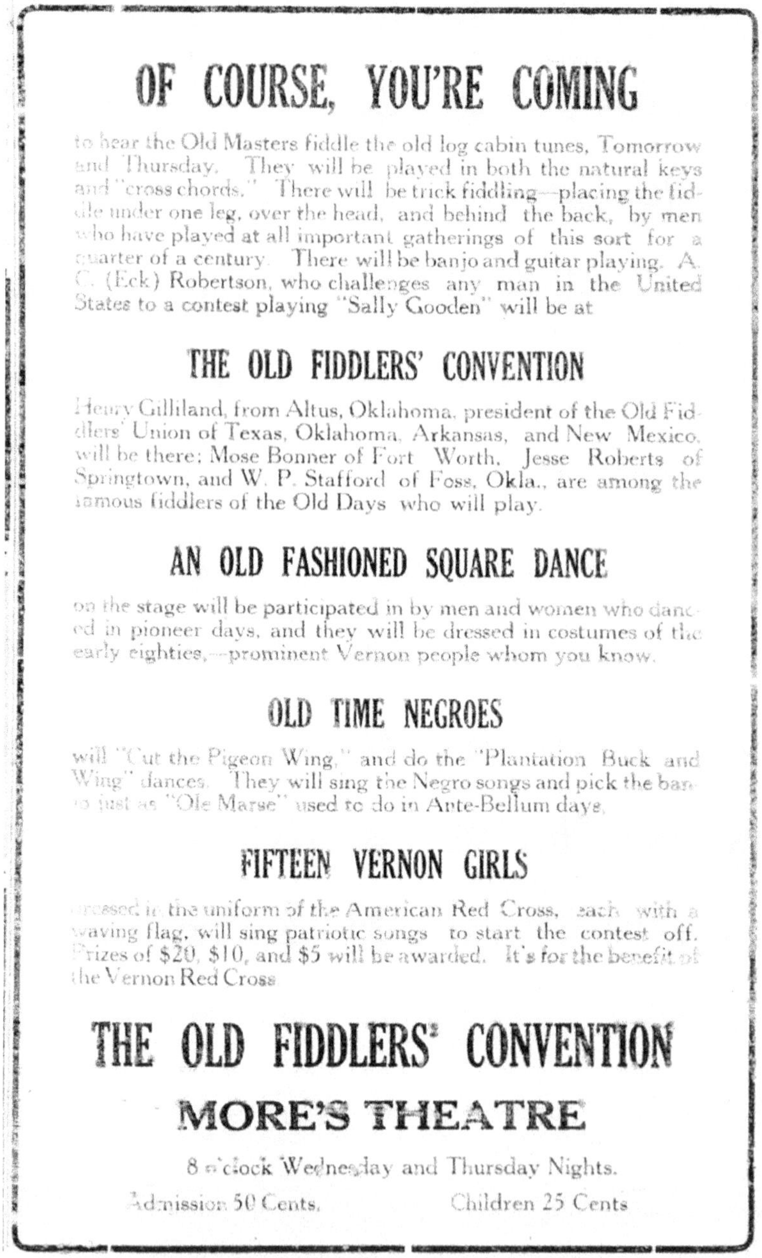

> **OF COURSE, YOU'RE COMING**
>
> to hear the Old Masters fiddle the old log cabin tunes, Tomorrow and Thursday. They will be played in both the natural keys and "cross chords." There will be trick fiddling—placing the fiddle under one leg, over the head, and behind the back, by men who have played at all important gatherings of this sort for a quarter of a century. There will be banjo and guitar playing. A. C. (Eck) Robertson, who challenges any man in the United States to a contest playing "Sally Gooden" will be at
>
> **THE OLD FIDDLERS' CONVENTION**
>
> Henry Gilliland, from Altus, Oklahoma, president of the Old Fiddlers' Union of Texas, Oklahoma, Arkansas, and New Mexico, will be there; Mose Bonner of Fort Worth, Jesse Roberts of Springtown, and W. P. Stafford of Foss, Okla., are among the famous fiddlers of the Old Days who will play.
>
> **AN OLD FASHIONED SQUARE DANCE**
>
> on the stage will be participated in by men and women who danced in pioneer days, and they will be dressed in costumes of the early eighties,—prominent Vernon people whom you know.
>
> **OLD TIME NEGROES**
>
> will "Cut the Pigeon Wing," and do the "Plantation Buck and Wing" dances. They will sing the Negro songs and pick the banjo just as "Ole Marse" used to do in Ante-Bellum days.
>
> **FIFTEEN VERNON GIRLS**
>
> dressed in the uniform of the American Red Cross, each with a waving flag, will sing patriotic songs to start the contest off. Prizes of $20, $10, and $5 will be awarded. It's for the benefit of the Vernon Red Cross.
>
> **THE OLD FIDDLERS' CONVENTION**
>
> **MORE'S THEATRE**
>
> 8 o'clock Wednesday and Thursday Nights.
>
> Admission 50 Cents.   Children 25 Cents.

Figure 14. An ad for a festival centering on a fiddle contest printed in the *Vernon Record* on Jan. 22, 1918.

Theatre injects history-based nostalgic fun into the core of Vernon's social life. I built this chapter around this advertisement, focusing on the opening section declaring that Eck would be featured in the two-night event, that the fiddling the audience would hear was claimed to be both authentic and interesting, and especially on the second section of the ad announcing this "Old Fiddlers Convention." The remainder of the ad offers three vignettes presenting a summary of the socially stable context for the lively visual and auditory central spectacle of the fiddle contest. The last activity listed—actually the first portion of the program—was certainly appropriate at the time. The Red Cross grew greatly during World War I. When this fiddle contest took place, nearly a year of the fighting remained, and supporting the Red Cross was a popular and important cause. Dressing local girls in Red Cross uniforms illustrates what was then a common strategy—promoting events and swelling audiences by putting family members and neighbors on stage.

This incorporating of a parade of local "girls" in Red Cross outfits into a fiddle event reminds me of a pair of articles published in the *Vernon Record* (adjacent on the front page) a few years later, on Friday, April 13, 1923. The first reads as follows:

> PURE FOOD SHOW FASHION DISPLAY AND FIDDLE MELEE.
> Big Event Planned for Vernon with Living Models Displaying Late Styles.
> A pure food week under the auspices of the women's auxiliary of the Presbyterian Church is announced for the first week in May. The merchants of Vernon will have on display good eatable products of all descriptions.
> This show will be put on at the Hahn Building, south side of the square. A style show will be staged each night and the new fashions will be displayed on living models. Each afternoon a baby show will be given and prizes awarded for the best specimen of young America exhibited.
> Saturday afternoon an old fiddlers' jubilee will take place in the same building and all fiddlers who can play a "break down" are to be asked to come and play for the prizes to be awarded.
> Mrs. George Zachry of Greenville who has been in Vernon arranging for the details of the pure food and style show with its various side events, said before leaving yesterday she is confident it is going to be a big success. Such shows have been big drawing cards elsewhere, Mrs. Zachry said, and she expects to duplicate the success here.
> While the pure food part will be a big attraction, the fiddlers "melee" is expected to be one of the most interesting events ever staged here in the musical line. The style show with pretty Vernon girls as living models displaying the latest creations in dress from the street dresses to evening gowns and negligee is expected to be one of the most interesting events Vernon has ever had. A similar show was recently staged in Wichita Falls at one of the picture shows and drew overflowing crowds.

Again, the parents, friends, and classmates of the Vernon models likely formed a generous fraction of the audience. And again, the event supports a good cause, now the "pure foods" movement, which would culminate in the founding of the Food, Drug and Insecticide Administration within the Department of Agriculture just four years later (this would become the Food and Drug Administration in 1930).

Next to this article was one entitled "High School Girls Do Their Stuff":

> Vernon high school girls are going to step out on the evening of April 20. They are going to doll up in the fancy dresses they have learned to make and put on a style show, which according to indications is going to be one of the best ever put on by any school in Texas. It is the domestic art girls who are going to put on the show. They want to give the people of Vernon a chance to see what has been done in their department—just how much they have learned—and how much they appreciate the chance to learn domestic art work. The costumes to be worn at the art review will represent the old time family album with all the styles of yester-year and on down to the modern. Each style will be shown as the pages to the album are turned and the old-timers can dwell in their memories of the days of long ago when they went courting the girl in the hoop skirts or the girl in the empire and so on.

That article announced yet another event that showcased Vernon high school girls, this time to advertise their school program in sewing. Once again, the present and past are gathered up, here through the students having made outfits from both their own and earlier generations. Returning to the ad for the early 1918 entertainment, we see something similar happening with the advertised square dance. The pioneer days were not long in the past—just a few decades previous in the Panhandle—so that the dancers wearing clothes of the resonating past were people who had lived that past. Townsfolk who were, for instance, twenty years old in 1882, soon after buffalo hunting yielded to ranching in Wilbarger County, were just fifty-six when the advertised event took place. These "prominent Vernon people" were still spry enough to dance, able to deploy their older bodies (and solid status in the community) to remind us of the past, to evoke recent history that was concrete and valued and yet ready to be memorialized.

The only part of the composite event not convincingly joining present and past in this 1918 entertainment (figure 14) was of course that of the "Old Time Negroes." Quite a few fiddle conventions from this era included such an act, the purpose of which was to invoke a corner of nostalgia that the Black performers certainly would not share. Only the past was presented here, and a willfully reinterpreted one.

The start of the ad clearly meant to invoke a corner of fairly recent history that already was infused with nostalgia: the *Old* Masters will—in person—fiddle the *old* log cabin tunes. The writers of the ad expected that many of their readers would welcome being told something intriguing about "old" fiddling, something that set fiddling apart from playing the violin in conventional ways, and, significantly, something that they either wouldn't know or that they would welcome being reminded of.

The sentence "They will be playing in both the natural keys and 'cross chords'" referred to tuning the fiddle in various ways. "Natural keys" indicated the normal violin tuning, one also common on fiddle, GDAE (low to high). The term "cross chords" refers to various tunings in which some deviation from GDAE is adopted in order to maximize resonance in specific keys, producing an increase in volume that is especially needed and especially effective when a fiddler is playing alone for a dance. In the tuning ADAE, the fact that the lowest string has been adjusted up a step to a makes that tuning especially useful in the key of D, since the pitch a is the dominant (fifth pitch) in that key. That low a is then very handy for extra sound both when bowed as a drone (simultaneously with a melody note on an adjacent string, in the simplest possible "double stop") and through sympathetic resonance, when the vibration of the air created by a bowed pitch sets another string very lightly in motion, a string whose pitch is in a logical mathematical relationship with that of the bowed note.

Another tuning, AEAE, works well for the key of A; Eck always played "Sally Goodin" in that key (as do almost all modern fiddlers), but not always in this tuning. He employed this specific tuning for his 1922 recorded performance; he could also perform it in normal tuning, as do almost all fiddlers today. And he used other, rarer tunings for specific pieces that were novelty numbers partly due to their being in those uncommon "open" tunings. For instance, playing in a tuning even more specific to the key of A, that is, AEAC♯, allows more open-string double stopping and also left-hand plucking of the strings. What is most significant for our purposes is that the use of these "cross chords" was and remains ubiquitous in Southeastern fiddle styles, but would become rare in Texas fiddling as it would develop. Hearing playing in "cross chords" represents early Texas fiddling as not yet very differentiated from other southern fiddling. Eck told John Fahey that "all the old guys played in open tunings. They're all gone; I'm the only one left" (1995, 32).

In fact, "Sally Goodin," Eck's signature piece both in his own time and within his legacy today, represents a combination of style features that now have multiple, actually conflicting geographic associations. It is remarkable in how much variation it features. That sheer amount of artistry and effort invested in variation would become the most distinctive feature of contemporary Texas style. However, both the fact that Eck played this piece with his fiddle tuned to AEAE and the near constant double-stopping he employed point instead to the melody's roots in the Southeast. I will further explore this complex of factors in chapter 5.

Trick fiddling, mentioned early in the 1918 ad, was a set of skills Eck had learned during his travels in Indian Territory with minstrel/vaudeville musicians during his teens, and which would remain an important ingredient of many of his solo performances. For instance, an ad published in 1927 represented a combination of activities Eck had pursued for decades

> **ADDED ATTRACTIONS**
> **At The Gem**
> THURSDAY ONLY
> A. C. (Eck) Robertson
> IN PERSON
> With his $10,000 Violin
> World's champion Cowboy Fiddler
> Victor Record Making Artist
> Popular Radio Artist
> PRODUCES
> Old time tunes—Trick and Stunt Fiddling.
> He makes the violin say words that anyone can understand
> **"The Flaming Forest"**
> **and Comedy.**
> 10c————————25c

Figure 15. This ad, printed on Jan. 27, 1927, in the Edmond, Oklahoma, *Enterprise*, shows Eck touting his many accomplishments as a performer; he was in town primarily to furnish the music for a silent movie, *The Flaming Forest*.

(figure 15). He was playing at The Gem, which was then Edmond, Oklahoma's youngest theater screening silent movies (Edmond is on the north side of Oklahoma City). *The Flaming Forest* and the "Comedy" were two different features to be aired during the evening. In *The Flaming Forest*, Eck would be doing again what he had begun doing in his teens, often in company with Nettie: furnishing the music backdrop for a silent movie. This film, made in 1926, was a hit movie based on the book of the same name by popular and prolific writer James Oliver Curwood (first published in 1921). It's a Canadian Mountie adventure replete with heroes and villains, generous servings of gunfire, plenty of excruciating longing alternating with a battery of other extreme emotions, and a climactic forest fire—a real check-all-of-the-boxes action melodrama. That night's accompanying "Comedy" may have been some self-contained minstrel/vaudeville act, but may instead have just characterized Eck's separate act of trick fiddling.

DR. HOWARD AND THE VERNON FIDDLERS

Now I will turn to the second part of the 1918 ad (figure 14), the part bearing the heading THE OLD FIDDLERS' CONVENTION. Eck competed in literally hundreds of fiddle contests, and did well enough at them to make his adopted title "The World's Champion Fiddler" plausible; this phrase would be inscribed on his gravestone. Much of his public fiddling done while living in Vernon was with a trio called the Vernon Fiddlers, an ensemble led by the eccentric and flamboyant town physician, Dr. A. P. Howard (Abner Perry Howard). As a musician, Dr. Howard was almost certainly not on the same high level as the other long-term members, Eck and a left-handed fiddler named Lewis Franklin (who did not belong to the family of much more famous fiddlers named Franklin who were based in East Texas). But Dr. Howard was eloquent and affluent; Eck later referred to him as his "main master of ceremonies" (Seeger interview, 1963). One particular competitive occasion featuring the Vernon Fiddlers was publicized in great detail in a pair of articles in the *Vernon Record*. The first of these articles appeared at the bottom of the front page of that newspaper on September 12, 1919. I will give the complete text of the article because it offers a good picture of the flowery and aggressive flavor of Dr. Howard's rhetoric and of his love of fiddling.

> **WILL FIDDLE IN GEORGIA. Vernon Musicians Going to Confederate Reunion in Atlanta Next Month to Bring Home Honors.**
>
> Vernon Fiddlers will invade the Old South next month when Dr. A. P. Howard, Eck Robertson and Louis Franklin go to Atlanta, Georgia to attend the Confederate Reunion. Uncle Henry Gilliland of Altus, Okla., president of the Old Fiddlers' Association of four states, Mose Bonner and J. K. P. Harris of Maryneal will also go along in the Texas party.
>
> "Georgia fiddlers are lined up and have challenged the world," says Dr. A. P. Howard. "Old John Carson has been playing in North Georgia for forty years, and they think he is the best fiddler in the world. It is up to us to 'show them.'"
>
> Dr. Howard insists that his party [here, he means specifically Eck] can beat the world playing "Sally Gooden," and he says if necessary the Texans have $100,000 to back up this belief. Fiddles worth $45,000 will be carried to Atlanta, Dr. Howard says.

The second, much longer article appeared in that paper on October 14, 1919, on pages 1–2:

> **VERNON FIDDLERS CAN'T FIND PLACE TO MEET GEORGIANS**
> **No Place Available in Atlanta That Was Big Enough For Combat They Expected to Stage—Dr. Howard Challenged Easterners to Come to Texas, Expenses Paid if They Won.**
>
> Atlanta, Ga. and the Confederate Reunion are paying considerable attention to the fiddlers from Texas. The party includes Dr. A. P. Howard, Eck Robertson, and Louis Franklin of Vernon; John W. Barnes and Mose Bonner of Fort Worth; Henry C. Gilliland of Altus, Okla., and George F. Barnes, champion banjo picker.

Their pictures are shown in Friday's *Atlanta Constitution*, along with that of Fiddling John Carson, champion of Georgia, and they were said to be carrying $40,000 worth of fiddles. The following is taken from *The Constitution* of that date:

"They wouldn't let us pull off the big battle in the Auditorium," declared Dr. A. P. Howard, millionaire leader of the braves from the west, "and there is no other place in this town big enough for a scrap like my boys were going to put up. So we decided to issue a challenge to all fiddlers to meet us in Texas, expenses paid by us if we lose, and you can back on it that we don't make any foolish promises."

"Fiddling John" Carson, the leader of the Georgia fiddlers, was crestfallen Thursday morning over the fact that no place could be found in which to stage the fiddling bout. "Of course they have fine fiddlers," said John, "but we have fine fiddlers, too, and were much in hopes that we would have a chance to show them some real fiddling."

Thursday's *Atlanta Constitution* had the challenge from the Texans and the following writeup:

Issuing a challenge to all artists of the horsehair bow in the Sunny South, Dr. A. P. Howard, a millionaire of Texas, has arrived in Atlanta with a $25,000 fiddle, and a band of confederate veterans, Indian fighters, cowpunchers and former gunmen, all of whom have won their laurels on the musical battle grounds of the west.

Armed with his Stradivarius violin, Dr. Howard proposes to lead his bowmen against an equal number of southern fiddlers, under the leadership of "Fiddlin'" John Carson, champion of Georgia, and he freely declares that when east meets west before the big gathering of confederate veterans at the Auditorium tonight, no one present will doubt that a real scrap is in progress.

Dr. Howard declares his men are all undisputed champions of their several western states, and he is confident of their ability to win hands down against the fiddlers of the east.

"All we ask is a range big enough for a battleground, a place big enough sidewise to bring off the big tuneful scrap, and we promise the people of this city the most interestin' contest since the battle of Atlanta," said he. "We challenge the whole south for fiddlin' and banjo pickin'—anybody that can pull horsehair across catgut. We have our stingers out and are here to win or lose, but we don't expect to go back to Texas without some Georgia Scalps."

Carson Retorts

"Fiddling" John Carson, who is the champion of Georgia, has been placed on the defensive because of the invasion of his precincts because of the invasion of the western fiddlers. He heard the defiance of his antagonist, and spit out his quid to make the following retort:

"That's all right. That Texas bunch may beat us branding horses and riding steers, but when it comes to making corn likker, and coaxin' real music out of a fiddle, they'll have to be goin' some. We have heard about yo' $25,000 fiddle, too, but, Doc, hit ain't what they cost, it's how you play 'em."

Then both leaders named the men who would stand behind them in the big contest, and the war was on. Nothing is left to do but to settle the rules of battle and name the judges.

Visiting Fiddlers.

Dr. Howard then named the following members of his band, with the titles they have won:

Henry C. Gilliland, of Altus, Oklahoma, 74 years of age, and a famous Indian fighter of the frontier days. He is also the president of the Fiddlers' Association of Texas, Oklahoma, New Mexico, and Arkansas, and one of the champion fiddlers of the south.

Mr. Barnes, a confederate veteran of Fort Worth, Texas, and champion, 67-year-old fiddler.

Comanche Frank [Lewis Franklin], one-eighth Comanche Indian, left-handed champion fiddler of the United States, who challenges all comers to left-handed fiddling.

"Sallie" [Eck] Robertson, who is claimed to be the world's best breakdown fiddler of the country. "In fact," declared Dr. Howard, "there is a bet of $1000 already up on this man, and we can accommodate any man with money. We will give all the action any one wants on one or a hundred tunes.

Frank Barnes, banjo picker, who challenges the whole country for banjo picking, either "single-handed or solo playing."

For buck and wing dancing, M. J. Bonner, 75 years old, of Fort Worth, Texas, is pitted against any man in the United States his age.

Naming the men who would aid him in the big musical scrap against the westerners, "Fiddling" John Carson told off [sic] the following Georgia fiddlers, who have gathered in the city for the syncopated fray:

"Long Tom" Deal, Gid Tanner, "Shorty" Harper, "Laughing Ben" Singer, "Big Earl" Johnston, of Rabun county, Bill Williams of Talking Rock, "Uncle" Bill Byers of Ball Ground, "Banjo Pickin' Bill" from Cedartown, "Shorty" Blackwell of Columbus, and "Kid the Fiddler," "who is only 17 years old, but who pulls some bow."

Rules of Contest

The rules of the contest, as framed so far, include "Honest to God Fiddlin," the young men 'gainst the old, the result being left to three judges, who will be named from three states.

Dr. A. P. Howard, who is leading the western fiddlers, and who presents the striking appearance of a movie actor, comes from Vernon, Texas, where he recently struck an oil gusher. A lover of fiddles, he has a number of very valuable instruments, some of which are of the rarest makes. "I resent that word violin," said he, "because it makes me think of Ber-lin."

Dr. Howard then told of the $25,000 instrument he has brought with him to the city, a genuine "Strad." This violin is very old, and was found several years ago in the attic of an old Norway barn, where it was roughly wrapped in a ragged bundle.

Dr. Howard is spoken of by the members of his musical band as a man of extreme generosity, and his followers claim that he insists upon seeing them through the big contest that is to be staged against the Georgia fiddlers, paying all expenses and seeing that all are made comfortable.

Thus, this remarkably detailed and informative early newspaper article about a fiddle competition concerned an event that would not take place! But the publicity surrounding it is rich in information about the fiddling environment in Texas of that time, and certainly about Eck and the fiddlers whom he got to know in Vernon. Eck spent a great deal of time and shared several highly publicized trips with that flamboyant leader of the Vernon Fiddlers, Dr. Abner Perry Howard Jr. (born Feb. 27, 1870, Longview, TX; died Feb. 17, 1952, Vernon, TX). One of Howard's daughters wrote a memorial that is now available on findagrave.com: "Dr. A. P. Howard was a very colorful character, having the whitest hair and the largest diamond in all Wilbarger County. He played the violin with a band, graduated from Tulane University New Orleans in 1903, practiced medicine in several cities in Texas, often trading his services for chickens. He was a wonderfully interesting person."

Dr. Howard's birthplace of Longview is 130 miles east of Dallas; like Eck, he was a transplant from the formerly fertile lands of East Texas to the even more challenging agricultural environment of the Panhandle. The 1870 census notes that Howard was the youngest of eight surviving siblings, and that his father was a farmer. We cannot find him in the 1890 census (since most of that census was lost to fire) nor in that of 1900; he was then studying medicine at Tulane. By 1910 he had become the town physician in Vernon. His wife Lizzie owned their house; they had three daughters and a son. The name he gave to the census taker in 1910 was a flippant fiction: "Admiral P. Howard." The family's houses in 1910, 1920, and 1930 were respectively on Pease St., E. Wilbarger St., and finally at 1718 Bowie St.—all nice downtown locations, probably within two blocks of each other (none of the buildings survive). The 1930 census assessed the Bowie Street house as being worth $5,000, which was on a par with houses owned by other Vernon worthies—a furniture store owner, a grocer, a painter, a blacksmith. Thus, this was a good middle-class home, perhaps not measuring up to what we would expect for the town doctor, but substantial and respectable. Dr. Howard spent quite a bit supporting the

Vernon Fiddlers, which became a costly hobby. The 1920s were the peak of his affluence and of his activity talking about fiddling and playing with Eck and with Lewis Franklin. That 1930 census notes that he was retired, and that a lodger, one J. A. Pressley (aged forty-five), was in "general practice," doubtless having taken over Howard's function as town doctor. But Howard could not afford to stay completely retired: the 1940 census lists him as an office worker in a drug store.

Dr. Howard was certainly a flashy character, and evidently quite a generous patron of fiddling in Vernon. He hosted both jams and more formal fiddling events on the porch of his home, and financed trips taken by the Vernon Fiddlers; dabbling in the oil business seems to have worked out for him. Was it unusual for him to claim to own very valuable violins? Newspaper articles about both fiddlers and violinists frequently specified high values for instruments. On several occasions when violinist David Rubinoff was mentioned in Texas newspapers, his playing a "$100,000 Stradivarius" was specified (for example, *Amarillo Daily News*, December 8, 1939). Let us keep in mind that the Stradivarius "worth $25,000" that Howard owned "had been found several years ago in the attic of an old Norway barn" (*Vernon Record*, October 14, 1919, 1–2). Ole Evensen, an immigrant farmer living in Olustee, OK—about thirty miles north of Vernon—had worked on violins in his native Norway, and stayed with Howard in Vernon on occasion (*Vernon Record*, April 2, 1918). It's tempting to think that Evensen cleared a substantial profit by selling a Black Forest Strad copy to Howard (that part of Germany was rich in luthiers). We will visit Evensen again later in this book.

Fox News came to Vernon in 1922—supposedly to film the Vernon fiddlers playing on Howard's porch (all three fiddlers wearing cowboy garb). A reporter for the *Vernon Record* said that Howard was playing a violin made by "Nicolaus Amatus" (Nicola Amati) "valued at $20,000" (March 21, 1922, 3). In addition, Eck was playing his [probably Sears copy of] Stainer, and Lewis Franklin a "Cordavora." But the connection between Ole Evensen and Dr. Howard must have been behind this last instrument, which in a previous article was said to have been owned by Howard. This earlier article is reproduced in figure 16. Howard waxed eloquent about two of his instruments in the last two paragraphs of that essay, and used the interview as an opportunity to echo several of his themes:

> Prof. Carl Venth was a guest at my home last spring and said they were first class, and would pass any musical conservatory in the world. I may add that he liked the "Strad" better than he did the Amati. The incentive of this letter is to let all those who are interested in violins and "fiddling" that Vernon has, we thing [sic], the best "fiddles" and "fiddlers" of any place in Texas. Therefore I suggest a contest to see who really is the best fiddler playing the old-time tunes. I have only two here besides myself, and we

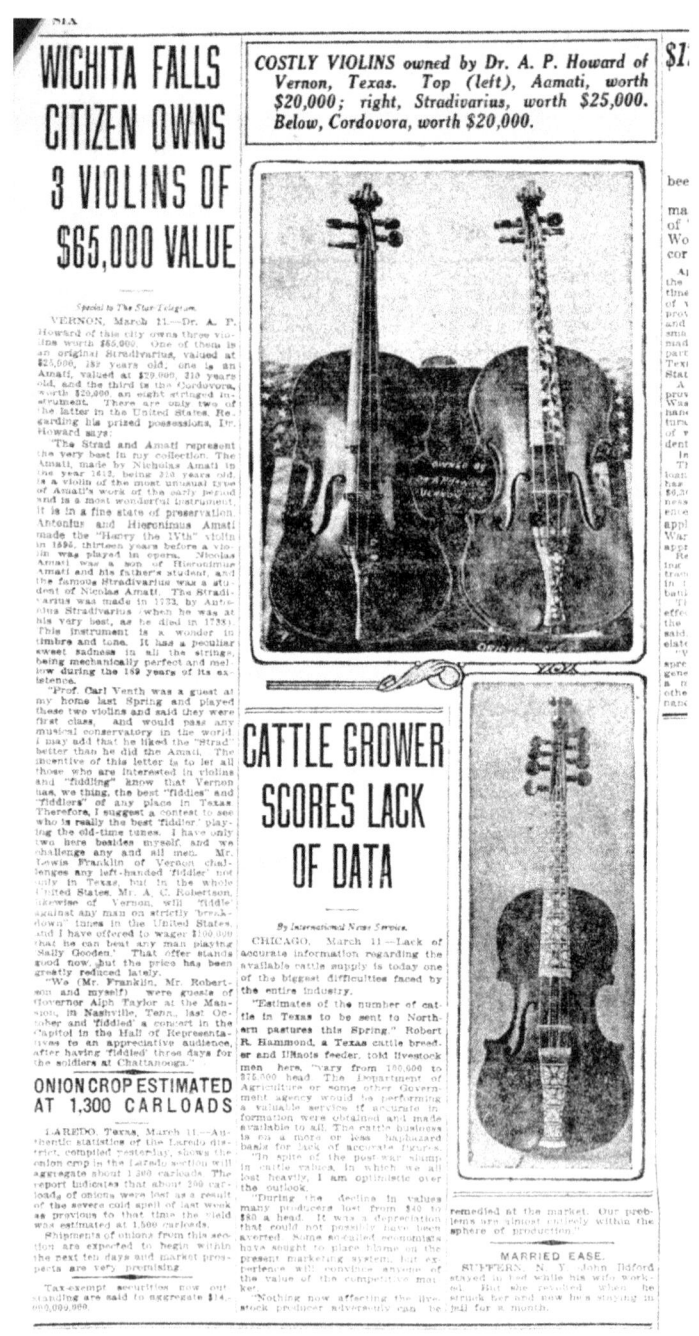

Figure 16. Violins belonging to Dr. A. P. Howard of Vernon. This town physician and oil mogul led the Vernon Fiddlers during the time Eck lived in Vernon (*Fort Worth Texas Star-Telegram*, March 12, 1922).

challenge any and all men. Mr. Lewis Franklin of Vernon challenges any left-handed fiddler not only in Texas, but in the whole United States. Mr. A. C. Robertson, likewise of Vernon, will fiddle against any man strictly on "breakdown" tunes in the United States, and I have offered to wager $100,000 that he can beat any man playing "Sally Gooden." That offer stands good now, but the price has been greatly reduced lately.

We (Mr. Franklin, Mr. Robertson, and myself) were guests of Governor Alph Taylor at the Mansion, in Nashville, Tenn., last October, and "fiddled" a concert in the Capitol in the Hall of Representatives to an appreciative audience, after having "fiddled" three days for the soldiers at Chattanooga.

I suppose that there is a miniscule chance that the two violins Howard chose to mention in the interview were legitimate examples of the fine work of Amati and Stradivari, but more likely that these loftily named instruments were among the plenty of dutiful, fairly convincing copies that were coming out of southern Germany at that time. However, it is the third instrument, the "Cordovora," that remains the most intriguing. I don't know where Howard got the sobriquet "Cordovora" for what is decorated and equipped in the manner of a *hardingfele* (Hardanger fiddle), a Norwegian cousin of the violin. Howard must have gotten his hardingfele from Norwegian immigrant Evensen. Did Howard ever learn to play it? Probably not; that is likely why it was soon passed on to a better fiddler in the group. That fiddler, the third regular member of the Vernon Fiddlers, Lewis Franklin, was well known as a musician; I never learned of any other profession he pursued. Franklin competed in plenty of fiddle contests, traveled with the Vernon Fiddlers in the well-publicized 1919 trip (in the article just cited, it must have been he who was referred to as "Comanche Frank," a "one-eighth Comanche left-handed fiddler"). Franklin traveled with Dr. Howard and Eck to other Confederate reunions. He was inactive for some time after 1937, after he shot his landlady in Chillicothe (seventeen miles northwest of Vernon). She was a childless widow running a small boarding house; a dispute over his borrowing her car had escalated into violence. Franklin was sentenced to life for the murder (*Quanah Tribune Chief*, October 15, 1937), but was again competing in fiddle contests by 1953 (*Lubbock Avalanche Journal*, June 21, 1953). He had been among the oldest ten of some 2,500 prisoners in jail in Huntsville. His parole may have been inspired by his age (in the 1940 census of the prison, he was said to have been sixty-seven years old) and his frailty (in his trial, his defense was based on his allegedly having paresis, a mild paralysis that affected his judgment [*Quanah Tribune Chief*, October 15, 1937]).

The article about the affair constitutes the most substantial writing about Franklin. Much of the reportage concerns Franklin's crime and the arrest process. Here is the lengthy title of this contribution, and the tiny bit left of the article after the details of the shooting and its aftermath are excised:

Lewis Franklin Charged in Chillicothe Slaying
　WIDELY KNOWN MUSICIAN IS HELD IN CASE
　Mrs. Cora Houston Slain Following Quarrel with Man. Victim Was Resident of Hardemon County for Past 30 Years.

Mrs. Houston . . . had operated a boarding house where Franklin had been a resident for the past several years. . . .

Franklin is a widely known musician in this section. He has resided in Wilbarger and Hardeman counties for many years. Franklin has been in demand for many square dance orchestras throughout his life. He plays the violin with his left hand. . . . Sam Hysmith, a friend of Mrs. Houston . . . told them a quarrel between Mrs. Houston and Franklin preceded the affray. Hysmith and Franklin had just returned from Vernon where they had gone in Mrs. Houston's automobile, Hysmith said, and it was about this that the quarrel was said to have begun."

ECK AT CONFEDERATE REUNIONS AND AT THE TRI-STATE FAIR

The lengthily advertised 1919 Atlanta trip that in the end did not result in a direct contest of the Vernon Fiddlers (and friends) versus John Carson and his fleet of Georgia fiddlers had a significant, contrasting initial purpose. The Vernon contingent played at the annual meeting of the United Confederate Veterans, held that year in Atlanta. This organization was a late nineteenth-century conflation of smaller Confederate clubs. It flourished from 1890 through about 1930, sponsoring annual meetings in different southern cities, with a last small gathering being held in 1951. Each of these meetings drew tens of thousands of veterans in the early years, and more tens of thousands of relatives and friends. The gatherings featured ceremonies during the day that were stuffed with rhetoric that, on the one hand, celebrated national unity but, without obvious irony, reiterated confederate dogma and justifications. Music punctuated the speeches. Days started with a trumpet call, brass band renditions of "Dixie," and a group called the Confederate Choir singing standards such as "Tenting Tonight." The thirtieth reunion was also regaled by church choirs from the host city, Houston, singing these hymns: "How Firm a Foundation," "Lead, Kindly Light," and "God Be With You Till We Meet Again" (United Confederate Veterans 1920, 3–5).

Every evening during these reunions ended with a dance—that is when Eck and various fellow fiddlers took the stage. He went with Dr. Howard to the reunion in 1918 in Tulsa, Oklahoma. The *Vernon Record* celebrated their return: "Dr. A. P. Howard and A. C. Robertson returned Wednesday from Wichita, Kansas, where they played at the opening of the Kansas Wheat Show, an event which Dr. Howard says draws many thousands of visitors. They also played for the Ex-Confederates at Tulsa, Okla. 'Old Soldiers danced the Virginia Reel, had 'buck and wing' contests, and acted like youngsters in general when we got to playing,' Dr. Howard says. The two men brought home a gold signet ring each, which was given them for fiddling 'Arkansas Traveler' and 'Billy in the Low Grounds'" (October 8, 1918). (Please remember that the spellings "Arkansas Traveler" and "Arkansas Traveller" are both correct and both often found. I will replicate how that title appears in each source quoted.)

Eck, Dr. Howard, and Lewis Franklin went to the 1919 reunion and to the 1921 reunion, which was in Chattanooga, Tennessee. The total party from Vernon and the rest of Wilbarger County on that trip was about fifty veterans, family members, and miscellaneous other participants including these three fiddlers. On the train to Chattanooga, they met, socialized, and played tunes with a notable fellow passenger, Governor Alf Taylor of Tennessee, also a fiddler (and a loud talker about fiddling, too, along the lines of Dr. Howard; *Vernon Record*, October 25, 1921). At the reunion, Governor Taylor recruited an eighty-year-old veteran to accompany the four fiddlers on piano. The Governor led off with "Dixie"; the last tune was "Arkansaw Traveller" (*Vernon Record*, November 4, 1921).

Eck and veteran Henry Gilliland fiddled at the 1922 Confederate Reunion in Richmond. It was in connection with this journey that Eck and Gilliland traveled to New York. Their pair of brief recording sessions with Victor—on June 30 and July 1—were described in the Victor catalog of April 1923 (page 8; Victor was evidently not in a big hurry to market the results):

> One day, not so many months ago, two Southwesterners blew into our laboratory and told us they could play the fiddle. Now we know an awful lot of people who can play fiddle, so we weren't impressed. Here is their first record. Eck made "Sallie Gooden" alone—a medley of jigs and reels, in the very best style of the travelling cowboy fiddler, with almost continuous double stopping, one string being used for a kind of bag-pipe drone bass, and the other to carry the melody. In both numbers there is no accompaniment, none being needed. In the "Arkansas Traveller," you will realize that they are two of a kind, for Gilliland gets to it in as business-like a style as his partner.

Gilliland wore his Confederate uniform for the trip to New York and for meeting with the Victor authorities, then donned his Altus, Oklahoma, judge's suit for the Victor catalog photo. He was asserting two aspects of his identity outside of his musical activity. Eck wore what had become his usual performing clothes, a cowboy outfit. How had that fit with the Confederate event in Richmond? In fact, Confederate gatherings in the Texas Panhandle had long been also infused with the cowboy theme. The first all-Panhandle Confederate veterans reunion took place in 1893. The continuation of that event in 1899 was called a "Confederate and Cowboy Reunion," and advertised as "the best yet, with free grass, water, and music by the [Amarillo] Brass Band." Starting in 1901, such joint-themed reunions were held near Canyon (thirty miles south of Amarillo) on the T-Anchor Ranch, then were moved to the Opera House of Glenwood Park until the Opera House burned in 1915 (Key 1972, 234).

The era of cowboy-led cattle drives in the Panhandle was short and not so far in the past—the mid-1870s through mid-1890s (the early 1870s had been devoted primarily to hunting buffalo). But in the Panhandle, as everywhere in the west, cowboy memories and the cowboy image were every bit as powerful as the reality had been fleeting. And that image had quite a bit in common with that of the confederate soldier—danger and privation eased by practical alliances and comradeship with other strong men. Nostalgia for the recent past of the cowboy and nostalgia for the more distant past of the southern soldier were compatible feelings, and meshed easily in practice. Fiddlers at these events—many or most of them senior citizens—and the older members of their audiences may have been hearkening back simultaneously to profoundly misty early times, but certainly were also revisiting their own young days. Of course, when accomplishing this, they exaggerated and filtered their memories in the inevitable and psychologically handy patterns of nostalgia, but there was an actual personal connection with some of the referenced past on the part of many of the older celebrants.

The rules of the grand fiddle face-off in Atlanta that didn't happen didn't occupy much of the rhetoric circulating about that prospective contest. Only one description of style did concern authenticity—it would be "Honest to God Fiddlin'"—and another phrase concerned preventing favoritism in awarding scores: "the result being left to three judges, who will be named from three states." Both factors were in line with the time; these early fiddle contests relied on multiple compatible opinions of what good fiddling sounded like, and audiences were wary of judging that might be unfair due to personal connections or community loyalties.

An article published in the *Houston Daily Post* of December 9, 1899, described an upcoming contest:

COMBAT OF FIDDLERS.
Old Musicians will Appear at the Real Estate Convention.

Fort Worth, Texas, Dec. 8.—as per announcement sent out some days ago, the secretary of the Texas State Real Estate convention is arranging for a grand reunion and concert of fiddlers to be pulled off during their convention in Fort Worth, January 16 and 17 next. All lovers of the string and bow over the State are invited to attend and participate in the affair. The evening of the first day of the convention is the time fixed and the audience will no doubt be well entertained for an hour or so, after which the regular order of business will proceed.

There will be prizes for the best player of all the old tunes, for the tallest fiddler, the shortest fiddler, the fattest fiddler, for the leanest fiddler, the oldest and the youngest, the one playing the oldest violin, the one playing in the greatest number of positions, the one with the biggest feet, the one dancing best to his own music.

Three judges selected from the audience will decide the contest. All those who may enter the contest will please send in their names as early as possible.

Contests near Vernon during the 1920s were of various sizes and levels of formality; Eck participated in many. I will cite three contrasting examples. First, from the *Vernon Record*, July 18, 1922, 19: "Ice Cream Supper at Rayland Thursday Night." Dr. Howard and Eck were hired to entertain at this event, which, like a supper two weeks earlier, included a fiddle contest (not described further; it must have been small—Rayland is a neighborhood about twenty miles WSW of Vernon). Second, also mentioned in the *Vernon Record*, March 23, 1923, 2: "Famous Fiddlers Back from Tour. Met with Success in Contest with Fiddlers from Other Towns." This article reports that the "Dixie Fiddlers" (the Vernon Fiddlers, renamed) were in Cleburne for a faceoff with "Sam Peacock and his gang of bow-pullers in the local Carnegie Library." Peacock, a barber living in Cleburne, led "Smith's Garage Fiddle Band," which made the first recording of "Beaumont Rag." The author of the article noted that "several old timers . . . proved they had not forgotten how to shake a wicked foot." Third, here is an announcement that mentions a contest broadcast on radio (*Vernon Daily Record* (January 1, 1926, 1):

Vernon Fiddlers Send Challenge Three Winners

Vernon's Dixie Fiddlers are challenging the winners in the big fiddle contest that took place over the radio New Year's Eve, New Years at the Jefferson City, Mo. Radio station WOS according to Dr. A. P. Howard, manager of the local artists.

Sixty-three fiddlers played in the big contest Thursday night, and the winners are to be decided by vote of the radio fans. The Doctor is sure that his Dixie Fiddlers can beat them at every turn.

All the old tunes of long ago were heard over the radio, and many listened in for the old time dance program. Telegrams were received from all over the United States and requests for old square dance music were received.

The following telegram was sent to the Jefferson Station by Dr. Howard:

"Program good. We vote for No. 18, 'Mosquito Parade.' Play 'Rag Time Annie.' We challenge the three winners of the contest, also Henry Ford's fiddler, of Maine, and Bob Pyron of Battle Creek, Mich., for a duel in the last ditch, with the fiddle and the bow.

THE DIXIE FIDDLERS

Dr. A. P. Howard, Mgr."

The longest newspaper articles concerning Panhandle fiddle contests of this era advertised or commented on the Tri-State Fair, held in Amarillo in 1928. Contest publicity emphasized the historical link between cowboy life and fiddling. These articles, which are so packed with fascinating information that I cannot resist reproducing them in full, appeared in the *Amarillo Daily News*, the first on March 13, 1928:

OLD FIDDLERS' CONTEST HERE WILL BE GREAT

COWBOYS OF YEARS AGO HAD CHANCE TO LEARN, SAYS DR. O. H. LOYD

A letter giving detailed plans for the Old Fiddlers' contest, which will be held here March 20, under auspices of the Tri-State Fair association, has been received by The News-Globe from Dr. O. H. Loyd of Vega, who will direct the program.

Dr. Loyd declares that the program will consist of a real demonstration of "old-time fiddling" such as Panhandle people have not heard since the days of the cowboys. He also lauds the Amarillo Tri-State exposition as a worthy institution and encourages Panhandle people to support it. His letter in full follows:

"The All-Panhandle Old Fiddlers' contest which is being held in the city auditorium at Amarillo on Tuesday night, March 20, is sponsored by officials of the Tri-State Fair association, and the proceeds will go to aid in paying off the indebtedness of that institution.

Most of the Panhandle counties are taking an active interest in the old fiddlers' contest and will, by elimination contests or otherwise, send the very best fiddlers in every interested county to compete, thereby giving those who attend an opportunity to hear in one evening all the real old fiddlers in this whole country.

Some Real Fiddling.

And if one ever heard "fiddling," he will hear it that night. The cowboys who were youths twenty to forty years ago are old men now. As young men, their only companion many a lonely night was an old violin. And when they sat and looked at the bare walls of their little huts or dugouts, they heard their fiddles talk as they could not have done had company been present.

These conditions developed some of the best fiddlers that on the Plains ever attempted to draw a bow. They played for the old square dance to which lads and lassies would ride bucking broncs as far as fifty miles to attend. Where is there an old cowboy who does not remember these dances and long to be at one again.

Cattlemen who attend the convention in Amarillo next week can not go back to those days, but these fiddlers will bring back memories to them that will be worthwhile.

This entertainment will not be staged as an up-to-the-minute city affair, but will be conducted as an oldtime, cowboy, frontline contest such as has never been attempted and which probably will never again have an equal. Some of these old fiddlers were contemporaries of Bob and Alf Taylor of Tennessee fame, and had opportunity offered would have likely been as famous as they, although these men fiddled themselves into the highest places their state had to offer.

Many Are Broadcast.

Many old fiddlers' contests have gone out over the air recently. But none will equal the one on March 20, because these fiddlers will be seen and heard. The crowds will inspire the best that is in each contestant, and premiums as high as $100 for first prize will somewhat compensate that [sic] who fiddle. It will be a great program for the artist and the hearer.

Selections played will be the real folk songs of the past generations.

Every person who is interested in the development of this great Panhandle country should lend every possible assistance to the men who are so liberally giving of their time and energy to make a success of the Tri-State fair, and should, therefore, make it a point to attend the old fiddlers' contest.

The Tri-State fair will someday mean to Amarillo what the Dallas State fair has meant to Dallas. Nearly forty years ago a few of the far-seeing men of Dallas organized the corporation that sponsored the Dallas fair and struggled to keep it alive when many criticized them for the undertaking. It has been one of the greatest factors in building a city of Dallas. The institution today is self-supporting. It has one of the finest parks in the South, and the fair is the greatest state fair in the United States.

Win Numerous Prizes.

There is not a county in the state that has not at some time brought home ribbons from the Dallas fair that had a tendency to stimulate the home people to greater efforts. The exhibits have advertised the counties to the outside world in a manner that could not have been accomplished in any other way.

As an example, Oldham county last year exhibited its apples from Old Tascosa, winning blue ribbons as fast as they have been shown. As a result of this, some day apple orchards will be planted along the Canadian River that will feed the Southwest on the most delicious apples that can be found.

What Dallas has done with her fair, Amarillo can do with the Tri-State fair, especially when approximately 75 per cent of all the blue ribbons given at the Dallas fair come to the Panhandle.

From the *Amarillo Daily News*, March 14, 1928:

DR. LOYD TELLS RADIO FANS OF FIDDLING DAYS
   TWO ADDRESSES ON AIR ADVERTISE CONTEST TO BE HELD HERE SOON.

Dr. O. H. Loyd of Vega, director of the Tri-State fair and who will have charge of the Old Fiddlers' contest to be held under auspices of the fair association in the Auditorium on March 20, spoke over two Amarillo radio stations yesterday.

At 10 o'clock Dr. Loyd talked on the contest and the fair on Station KGRS and at noon from Station WDAG.

His radio speech, in part, follows:

"The Old Fiddlers' contest, which is to be held in the Auditorium at Amarillo Tuesday night, had its birth in the fertile brains of the Amarillo Board of City Development. It is now taken over and sponsored by the Tri-State Fair Association. The receipts of this contest will go toward financing the fair association. Admission charges will be 50 cents, 75 cents and $1.

[urges support, citing example of success of fair in Dallas]

First: Each contestant will draw his place by lot before the program giving him his place number of appearance.

Second: Each contestant shall be 40 years old or over [adds: *but not over one hundred ten* in an edited version of these rules for this same contest given in the *Amarillo Sunday News Globe* on March 18, 9].

Third: Each contestant shall play one piece only, unless requested by the judges to play more, but each shall be required to have ready at least 5 selections [adds on Sunday: *for emergencies*].

Fourth: Each selection offered shall be not less than three minutes, nor longer than five minutes in length.

Fifth: Each contestant is to play old-fashioned music. Preferably quadrilles, as this is more closely associated with old time breakdown dance music.

Sixth: Each contestant is to be allowed not to exceed two accompanists.

Seven: In forming conclusions of the merit of each contestant, the judges shall use a percentage basis, taking 100 per cent as perfect [adds on Sunday: *and that no man is perfect*]. They shall judge each selection under its separate column, giving it the percentage that in their judgement it is entitled and the final total of these added percentages will show the winners in order. This shall be done by six men chosen in Amarillo, and will give what we believe to be the most just plan that could be had. If any ties should develop and the judges require then those who are tied for place shall play another selection, or until such tie is settled.

[Eight]: The judges shall at their discretion may use the applause of the audience in reaching a decision if it is deemed necessary.

Ninth: Applause of the audience shall have no influence over the judges, except in the stunt class, which will be settled in that way only [yes, contradicting rule #8].

Ten: Being an old fiddlers' contest, credit shall not be allowed to the modern jazz.

Eleven: Contortions of the body of the artist shall not be given undue credit, patting of feet, however, is justified.

Twelve: Each contestant shall furnish, by March 16, to Bob Emmett, fair secretary, information given his birth place, date of birth, his musical record, and latest available photos.

There shall be no appeal from the judges' decision.

Selections to be played by these men will be the real old folk songs of the past generation, and let me tell you in conclusion, that if you miss this entertainment that you will regret it, for the old boys are in proper trim to meet you.

An article the day of the contest noted that quite a few local merchants were adding goods from their stores to the cash prizes, as follows: Riggs Clothing Company, belt and buckle; Harry Holland, shirt; E. E. Finkles Electric company, pair cuff links; Amarillo Music company, fiddle bow; Diamond Shop, watch chain; Rubin's Toggery, tie; Panhandle Music Company, two old-time fiddle records; Great West Mill, 24-pound sack of Amaryllis flour; Ed Green, pair silk hose; E., H., and A. Davis, pair silk hose; Edwards Studio, photograph first winner; Hub Clothing company, belt and buckle; Kilough & Davis, shirt; Tolzien Music company, two old-time records; Red Star Milling company, 48 pounds flour, first, second, and third winners (*Amarillo Daily News*, March 28, 1928, 1 [!]).

The day after the contest, the results were announced. The winner was Louis [Lewis] Franklin of Wilbarger County, Eck's former companion in the Vernon Fiddlers. Concerning a subsequent contest, this article appeared in the *Amarillo Daily News*, April 28, 1928, 2:

Southpaw from New Mexico is Champ Fiddler

Thos. G. Crawford, of Carlsbad, Eddy co., N. M., Who handled the bow with his left hand, and braced the fiddle with his knee, was declared winner of the All-Panhandle Old Fiddlers' contest held at the city auditorium last night under auspices of the Tri-State Fair association.

Besides the cash prize of $100 for first place, Mr. Crawford is now champion fiddler of the Panhandle country, as near as a legitimate contest will decide. He played "Medley Hornpipe."

Babe Helton, Wheeler county entry, won second place and $50, and F. M. Beach of Hale County placed third. Other winners included W. E. Walling, Donley county; J. T. Marshall, Randall county; H. E. Welchel, Potter county; Babe Barker, Armstrong county; J. O. Kelly, Quay County, N. M., in the order named.

Eck Robertson, maker of Victor records and hailed as the champion fiddler of the world, arrived too late to enter competition. He was introduced, however, and together with his 9-year-old son, and gave a very popular demonstration of his fiddling ability. The Robertson chap carried off his banjo full of money that was raised among the listeners.

Felix [*sic*; this was Lewis] Franklin, winner of the recent contest held during the Cattlemen's convention, was another favorite absent.

The exhibition was considerably [considered] the greatest ever held in the Panhandle, and was well received by an audience of 2000.

"Another such exhibition could not be held any [other] place in the world," declared Dr. O. H. Floyd [Loyd], of Vega, director.

It was necessary for the fiddlers to play but one number each. Judges were selected from counties in the Panhandle who were not represented in the contest.

Stunt numbers were given by Hugh Roden of Amarillo and U. H. Bell of Vega. Mr. Roden gave an exhibition of fiddling that is seldom excelled on the vaudeville stage, playing the violin from more than a dozen different positions.

Popular numbers were given by Miss Anna Merrick, local violin instructor, who specializes in old-time fiddling.

Tom Connelly, candidate for the United States senate from Texas, was introduced from the stage and made a short talk.

Judges were: H. E. Hastings, Spearman; A. W. Allen, Stratford; C. P. Presley, Miami; Julius Weilding, Dumas; P. H. Hooks, Lubbock; P. D. Brown, Anson; P. H. Hooker, Lubbock; J. H. Dunning, Taboka; Lucky King, Post; and W. B. Knowles, Guymon.

The contestants and the numbers they played are given below:

> Charles Gouce, Parma County, "Drunkard's Hiccups."*
> J. T. Marshall, Randall county, "Fisher's Hornpipe."*
> E. W. Jackson, Swisher county, "Forked Deer."*
> John S. Ray, Crosby county, "Cotton-Eyed Joe."
> Jim Chapman, Deaf Smith county, "Fisher's Hornpipe."*
> Louis J. Propps, Roosevelt county, New Mexico, "Sally Goodin."*
> P. M. Beach, Hale county, "Tom and Jerry."*
> W. E. Walling, Donley county, "Arkansaw Traveler."*
> W. C. Massy, Chaves county, New Mexico, "Pretty Polly Ann."
> Milt Trout, Castro county, "Cattle in the Cane Break."*
> H. E. Whelchel, Potter county, "Sally Goodin."*
> J. O. Kelly, Quay county, New Mexico, "Stay All Night, Then Stay A Little Longer."
> Babe Barket, Armstrong county, "Tom and Jerry."*
> Babe Heleton, Wheeler county, "Jenny Nettle."
> W. D. Fulton, Ochiltree county, "Irish Washerwoman."*
> Joe McPherson, Lincoln county, New Mexico, "The Lone Star Trail."
> Thomas G. Crawford, Eddy county, New Mexico, "Medley Hornpipe."
> M. Murray, Collingsworth county, "Arkansaw Traveller."*
> R. I. Hunter, Dawson county, "Where are you Going, My Pretty Gal."

Eck played many of these tunes cited in this list. I placed an asterisk immediately after the name of each tune that I know to have been in his capacious repertoire. We see that Eck's choices of tunes to cultivate, his active repertoire, was right on target for fiddling at contests of his time and place. These events would remain a focus for his fiddling. The "Vernon Fiddlers" had been more of a club of allies than an ensemble in which each member had a complementary role during performances. At this point in his life, Eck was best known not as a band member, but rather as a solo fiddler, indeed a "champion" fiddler.

Figure 17. The Robertson family band, as constituted in early 1931. This ad was for a square dance (and likely concert before the dance) to be held at the University Club in Amarillo.

– Chapter 3 –

THE ROBERTSON FAMILY IN BORGER, THEN ECK IN AMARILLO

Eck and his family moved several times in short order during the mid- to late 1920s. A newspaper article published in the young town of Borger in May 1927 included the remark that he "still maintained Clarendon as his home" (*Borger Daily Herald*, May 17, 1927, 3). In that city, about 120 miles WNW of Vernon—on the direct route to Amarillo—he sold pianos of various types and pump organs, with the aid of his brother Vird. A fiddle contest announcement in early 1928 has him residing in Altus, Oklahoma, about thirty miles north of Vernon (*Amarillo Daily News*, April 26, 1928, 4), a town which also had been the home of Henry Gilliland, the much older fiddler and Confederate veteran with whom he had traveled to New York and made his very earliest commercial recordings. Altus is also quite near the land owned by Norwegian immigrant farmer and violin repairman Ole Evensen. In early 1929, Eck was residing in Lubbock again (*Lubbock Morning Avalanche*, March 5, 1929, 5). Then the 1930 census finds the family in Dallas, and identifies Eck as a "musician" in an "orchestra" (figure 18). An address was specified—4020 Swiss Avenue. I was pleased to come upon such precise information—might it be possible to visit a place where the Robertsons had lived? No. That address now rests, unused, somewhere within a parking lot for the Swiss Tower Apartments—housing for married students (and single students who are parents) working their way through Dallas Theological Seminary. We don't know what kind of "orchestra" Eck had joined in Dallas; my best guess would be that this would have been a dance band of perhaps six to ten members. In any case, the work—and the retreat to East Texas—was fleeting.

In 1931 the family was again in the Panhandle, but now in Borger, a particular sort of twentieth-century frontier town—an oil boom town—located about fifty miles northeast of Amarillo. An article in the *Borger Daily Herald* of Friday, May 18, 1928, 2, tells of an early visit Eck made to the area, during which he gave a concert and perhaps considered this area as a place to which to relocate, since his music store in Clarendon had

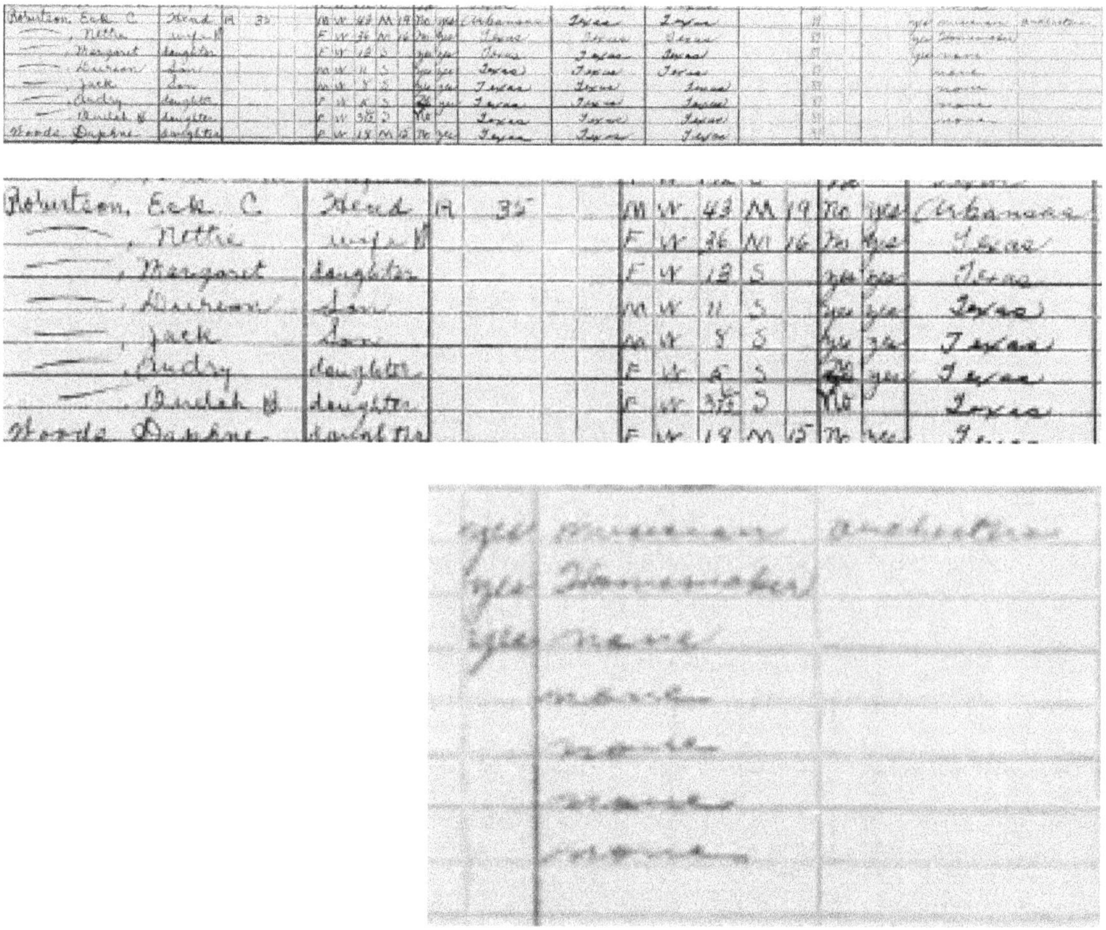

Robertson, Eck C.	Head	R	35	M	W	43	M	19	No	yes	Arkansas	yes	musician orchestra
—, Nettie	wife H			F	W	36	M	16	No	yes	Texas	yes	Homemaker
—, Margaret	daughter			F	W	13	S		yes	yes	Texas	yes	none
—, Harrison	Son			M	W	11	S		yes	yes	Texas		none
—, Jack	Son			M	W	8	S		yes	yes	Texas		none
—, Audry	daughter			F	W	6	S		yes	yes	Texas		none
—, Beulah M.	daughter			F	W	3 5/12	S		No		Texas		none
Woods, Daphne	daughter			F	W	18	M	15	No	yes	Texas		

Figure 18. The Robertson family in the 1930 census, living in Dallas; widescreen above closeups of left and then right sides of entry.

failed. Because Eck was interviewed for this extended article, and since he vigorously guided the course of any interview, his choices of topics for this article help flesh out the picture of what he then considered significant in his career. He was about to perform in Stinnett, a very small town a dozen miles north of Borger, at a concert under the auspices of the local Campfire Girls. The reporter penning the article stated that Eck was in the area to visit his daughter Odessa, who lived in Stinnett; she had married Caleb Owenby, a local tailor. In the course of the conversation, Eck noted that he was "not a violinist, [instead] just a fiddler." The reporter told his readers to expect to see Eck play "in more positions than imaginable"; this subcategory of trick fiddling was high on the list of thrills to come. Eck bragged that he had had the opportunity to perform in many prestigious settings, among them playing for the Oklahoma State Senate in 1927, when he had been in Oklahoma City for a four-day engagement at that city's Orpheum Theatre. He also presented a version of his oft-repeated story of making his first fiddle, on this occasion adding that the cat-hide top on the gourd instrument was eventually replaced with a pine board, and that he had obtained hair for his bow from the mane of a gray horse the family had owned. He mentioned his commercial recordings, and offered a short tune list that the *Daily Herald* reporter placed within a romanticized characterization of the fiddle repertoire:

> His best renditions and those that have won him fame and a living for a large family are the old time tunes such as "Turkey in the Straw," "Arkansaw Traveller," "Green Corn," "Billy in the Low Grounds," "Sally Goodin," and hundreds of others which have descended from the dim and distant past to the present without being written and without the knowledge of their origin other than the belief that they were inspired in the soul of fiddlers of hundreds of years ago.

Should the town of Borger as it flourished in the 1930s be thought of primarily as a notoriously rough-hewn boom town? Or was it a typical Plains city, that is, could it have near-instantaneously become parallel in demographics and behavior to the older towns around it? Enough drama filled its early story to attract both sober and sensationalist authors—respectively John T. White in "A Brief History of Hutchinson County, Texas" (1980) and Jane Snyder Agee in *Borger* (2012). I gathered up facts that both of these authors found notable for the following summary, and also encourage the reader to sample and enjoy the judiciously selected photographs and measured prose displayed at Hutchinson County's historical museum (made available in hutchinsoncountymuseum.org/stories/).

After the buffalo were largely extinct in the Panhandle, a few entrepreneurs realized that "if buffalo could survive, cattle could do well in the area" (White 1980, 16). Ranches bloomed. As late as 1890, what would soon become Hutchinson County was simply a huge grazing ground. In 1901, the county was officially organized, with a county seat of Plemons (populated by a single family bearing that name). In September 1918, the Panhandle's petrochemical boom began with a single successful well in Potter County (immediately south of Hutchinson County). In 1925 entrepreneurs A. P. "Ace" Borger and John R. Miller hatched a scheme for a new town; Ace Borger was experienced at this. The partners purchased 240 acres from a rancher, and mapped out a city. On March 8, 1926, the Borger Townsite Company opened for business, selling home and business lots advertised as being "in the heart of the Panhandle oil fields" (Henderson 1937, 21). Within ninety days, the population exceeded 35,000. The first train arrived on October 22. By that date, the town contained dozens of oil wells, thousands of cheap shacks, and a surfeit of saloons and whorehouses. But numerous school buildings and churches sprang up, too.

Eck relished describing the dark side of Borger, calling it "one of the roughest damn towns I ever saw in my life. Killings of all kinds going on there, and robberies and everything like that. Toughest damn place. And you hardly ever had a dance in a big hall there [when there] wouldn't be a big, bad fight—shoot and scrape or cut and scrape or something. Damnedest place I ever saw in the world at that time" (Seeger interview, 1963). Another citizen recalled "a bygone bar strip that rolled around the clock and caused midnight traffic jams" (Jaremko 2007).

The amount of corruption and violent crime in the brand new city was truly remarkable. Miller brought in a sheriff who was himself under indictment for murder in Oklahoma, Richard "Two-Gun Dick" Herwig, who ran his office essentially as a protection racket. Among Ace Borger's own focuses was operating a bank. After that enterprise failed, a bank employee murdered him. On September 13, 1929, courageous and honest District Attorney John A. Holmes was assassinated. Just two weeks later, on September 28, the governor declared martial law, and placed the Texas Rangers in charge of the city for an extended period (the first of two occasions when the Rangers would run the town). However, at the same time that rampant crime made the city infamous, many of the workers who flocked to the new town were solid citizens with families, men seeking prosperous but settled, civilized lives. It is true that young, single oil workers welcoming wild times packed many pages of the 1930 census, certainly enough of them to support a criminal populace tidily integrated with the city government. But complete families moving from other states filled other pages of the census. For instance, Harry V. Dice, a forty-two-year-old "driller," moved to Borger from West Virginia along with his wife and three children; and Therman J. Amos, a twenty-nine-year-old laborer, came with his wife and three young daughters from Arkansas. The Amos household included his wife's brother, Paul Pettigrew, aged twenty-two. Perhaps young Pettigrew was interested in participating in some wild moments, but the head of family listed in a neighboring entry, George Appel, a German tinner aged sixty-eight, likely was not (1930 Federal Census Texas>Hutchinson>Borger>District 0002). Laborer William R. Hunter, aged forty-three, was born in Texas, but had followed oil-related work in other states—the six Hunter kids were born in Oklahoma and Kansas. He and his wife Edith (aged thirty-nine, from Missouri) probably wanted a church to join, and certainly schools for their kids. In short, Borger was at least two cities in one, both a rough and raucous boom town and a placid, conservative village.

Could a traditional fiddler craft a career here as a performing musician? In 1937 Mary Henderson, a student at the young Texas Technological College (founded in 1925 in Lubbock), completed her master's thesis outlining "The History of Borger, Texas." She did not shrink from employing vivid prose, characterizing early Borger as "much like a festering sore upon the picturesque red hills of the Panhandle" (29) and "one of the most wicked little towns in the United States" (2). She mined an undated pamphlet written by local lawyer John H. White entitled "Borger at Night" that included a detailed description of the town's sonic environment:

> Noises of all sorts were to be heard. The pop of opening beer bottles—the roar of escaping gas from wells a few hundred feet away—the sound of the siren on an ambulance tearing by as fast as traffic would permit—the backfire of trucks and cars and occasional pistol shots—the indefinable jargon of human voices—a squabble between some man and woman, neither caring who heard—the clang of a lever from a slot machine—the continuous grinding away of an automatic piano—the blare of a half drunk jazz orchestra in one of the '49 dance halls ["49" referred to the spirit of the California Gold Rush of 1849]—the same old tune being constantly repeated on a phonograph—the struggle and cries of men fighting—the voices of "the law"—the whack of a pistol on some poor creature's head—the whine of some beggar wanting the price of a bed, but in most cases the money for another drink—all these and more sounds greeted the Borger night visitor in those days. (White n.d., quoted in Henderson 1937, 34)

Mr. White's lengthy roster of sounds regularly heard in the less reputable parts of town seems to been composed meticulously; it was intended to be not just colorful, but exhaustive. The sounds cited included numerous musical ingredients, but neither a fiddle nor a string band made it into White's voluminous list. At the same time, in the respectable part of town, a music club founded in 1928 performed versions of *Pinafore* (Gilbert and Sullivan's H. M. S. *Pinafore*) and *Carlotta* (probably one of the many adaptations of Gaston Leroux's 1910 novel *Le Fantôme de l'opéra*, *The Phantom of the Opera*; Henderson 1937, 77). These operettas probably had all female casts—unless the club stepped outside of its female membership for performers—and would have been accompanied on piano. In fact, pianos seemed to be everywhere, for sale, for rent, being played as often in civic clubs (Lions Club, PTA, Rotary Club, Twentieth-Century Club) as in night clubs, and so on. Already in late 1927, two piano teachers had advertised their services (*Borger Daily Herald*, September 18, 1927, 5 and October 7, 1927, 2) and a piano tuner had visited from Denver (*Borger Daily Herald*, August 15, 1927, 4).

By this time, records were being sold in Borger's music stores, and entertainment venues were busy—a seven-piece band called the Mohawk Aces were in residence at the Tokio Club (*Borger Daily Herald*, May 8, 1927, 4), run by Mattie Castlebury, an associate of Ace Borger who also maintained a fleet of women paid by the dance at her other club, The White Way. Were her regular protestations claiming that dancing was the extent of their professional activity valid? The Texas Rangers who were trying to eliminate criminal elements from the city thought not: they convinced

Castlebury to leave Borger in 1929. Nevertheless, members of her club's main musical ensemble, the Mohawk Aces, still appeared in the 1930 census of Borger. In many of their frequent stints at the Tokio Club, the Aces constituted the resident band that "battled" (took turns with) other guest jazz-oriented similarly-sized dance bands, including the Jazz Pirates Girl Band (*Pampa Daily News*, January 29, 1929), Blue Devils of Denver (*Pampa Daily News*, April 19, 1929), Oklahoma Vagabonds, and Amarillo Blue Boys. In short, this young, Janus-faced town supported not just a variety of musical activities in disreputable quarters, but also a rich, fully developed roster of activities in the cultivated sphere. In terms of the arts, Borger was never any kind of frontier, but rather a swiftly assembled fully mature city, at once comprehensively wicked and just as insistently virtuous. But traditional fiddling was not daily fare in either social environment.

Eck's professional activities did not find their way into books written about Borger, but do appear piecemeal in the *Borger Daily Herald* and other Panhandle newspapers, and in city directories. His most regular income was from piano tuning and from various chores involving bowed and plucked stringed instruments. In the city directory of 1934, he appeared as a "violinist" living in the "Mojo Apartments." But by 1936–37, he was listed instead as a "piano tuner" residing at 711 W. Monroe. He ran an ad in the *Borger Daily Herald* from October 25 through October 30, 1942, that read: "Notice: Eck Robertson, piano tuning, violin repairing, bow rehairing, 35 years' experience. Music teacher references. 310 West Wilson. Phone 646" (October 25, 7). This was after the family's initial stay in Borger, and also after he had lived in turn in Amarillo and Panhandle for a year or so; the ad announced a *return* to easy access to his services in Borger. The legions of pianos in use in Borger apparently kept him busy enough, and yielded sufficient income to support his family. But this was never where his heart lay. His realistic reclassification of his profession in successive volumes of the City Directory from "violinist" to "piano tuner" must have hurt. He would eventually face the inevitability of changing musical fashions, and would found a dance band likely resembling the Mohawk Aces in both personnel and repertoire, but this hadn't yet happened during the family's stint in Borger in the 1930s.

Back in the 1920s, when the Robertson family lived in Vernon, Eck's activity as a performer had been in two streams—as a soloist in fiddle contests and as a team member in the Vernon Fiddlers (later called the Dixie Fiddlers), the trio led by Dr. A. P. Howard. Eck and third member Lewis Franklin benefitted then from Howard's apparently tireless (and ineluctably loud) promotion of the group, and they must have welcomed his financial support of their travel. But I wonder if some friction seeped into the relationship between Howard and the others. Eck and Franklin did well at contests, but Howard's name rarely appears in competitor lists. His being the bombastic spokesman and administrative leader of the group—despite not being a strong performer—may have palled. In any case, Eck and his family left Vernon, made a handful of brief stops, and then settled in Borger. Eck continued to win prizes in fiddle contests, but his ensemble work was now as fiddler in and leader of the five-person family band. His wife Nettie had long served as an effective guitar accompanist, and several of their children had talent. When Eck returned to the recording studio in 1929, it would be with his family backing him.

ECK AND HIS FAMILY BAND

Eck's first public performances with family members other than his wife that are mentioned in surviving newspapers were with his elder son Dueron, who was generally billed as "Eck Jr." The two of them attended a contest in Amarillo in April 1928. As described in chapter 2, they arrived too late for the competition itself, but gathered up donations that rewarded the supplemental entertainment they presented (*Amarillo Daily News*, April 28, 1928, 2). The reporter waxing eloquent about the program in the Rex Theater in Stinnett the next month described "Eck Jr." as being half the show (*Borger Daily Herald*, May 18, 1928, 2). At the major contest at the Tri-State Fair in Amarillo the next year, Eck took first place with Dueron accompanying him (*Amarillo Daily News*, March 8, 1929, 1). Dueron would play tenor banjo in the family band; perhaps he accompanied Eck on this instrument at these contests.

What percentage of such events do we know about? The major Panhandle newspapers of the day have survived pretty well; I would guess that we can read about half or more of the events deemed worth advertising in them. However, plenty more playing for pay took place—making music for private parties, adding music to numerous silent movies, joining in contests at smaller venues in towns lacking newspapers, and so on. Eck, accompanied by either Nettie or increasingly Dueron, was playing regularly, and making some money doing so, even though the bulk of the family income came from piano tuning and the repairing of pianos and miscellaneous stringed instruments.

An article in the *Amarillo Daily News* in March 1929 advertised a fiddle program to take place in the municipal auditorium. The beginning of the article narrated an argument over the authorship of the "Amarillo Waltz"— was it Eck or not? This wasn't much of a controversy—there were two tunes with this title. After dismissing this non-topic, the reporter continued:

> Mr. Robertson is one of 12 old-time fiddlers who will take part in the special program at the Municipal Auditorium on March 27. He will be assisted by Eck, Jr., his ten-year-old son, who is a tenor and a banjo player [the reporter should have written "tenor banjo player"]. Miss Daphne, one

of his daughters, plays the guitar or mandolin and Miss Marguerite is a 12-year-old novelty dancer. Mrs. Robertson plays the guitar and the piano [Following those specifications, we can identify the family members in Figure 17 as, left to right, Nettie, Marguerite, Eck, Dueron, and Daphne].

Mr. Robertson suggested this snappy program for his family of five: "The Arkansas Traveller, [played by the] entire family; Amarillo Waltz, Barnyard Blues or Cackling Chicken; Eck, Jr. in song and banjo solo; Sally Goodin; Around the World on a Dime, Song; My Experiences on a Ranch [either a monologue or a skit with Dueron]; Done Gone, banjo and violin; Kelly Waltz; Pop Goes the Weasel; Waggoner; Novelty Dancing, by Miss Marguerite, [with] music by the entire family. (*Amarillo Daily News*, March 22, 1929, 3)

Most of the publicity of family performances is from 1929–31. The Robertsons were playing at events such as the concert in Stinnett, and making appearances as special entertainment at fiddle contests in which Eck was competing. I expect that the family band concertized briefly between competition brackets at those contests, in what is still an occasional daily format for such events. During those years, the Robertsons were the main such act in their part of the plains. William Rodgers and Hugh Roden, multi-instrumentalists and trick fiddlers, were the only alternative entertainment mentioned regularly in the *Amarillo Daily News*. In the Robertson family's live performances, young Dueron was especially important. He played his tenor banjo with verve, and loomed large in publicity of the band because he was viewed as a child prodigy, a role that has appealed to audiences for centuries. He must have been competent, though he seems not to have sought a career in music. He was intelligent and a hard worker, clearly destined for success in mainstream society. When Dueron transitioned into his own adult life and away from the music profession, the family band was done.

The last publicity for the family ensemble that I have seen was for a concert at the Robertson kids' high school in Borger in 1937. This short notice appeared in the *Amarillo Daily News*: "Hutchinson School Program is Tuesday. The variety program will feature Roy Rodgers and his accordion, novelty numbers on the handsaw, harmonica, tea-kettle, bottles and whistling numbers; Audrey Robertson tap-dancing; Dueron Robertson on the banjo, and Eck Robertson in several trick fiddling stunts" (March 8, 1937, 2). This program appears to have been shaped just like those given during breaks from competition at the Tri-State Contests. In addition, William Rodgers presented his one-man-band act (he had often collaborated with Hugh Roden at the Tri-State Fair; he would frequently work with Eck in the future).

I expect that we should imagine the last version of the Robertson family band as now being constituted much as pictured in figure 17, but with

Figure 19. Dueron Robertson, Eck and Nettie's elder son, decorated pilot in World War II.

Marguerite now grown and taking on Daphne's role (Daphne had married and left town), and with Audrey replacing Marguerite in the role of cute young dancer. And Dueron had become a young adult; he would graduate from high school the next year, the first in the family to do so.

In the 1930s and early 1940s, Eck and Nettie's marriage gradually unraveled. Their children grew up and moved away on a natural, predictable schedule. Eck toured alone and faced various temptations (Seeger interview). Dueron, who had become a star in high school as a staunch member of both the debate and football teams, launched into a respectable middle-class life outside of the immediate family orbit. After graduation he was able to find work in the oil business in Borger, which thrived even during the Great Depression, and he eventually settled into a white-collar job with the Republic Supplies Company (*Borger Daily Herald*, July 9, 1944, 1). By 1938 he was a prominent member of Borger's First Christian Church, belonged to its "Christian Endeavor" social and activist group, sang in a trio during some services, and even delivered invocations occasionally (*Borger Daily Herald*, May 1, 1941, 3).

World War II arrived. By mid-1942, Dueron and his younger brother Jack were in the armed services (*Borger Daily Herald*, November 15, 1942, 6, 10). Dueron joined the Air Force, and entered flight training in Phoenix. He married an Arizona girl on May 20, 1943, the day he received his commission (*Borger Daily Herald*, January 31, 1943, 10). He arrived in France in March 1944, flew a dozen hazardous missions, was promoted to first lieutenant, and was awarded the Air Medal (figure 19). He was flight leader of a P-38 Flight Group of the Allied Expeditionary Air Force when his plane did not return from a mission over Cherbourg. He was reported MIA in June 1944, two weeks after D-Day, and eventually presumed dead (*Borger Daily Herald*, June 9, 1944, and August 8, 1945). Eck could never quite face this then-all-too-commonplace tragedy, and gave credence to a conspiracy theory holding that Dueron might still be alive, but in some sort of confinement in Russia (Riggs/Nagy interview, 1962).

We don't know what combination of professional and personal stresses led to Eck and Nettie parting ways. Eck's own summary was short and straightforward: "That World War II is what separated us" (Seeger interview, 1963). The first surviving evidence of their parting is dramatic. The 1940 census found Eck boarding at the Mitchell House, a hotel in Amarillo (figure 20). But Nettie and the children who were still minors (plus a pair of grandchildren; their daughter Daphne had died) were residing in

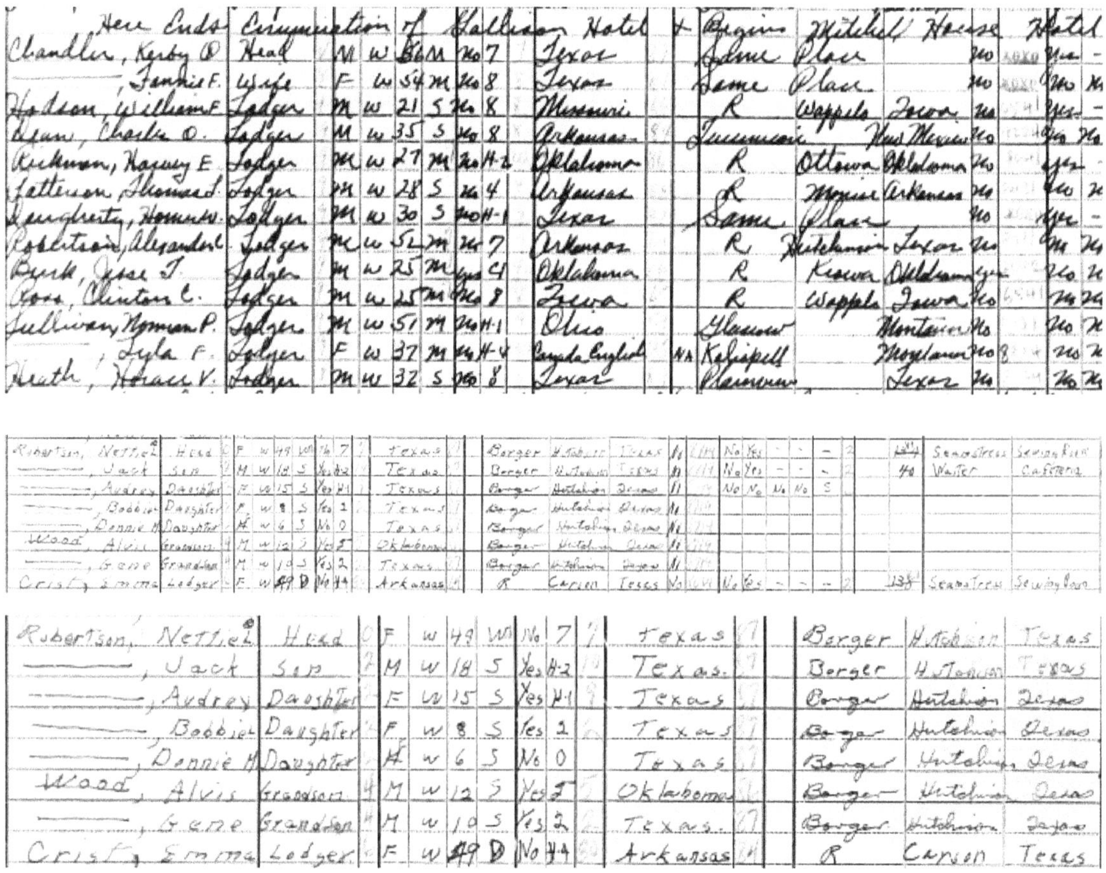

Here Ends Enumeration of Hallison Hotel & Begins Mitchell House Hotel

Chandler, Kerby D	Head	M	W	56	M	No	7	Texas	Same Place		No	Yes
, Fannie F.	Wife	F	W	54	M	No	8	Texas	Same Place		No	No
Hodson, William F	Lodger	M	W	21	S	No	8	Missouri	R	Wapello Iowa	No	Yes
Dean, Charles O.	Lodger	M	W	35	S	No	8	Arkansas	Tucumcari	New Mexico	No	No
Rickman, Harvey E	Lodger	M	W	27	M	No	H-2	Oklahoma	R	Ottawa Oklahoma	No	Yes
Patterson, Thomas	Lodger	M	W	28	S	No	4	Arkansas	R	Monroe Arkansas	No	No
Daugherty, Homer W.	Lodger	M	W	30	S	No	H-1	Texas	Same Place		No	Yes
Robertson, Alexander	Lodger	M	W	52	M	No	7	Arkansas	R	Hutchinson Texas	No	No
Burk, Jesse T.	Lodger	M	W	25	M	Yes	4	Oklahoma	R	Kiowa Oklahoma	Yes	No
Ross, Clinton C.	Lodger	M	W	25	M	No	8	Iowa	R	Wapello Iowa	No	No
Sullivan, Norman P.	Lodger	M	W	51	M	No	H-1	Ohio	Glasgow	Montana	No	No
, Lyla F.	Lodger	F	W	37	M	No	H-4	Canada English	Kalispell	Montana	No	No
Heath, Horace V.	Lodger	M	W	32	S	No	8	Texas	Plainview	Texas	No	No

Robertson, Nettie L	Head	F	W	49	Wd	No	7	Texas	Borger	Hutchinson	Texas
, Jack	Son	M	W	18	S	Yes	H-2	Texas	Borger	Hutchinson	Texas
, Audrey	Daughter	F	W	15	S	Yes	H-1	Texas	Borger	Hutchinson	Texas
, Bobbie	Daughter	F	W	8	S	Yes	2	Texas	Borger	Hutchinson	Texas
, Donnie M	Daughter	F	W	6	S	No	0	Texas	Borger	Hutchinson	Texas
Wood, Alvis	Grandson	M	W	12	S	Yes	5	Oklahoma	Borger	Hutchinson	Texas
, Gene	Grandson	M	W	10	S	Yes	2	Texas	Borger	Hutchinson	Texas
Crist, Emma	Lodger	F	W	49	D	No	H-4	Arkansas	R	Carson	Texas

Figure 20. The Robertsons in the 1940 census. The first photo shows Eck in an Amarillo boarding house, the other two pictures are the widescreen and closeup views of the entry showing Nettie and the children (and two grandchildren) in the nearby village of Panhandle.

Panhandle, a small town about thirty miles east and a bit north of Amarillo, and twenty-three miles due south of Borger. In that census, Nettie emphatically declared herself a widow, and was listed as a "head of family." She and a female boarder were now professionally employed, working in a program for seamstresses sponsored by the New Deal. At some point—perhaps after Dueron's death—Eck and Nettie reunited for a few years, living together in Panhandle and then in Amarillo, in the Pantex Villages, a 360-unit apartment complex built for the employees for the Pantex Ordnance Plant; Nettie worked at that plant (*Amarillo Daily News*, November 11, 1945). But she eventually left for good. The 1950 census lists her as a lodger in Lubbock, again "widowed," classified as a housekeeper, living next door to the presumably more substantial home of one Robert C. Hash, a receiving clerk in a retail department store (his address: 1402 Ave. L). Prose memorials solicited and distributed by a Vernon funeral home when Eck's father died—the James Leander Robertson ceremony—included many short biographies of Robertson family members. Nettie was never mentioned, quite conspicuously (see findagrave.com/memorial/111859303/james-leander-robertson).

ECK IN AMARILLO

Eck would be single and based in Amarillo for most of the rest of his life. He did create a contemporary dance band, the Sleep Disturbers, and had other chances to play professionally, though his main public venues were now fiddle contests. He settled into his established career as piano tuner and stringed instrument repairman.

The rest of Eck's story falls into two tracks, one as told through newspaper articles documenting his participation in contests or festivals, and the other in interviews conducted by fellow musicians, many of whom were also folklorists or ethnomusicologists. The pertinent newspaper articles from the late 1940s forward are few enough that I have room to cite most that I have seen, most from the *Amarillo Daily News*, the *Lubbock Morning Avalanche*, or the *Lubbock Avalanche Journal*. For these notices, I give the date and page number, the name of the newspaper, the article's title, and a quote and/or pertinent fact or two from each.

April 29, 1947, *Amarillo Daily News*, 2. **Fiddlers Contest Ticket Sale Opens**. "Only recognized old-timey tunes will be played. . . . We'll tolerate none of this boogey-woogey or hopped-up jazz." Each participant was required to be ready to play at least four tunes. Eck, one of ten contestants signed up at this point, was listed as living in Amarillo. Supplementary entertainment was furnished by "two sets of fancy-stepping square dancers," the Cowboy Set and the Chicken Feed Set.

Figure 21. Eck in his shop in Amarillo (date unknown). Photo courtesy of Panhandle-Plains Historical Museum. Used by permission.

May 30, 1947, *Amarillo Daily News*, 27–28. An advertisement: "DANCE!! Sat. May 31 8:30pm. Music by Gertrude's Western Band, Eck Robertson, Fiddler. The Sundown. 6 Miles North on Fillmore on West Side of Highway. SPECIALIZING IN SQUARES, WALTZES AND SCHOTTISCHES."

August 26, 1948, *Amarillo Daily News*, 1–2. **Range Riders on Memory Lane** (Western Cowpunchers Association BBQ and Convention). Music provided by A. C. "Eck" Robertson and The Sleep Disturbers. "Limbs that rested all year long, after long years spent in the saddle, swung out with all the vigor of youth to square dance, schottische, two step, and waltz. . . . It was a day for renewal of acquaintance and friendships begun long, long ago, before Amarillo was a town and when, as one old timer put it, 'this section was nothing but grass belly-deep on a 15-hand horse. It was a day for conversations that began with 'Do you remember when . . .' the cowboys and their gals danced till late. . . .'"

The Sleep Disturbers had been briefly mentioned in an earlier article (*Amarillo Daily News*, March 7, 1947, 6):

'Dopey the Puppet' to Share Spotlight at Revue Tonight. William "Schnozz" Dunn and his hand puppet, "Dopey," will be one of the feature attractions of the American Legion Show, "Gay Nineties Revue," opening at 8:15 o'clock tonight, Municipal Auditorium [four paragraphs about Dunn and Dopey follow].

Entertainment in a musical manner will be given by Jeanne Caroll, musical songbird for Dick Morton's orchestra; the Marshall sisters, Helen, Lois, and Jean; Blackburn-Shaw Quartet; Eck Robertson's "Sleep Disturbers"; pupils of Dixie Dice, Nib Noble's orchestra assisted by Rodney Duling; Johnny West and Frances Irvin; and Julia Dean Evans' A Capella Choir.

Show proceeds will go to the American Legion Building Fund.

September 9, 1950, *Amarillo Daily News*, 57. **7000 Watch Floyd County Fair Parade**. This county fair, held in county seat Lockney, about ninety-seven miles south of Amarillo and fifty-seven miles north of Lubbock, included a fiddle contest and jamboree. "Eck Robertson, 73, of Amarillo placed first [among] fiddlers aged 65 and older." There were forty-five contestants, one of them a woman, playing before an estimated 600 audience members, in a tent. The contest lasted from 4:30pm until after 10pm; the fiddlers must not have played very many tunes each.

July 5, 1952, *Lubbock Morning Avalanche*, 11. **Celebrations Over Area Mark Fourth. 8,000 Spectators Jam Hale Center**. (The population of Hale Center was only about 2,000). The first prize of $50 was won by Cal Brown, aged seventy-one. Eck (listed as aged sixty-four, and living in Amarillo) won the second prize of $30. Jack Mears, a plumber at employed at Texas Tech, won third prize; he and Eck were regular winners at area fiddle contests during this period. This festival also featured what was called a beard-growing contest (for finished achievements, rather than for on-the-spot cultivation). The article included a photograph of Eck playing "Listen to the Mockingbird," a picture not clear enough for reproduction but capturing him in a conventional playing stance, not contorted for this trick fiddle tune.

October 15, 1952, *Amarillo Daily News*, 63. **Gray County Gets Unexpected Birthday Greeting. 50th anniversary celebrated with Jubilee-Fandangle**. This festival included a fiddle contest won by Eck, who was listed as residing in Amarillo. Pampa, site of the festival, is about sixty miles from Amarillo.

June 21, 1953, *Lubbock Avalanche Journal*, 7. **Hale Center is "Tuning Up" for Second Fiddle Contest**. A total of $350 in cash prizes were specified. "A $150 cash prize and trophy will be awarded in the open division compared to $125 awarded to the world champion fiddler at Crockett last week." The runner up would get $50. In the ladies division first and second prize would be $50 and $25. The same amounts would hold for fiddlers aged at least seventy-five. Televised on WBAP-TV, Fort Worth. Done in connection with annual July 4 homecoming celebration. The first time this contest was held (the previous year), Uncle Cal Brown of Plainview beat Eck (in which division, we do not learn). Early registrants for the contest include Eck and also his former "Vernon Fiddlers" companion Lewis Franklin, now living in Vernon, apparently paroled.

June 28, 1953, *Lubbock Avalanche Journal*, 4. **A. J. Mears Enters Fiddling Contest**. (Mears had won the "World Fiddle Championship" in Crockett, Texas that year; I haven't seen any evidence that Eck ever competed in Crockett.) Others registered to compete included master fiddlers of a younger generation: Vernon and Norman Soloman, Major and Louis Franklin (not the much older Lewis Franklin of Vernon), Benny Thomasson, Bartow Riley, and, among the senior players, Eck.

June 30, 1953, *Amarillo Daily News*, 5. **Fiddle Battle Set Saturday** (in Hale City, on July 4, the same contest described in the entry above). "Uncle Cal Brown, of Plainview ... outplayed Eck and Uncle Jack [Mears] the previous year." The reporter expected contestants from Texas, New Mexico, Oklahoma, Arkansas, and Missouri, and also anticipated that the event would be aired on both radio and television.

July 2, 1953, *Lubbock Morning Avalanche*, 25. **Area Tournament of Top Fiddlers Saturday**. This article linked competitors with tunes they liked. The oldest fiddler as of this date was "William Eckles, 88, of Roaring Springs. He likes 'Over the Waves,' 'College Hornpipe,' and 'Ragtime Annie.' Tom Michael, 80, of Sweetwater, likes 'Fisher's Hornpipe,' 'Butterfly Hornpipe,' and 'Wagoner.' The youngest registrants of this date were Sonny Curtis, 16, of Meadow and Bob Zellner, 10, of Hereford, who likes 'Devil's Dream,' 'Black Mountain Rag,' and 'Orange Blossom Special.' J. C. (Uncle Cal) Brown, the defending champion, 72, likes 'Wagner,' 'Bill Cheatum,' and 'Paddy on the Turnpike.' Eck Robertson, Amarillo, 65, likes 'Sally Gooden,' 'Sally Johnson,' 'Leather Britches,' and [various] hornpipes. A. J. Mears, Lubbock, 60, likes '[Done] Gone, and 'Cattle in the Cane Brake.'" Among the others registered we again see Lewis Franklin, seventy-eight, of Vernon.

July 5, 1953, *Lubbock Avalanche Journal*, 23. **Reunion Jams Hale Center**. This "Fiddlers of Hale Center Reunion" lasted "from early morning until late [that night]." First prize went to Tom Mitchell of Sweetwater, second prize to Lewis Franklin of Roaring Springs, and third to Eck. Franklin apparently retained his skill during his lengthy stay in the prison in Huntsville.

From Hale Center, it is about 165 miles to Sweetwater, ninety miles to Amarillo, and seventy-five miles to Roaring Springs. By this time, roads were better and more people owned cars; fiddlers often travelled much further to contests than had the participants in the 1900 Brenham contest discussed in the first chapter of this book. This may seem obvious, but it matters. By the 1950s, there were far fewer fiddlers per capita, but contests could still be well stocked with skilled players simply because travel had become much easier.

June 23, 1954, *Lubbock Morning Avalanche*, 19. **Tournament of Fiddlers Set At Hale Center**. This article about the next year's contest in Hale Center emphasized the prospect of having eighty-nine-year-old "diminutive" bridegroom William Eckles of Roaring Springs participate. Eck also registered. There were three competition brackets defined by age: for fiddlers less than twenty-five years old, those aged twenty-five through fifty, and those over fifty. This presages current practice of having three age-defined competition brackets, though nowadays the youngest group may be less than sixteen years old—and the oldest group over sixty-five; good health and physical condition is now apt to last longer.

July 4, 1954, *Lubbock Avalanche Journal*, 1, 10. **10,000 Hear Old Fiddlers**. This article was accompanied by a photograph of fiddler Major Franklin (listed as residing in Muleshoe, perhaps in error), guitarist O[mega] Burden, fiddler Eck Robertson, and fiddler Benny Thomasson (who lived in Arlington). The beneficiary of the event was vaguely specified: "Hale Center community projects." The reporter narrated an instructive sequence:

> Franklin was first in the finals with the immortal "Sally Goodin." Then came Thomasson, who also played "Sally Goodin."
>
> "Well, sir," said Eck as he stepped up to the mike, "Guess I'll have to show them youngsters how to play 'Sally Goodin.'"
>
> Judges, not satisfied, put the finalists through their paces three times before selecting a winner. Thomasson and Franklin split the pot—after an announcement that Eck was the star of one of the very first recordings of "Sally Goodin."
>
> As the money was handed out, Eck plucked happily on the fiddle and admitted: Benny and Major are good friends of mine—and they're about the best fiddlers in the country. Then with a grin he added, I think those boys learned to play "Sally Goodin" from my record.
>
> Eck bounced back in the second round at the contest for fiddlers over fifty years of age, and won handily.

The reporter further noted that "Thomason [*sic*] and Franklin are 'sweet fiddlers' who play in the tradition popular nowadays. Eck, however, is 'just an old-time country fiddler.' Thus, while there may have been some gap between the younger fiddlers and Eck in fluency or intonation caused by the inevitable ravages of age, there was also an audible, significant difference in style. Thomasson, Franklin, and their contemporaries had incorporated influences from western swing that Eck did not assimilate, and these younger fiddlers' collective style had become the standard one.

July 1, 1958, *Lubbock Morning Avalanche*, 17. **Hale Center Test Expected to Draw Champion Fiddlers** (once again, for July 4). The event was predicted to again include Benny Thomasson and Norman Solomon. In the senior bracket, Eck had been "'nosed out' for two straight years" by Uncle Cal Brown, who was "too sick to participate this year." There were $700 in cash prizes. At this contest, the older fiddlers' division was announced to be for players aged sixty-five years or older, as is common today. I find it especially interesting that the first prize of $150 in the open division was matched with the same size prize in the senior division, a gesture I haven't heard about elsewhere.

July 2, 1958, *Amarillo Daily News*, 28. **Champion Fiddler to Defend Title**. The competitors included Norman Solomon, Benny Thomasson, and Eck, described as a "recording star of the hoe down era." Again, there was a separate division for fiddlers aged sixty-five and older; this was becoming the rule.

September 9, 1960, *Lubbock Avalanche Journal*, 76. **800 Turn Out for Floyd Co. Fair**. Forty-three men and one woman competed; Eck won the senior division, with his occasional nemesis Jack Mears in second place.

October 14, 1961, *Wichita Falls Times*, 14. **At State Fair, Lubbock Man Leads Fiddlers**. Sixty-eight-year-old Jesse [?] Mears won; he played "Leather Britches" and "Devil's Dream." "Second place went to Eck Robertson, 86 [incorrect], of Amarillo for his interpretation of 'Sally Goodin.'"

July 5, 1962, *Lubbock Avalanche Journal*, 77. **Thousands Jam Area Towns for Holiday Festivities** . . . parades, parties and picnics in Hale Center. The winner of the open division was James ["Texas Shorty"] Chancellor, nineteen, of Dallas. Other notable participants included Norman Solomon of Boyd, Vernon Solomon of Rhome, Louis Franklin of Whitewright (that is the younger fiddler by that name, the famous one), Bryant Houston of Dallas, and Carl Harwood of Tatum, New Mexico. The older fiddlers' division featured Frank McCraw (seventy-nine) of Macomb, Oklahoma, Eck (noted as being from Amarillo; awarded third prize), and Jack Mears of Lubbock. The youngest division included Byron Berline (seventeen) of Caldwell, Kansas, awarded second prize, and Mike Solomon (thirteen) and Rick Solomon (ten), of Rhome.

July 5, 1963, *Lubbock Avalanche Journal*, 59. **Only One Traffic Fatality Mars Area Celebrations. Thousands Turn Out**. That year, James Chancellor won first prize in the open division, while Eck triumphed in the senior division.

September 20, 1964, *Lubbock Avalanche Journal*, 10. **Floyd County Fair Lures 10,000**. Four thousand were present the day of the fiddle contest. There were "over twenty" contestants. In the competition bracket for fiddlers aged eighteen to thirty-five, Vernon Riddle of Lubbock took second; he had interviewed Eck in 1959, and learned many tunes from him. Eck won the senior division (for fiddlers over the age of sixty-four).

February 18, 1975, *Amarillo Daily News*, 28. Eck had died; "Survivors include one son, six daughters, one brother, 22 grandchildren and 9 great-grandchildren."

FOLKLORISTS FIND ECK

The handful of formal interviews of Eck or simply tune recording sessions took place within a short span of time late in his life, from 1959 through the 1960s. Folklore-interested musicians conducted most of these. One of them, John Cohen of the New Lost City Ramblers, summarized how this cluster of contacts developed, in an article published in *Sing Out!*:

> The diverse personalities and methods which were used to rediscover Eck Robertson after 35 years of relative obscurity also reveal the new techniques of folklore study being used by students today. First, people were impressed by his music heard on the Anthology compiled by Harry Smith . . . back in 1951. Then, more material was sought from record collectors and early catalogs. Ralph Rinzler talked to friends in Texas, trying to stimulate interest in locating Robertson. Segel Fry in Dallas heard mention of Eck in a newspaper article concerning a recent fiddle contest, and passed the word to Roger Abrahams, who is teaching English and Folklore at the University of Texas in Austin. Abrahams sent some of his students to Amarillo, and they had a long interview with Eck. This report was mimeographed and sent to Archie Green in Illinois, Ed Kahn in Los Angeles, Mike Seeger in New Jersey, and others, and was passed around at the Chicago Festival, where I saw it. En route to California last March, Tracy Schwarz and myself spent a day with Eck, talking, playing music, and recording him. Mike Seeger visited him a few months later. (1964, 57)

But the first surviving interview with Eck was not part of the stream of communications described by Cohen. It was instead a recording session done by a fellow fiddler, the transplanted South Carolinian named Vernon

Riddle (1935–2011; full name Harold Vernon Riddle). He was from the Spartanburg area, about seventy miles WSW of Charlotte, North Carolina. He grew up hearing fiddling in two settings, one situation in person from local mill workers, and the other the Grand Ole Opry, listened to avidly over the radio.

Riddle spent twenty years in the Air Force, stationed in Amarillo. He had begun fiddling as an adult at home in South Carolina, then completed much of his initial learning of technique in the mid- to late 1950s in Texas. He entered many fiddle contests (see the penultimate newspaper article above) and sought the tutelage of Eck and later of members of the next generation of Texas champions, notably Benny Thomasson and the Solomon brothers (see knowitall.org/photo/harold-vernon-riddle-photos-digital-traditions and https://www.slippery-hill.com>source>vernon-riddle).

The tape of Riddle's interview of Eck includes these tunes in this order; asterisks indicate performances transcribed for this book: "Kansas City Rag,"* "Wagoner's Hornpipe,"* "Brilliancy Medley," "Chadwick,"* "Snowbird in the Ashbank,"* "Cacklin' Hen,"* "Call of the Wild Goose"* (under the shortest of the various titles of this tune, "Lost Goose"), "Done Gone," "College Hornpipe,"* "Texas Wagoner," "Sally Johnson,"* "Say Old Man,"* "Leather Britches," "Cattle in the Cane," "Old Lime Rock,"* "Sally Goodin," "Tom and Jerry,"* "Grey Eagle,"* "Lost Indian,"* and, again, "Sally Goodin." This second take of "Sally Goodin" is prefaced by an announcement by Riddle, truncated on the tape: ". . . master of Amarillo, Eck Robertson himself, doing his all-time favorite, 'Sally Goodin.'" This suggests that Riddle and Eck were thinking about issuing a commercial recording, though we don't learn if that goal was ever pursued. The list of pieces doesn't seem to express any unusual preferences on Riddle's part in terms of types of tunes. These are tunes that he wanted to learn from Eck, or ones he thought would sell, or both.

A friend of urban folk enthusiast Pat Conte visited Eck, likely in the early 1970s. Conte doesn't recall which friend that was (email, Harry Bolick, Feb. 18, 2025). The friend recorded Eck playing "Fisher's Hornpipe,"* "College Hornpipe," "Dominion Hornpipe,"* "Durang's Hornpipe,"* "Over the Waves,"* "Billy in the Low Grounds,"* "Big Devil Medley,"* "Irish Washerwoman,"* "Soldier's Joy,"* "Mississippi Sawyer,"* "Forked Deer," "Rhubarb,"* and "Done Gone"* (see note below transcription; asterisks mark performances I transcribed). Conte kept the tape, and shared it widely. Many of the tunes on it reach back to the late 1700s in both oral tradition and popular music publication. The hornpipes and other tunes of this vintage ("Irish Washerwoman" and "Soldier's Joy") remained in use for square dances and similar events in rural New York. These are traditional melodies from Conte's own stomping ground in New York State, and likely constitute repertorial common ground between Conte, his friend, and Eck.

While Riddle and Conte's friend's contributions are groups of tunes recorded with little or no commentary, two interviews with Eck were exactly that, interviews. I have quoted considerably from that done by students of Roger Abrahams in 1962. The recording made by these students, Pat Riggs and Szabo Nagy, did include a pair of performances, one of a tune not named during the interview, but entitled elsewhere "Alf Taylor's Fox Chase," and the other of one of Eck's hits, "Beaumont Rag." My transcriptions of both of these tunes are from that interview.

The most substantial contact between Eck and musicians from outside of the Texas fiddle world was with members of the New Lost City Ramblers or arranged by members of that band. These meetings, mentioned by John Cohen in the paragraph excerpted from his *Sing Out!* article, were especially productive. They included the most extensive recordings of Eck playing and the greatest variety of topics explored in conversation, and led to opportunities for Eck to play at several folk festivals during the mid-1960s. Mike Seeger's papers, on deposit at the University of North Carolina, include recordings of these meetings. This material has been digitized, and is available to the public. Parts are more fully processed than are others; many tunes were recorded. I will simply list these tunes in the order they appear in those interviews.

SFC (Southern Folklore Collection) Audio Open Reel FT 20009/5602, June 1963, includes these tunes in this order: "College Hornpipe," "Bonaparte's Retreat," two unnamed tunes in the same unusual tuning (low DDAD),* "Say Old Man," "Lost Goose," "Turkey in the Straw [in C],"* "Get Up in the Cool," "Lost Indian," /5613: "Sally Johnson," "Soldier's Joy," "Billy in the Low Grounds," "Stumptown Stomp in Grand Saline," "Hell Among the Yearlings," "Brilliancy Medley," "Say Old Man," "Texas Wagoner," "Forked Deer," "Dusty Miller," "Sally Johnson," "Leather Britches," "Say Old Man," "Forked Deer," "Amarillo Waltz," "Borger Wiggle," "Sally Goodin," "Grigsby's Hornpipe," "Rye Whiskey," "Hawk Got a Chicken," "Snowbird in the Ashbank," "Grey Eagle."

While Eck was in Los Angeles in April 1964, he played with the New Lost City Ramblers at a coffee house called the Golden Vanity. SFC Audio Open Reel FT 20009/14273 contains the following tunes: "Brilliancy Medley," "Dusty Miller," "Beaumont Rag," "Apple Blossom," "Rhubarb," and "Grey Eagle." Conversation did not flag during the music, and just three titles are audible, "Dusty Miller," "Beaumont Rag," and "Grey Eagle." An audience member asked Eck if he knew "Orange Blossom Special." His curt reply: "No."

A number of tunes were selected by the New Lost City Ramblers for the LP album *Famous Cowboy Fiddler*. They are, in the order they appear on the album: "Texas Wagoner," "Stumptown Stomp," "Lost Indian," "Grigsby's Hornpipe," "Rye Whiskey," "Lost Goose," "Sally Johnson," "Billy in the Low Grounds," and "Beaumont Rag" (completes Side A), "Grey Eagle," "Dusty

Figure 22. A poster advertising a fiddle contest held in 1974 at the University of California, Santa Barbara, on deposit in the library of the Center for Popular Music, Middle Tennessee State University. The poster's designer borrowed the photograph of Eck from a 1923 Victor catalog.

Miller," "Hell Among the Yearlings," "Say Old Man, Can You Play a Fiddle?," "Get Up in the Cool," "Hawk Got the Chicken," unnamed tune in D, "Bonaparte's Retreat," "Forky Deer," and "Done Gone."

By the time these most lengthy interviews of Eck were taking place, the New Lost City Ramblers were important figures in the 1960s folk revival, and regular performers at, for example, the Newport Folk Festival. Eck was offered a spot at that festival; he performed right after his patrons and they accompanied his set. The version of Eck playing "Leather Britches" that I transcribed must have been a rehearsal for the festival performance. Before playing, Eck says, "This is Eck Robertson playing 'Leather Britches,' accompanied by the New Lost City Ramblers." Eck also played in a festival in Los Angeles; he kept his performer's badge from that occasion with his papers (those now on deposit at the Country Music Foundation).

The last extended interview of Eck was conducted by Earl V. Spielman in March 1969. Spielman found Eck to be beset by arthritis and quite unhappy, exhibiting an "undercurrent of despair and resentment." The setting was his Amarillo home, a "small two-room house, full of instruments in poor repair" (1972, 179).

Figure 22 is a photograph of a large poster advertising a fiddle contest in southern California that took place in 1974, a year before Eck's death. The picture of him reproduced on the poster is the most widely copied one of him. It's from the Victor catalog of 1923. It is a carefully composed image, illustrating his interpretation of cowboy wear, and with an American flag asserting patriotism. Aspects of Eck's performance technique appear too, notably that he holds the bow at the frog, thus controlling the bow more like an art violinist than an old-time player, this allowing long bow motions. And his left hand is in third position, illustrating his regular use of upper positions, now a feature of contest fiddling (he is fingering a high d).

Having an event scheduled in the 1970s illustrated with a photograph fifty years old helps bring home that Eck was viewed as a figure from the past rather than a contemporary entertainer. Eck had become a living representative of nostalgia.

Another window onto Eck's repertoire is offered in lists of tune titles that Eck penned, likely during the late 1930s or early 1940s, several of which must be set lists. A dozen such bits of paper, each approximately 5" by 7", rest in the Eck Robertson files of the library of the Country Music Foundation in Nashville (call number 1992.40.7.1–9). I photographed these barely-legible materials on July 6, 2021. The lists read as follows, with Eck's spellings and capitalizations retained:

> [p. 1, front]
> 1st [at top, centered]
> 1 Texas Wagoner, the Cacklin Chickens or Barnyard blues
> 2 when you and I were young Maggie
> 3 [number circled and crossed out] Beaumont Rag
> 4 the waltz you saved for me
> 5 Ole Faithful
> 6 Sally Gooden
> 7 Pop Goes the weasel
>
> [back side of p. 1]
> 1 [number circled and crossed out] Amarillo waltz
> 2 [number circled and crossed out] Cubianola Rag
> 3 Cacklin hen or Barnyard Blues
> 4 [number circled and crossed out] Say old man can you play fiddle
> 5 Pop Goes the weasel

1 [number circled and crossed out] Brown Kelley waltz
2 San Antonio Rose
3 [number circled and crossed out] Dominion Hornpipe
4 Pop Goes the weasel

[page 2]
[at top, centered:] 2nd
Loveless love
Some body loves you
Echo in the valley
In the valley of the moon
\when its lamp lighting time in the vally
when the moon comes over the mountain
Home on the Range
Nobodys darling but mine
maple on the hill
I saw your face in the moon
when Irsh eyes are Smiling
my cabin of dreams
My Darling hold me closer still
blue eyes
my wild Irsh rose
\Mexicana rose
\the waltz you saved for me
when I grow to old to dream
\Amarillo waltz
[slash mark \ to left circled and crossed out] Goodnight waltz
[back side of sheet is blank]

[page 3]
[at top of page, centered:] 3rd
\ Brown Kelly waltz
when the bloom is on the Sage
Old Faithful
The last Roundup
theres an empty cot in the bunk house
my exsperience on the ranch
I'm an old cowhand
you cant stop me from dreaming
Beach of balley balley
\The One Rose
sweet Heart of sigmachi
\Its a sin to tell a lie
Have you ever been lonely

Let me call you sweetheart
In the shade of the old Apple tree (Parides)
The Old Apple tree Populer
\There's a gold mine in the Sky
[back side of sheet is blank]

[page 4]
[at top, centered:] 4th
x [in circle] Beaumont Rag
x [in circle] Kansas City Rag
x [in circle] Dill Pickles Rag
x [in circle] Borger Wiggle
x [in circle] Just because
\Ranch O Grandi
x [in circle] my Frog aint no Bullfrog
x [in circle] Sadisfide
Rubies
x [in circle] G & E rag
x [in circle] Rag time Annie
x [in circle] Done Gone
my little girl
Down yonder
whats the reason Im not pleasing you
the Island of Capri
Sleepy time down south
Love letters in the sand
River stay away from my door
\whispering

[back side of p. 4:]
\there's a Gold mine in the Skie
\Old faithfull
\Alexanders Ragtime Band
\Dark town struters ball
Bully of the town
Tie me to your Apron strings

[page 5]
[at top, centered:] 5th
1 Home on the Range - G
2 [number circled and crossed with an x] Amarillo waltz - - G
3 [number circled and crossed with an x] Sally Johnson - - - G
4 [number crossed with a /] There's a Gold mine in the Skie G
5 when you and I were young G

6 [number circled and crossed with an x] Fishers Hornpipe - - - - D
7 Texas Wagoner - - - C
x [in a circle; this item squeezed in:] Extra Big Devil medley A
8 [number circled and crossed with an x] Sally Gooden - - - A
9 [number circled and crossed with an x] Lost Indian - - - A
10 [number circled and crossed with an x] Rye whiskey - - A
11 [number circled and crossed with an x] Beaumont Rag - - F
12 Old faithful - - F
13 Pop Goes the weasel – G
14 [number circled and crossed with an x] Say old man can you play
    a fiddle E
15 [number circled and crossed with an x] Cubianola glide B flat
16 [number circled and crossed with an x] Colege Hornpipe B flat
17 [number circled and crossed with an x] Done gone B flat G minor
[back side of page is blank]

[page 6; no label at top]
1 [number circled and crossed with an x] Beaumont Rag
2 Arkansas Traveler
3 [number circled and crossed with an x] Brown Kelly waltz
4 South of the Border
my experience on the Ranch
5 [number circled and crossed with an x] Brilancy medley
6 When you and I were young
7 Pop goes the weasel

[back of page 6, written oblong]
[at top right:] (2nd)
[forearm and finger pointing C:] Sally Goodin 3
x Rye whiskey 2
[forearm and finger pointing C:] Lost Indian——1
x Grey Eagle
4 Pop Goes the weasel
[circled x to left of forearm and finger pointing C:] Say old man can
    you play a fiddle 5
[circled x] Colledge Hornpipe
[forearm and finger pointing and circled x over the finger:] Fishers
    Hornpipe
[forearm and finger pointing and circled x over the finger:] Texas
    wagoner
[forearm and finger pointing and circled x over the finger:] Sally
    Johnson
[forearm and finger pointing:] Arkansas Traveler
[circled x] Big Devil medley

[circled x] Beaumont Rag
[circled x] Dusty Miller
[circled x] Brilancy

[page 7]
[at top, centered:] 7th [?]
Home on the range
Old Faithful
Be Nobodys Darling but mine
Mexicana rose
My exsperience on the ranch
Beaument Rag
Sally Goodin
you cant stop me from Dreaming
Pop Goes the weasel

[back side, upside down:]
Texas quickstep
want to go to meetin Uncle Joe
(Brilliantcy medley)
. . . Southern
(by Eck Robertson)

[page 8]
when the white azaleas are blooming - G
sweet litle Headache
little ser Echo
[circled x] whispering – B flat
There's a Goldmine in the skies G
when its lamp lighting time G
Dark town strutters ball F C or G
Old Faithful – F
[circled x] Beaumont Rag – F
[circled x] Amarillo waltz – G
[circled x] Kansas City Rag – D
[circled x] the Kelly waltz – G
[circled x] Borger wiggle – C
[circled x] Dill pickels – G
[circled x] Brown skin girl – G
Thers an Empty Cot in the Bunkhouse

[back of page 8]
Alexanders ragtime band – F
Drifting and Dreaming – F

Rain – F
Bear Barrell Polker – C and F
Dipsy Doodle – B flat
<u>Mexican Rose in F</u>
Ranch O Grandi – G
<u>The One Rose – B flat.</u>
Its a sin to tell a lie – C
Three little fishes – F
<u>Rubber Dollie – B flat</u>
Makes no difference now – F
<u>O Johnie – G.</u>
<u>South of the Border – G</u>
[circled x] Just Because C flat [C replaces some other letter that was erased]
[circled x] Amarillo waltz G
[circled x] Tears – F
The waltz you saved for me F
Cowboys yodle - G

[page 9]
[circled x] the negros Dream D
[circled x] Just Because C
Ranch O Grandia G
some of these days F
O Johnie F
Dark town strutters ball F
Alexanders ragtime band F
[circled x] Dill Pickles G & C
[circled x] Beaumont Rag F
[circled x] My frog F
[circled x] Sadisfide F
[circled x] Borger wiggle C
[circled x] Kansas City rag D
[circled x] Whispering B flat
[circled x] Tears waltz F
[circled x] Amarillo waltz G
[circled x] Brown Kelly waltz G
[circled x] Goodnight waltz C and F
the waltz you saved for me F
when I grow to old to dream F
the one Rose E flat

[back of p. 9]
my little girl C

x Down Yonder G
It makes no difference now G
Its a sin to tell a lie E flat
Rubber dollie A or B flat
Sanantonio Rose D and A
Mexicano rose B flat
Brown skin Girl G
nobodys Darling but mine G

_____

[is this a dividing line or an underlining of nobodys Darling?]
Gold mine in the Skie G
Home on the Range G
Old faithful F

In Eck's set lists just once, and not cited elsewhere as being played by him, are these titles: "Cacklin' Chickens," "G & E Rag," "The Island of Capri," "Love Letters in the Sand," "My Little Girl," "Rubies," "Sleepy Time Down South," "Texas Quickstep," "Uncle Joe," "Want to Go to Meeting," "What's the Reason I'm Not Pleasing You," and "You Can't Stop Me From Dreaming." ("Uncle Joe" likely equals "Want to Go to Meeting.")

These lists have contrasting characters that must reflect different purposes. The short lists that end with "Pop Goes the Weasel" are probably actual set lists, whether prospective or actually employed. These brief lists vary in numbers of pieces specified. Perhaps Eck was musing about playing opportunities during, for instance, breaks between competition brackets at contests, pauses to be filled with hired entertainment. He might be told that he had fifteen, or twenty, or thirty minutes to fill, and, with these set lists in hand, would be ready to match nicely balanced arrays of tunes with each of those amounts of time. The longer lists in which keys are identified were probably for members of the Sleep Disturbers; the personnel in that group likely fluctuated. And all performers know that lists of tunes that one knows are useful to jog memories. It is easy when on a stage to forget what one's options are! In any case, each of these scraps of paper meant enough to Eck that he kept them in his possession.

In Figure 23, which closes this chapter, I compare Eck's total known repertoire with the tunes known to have been played in the Brenham area during the well-documented fiddle contest of 1900, and with tunes mentioned in newspapers as having been played in Texas fiddle contests of the 1930s. I wish that I had more titles to place in the "1930s" middle column. Many a newspaper article reporting on a contest—whether coming up or having finished—contains names of competitors but no titles of tunes. For instance, I am sure that "Billy in the Low Grounds" was played in 1930s contests. Nevertheless, it's helpful to leaf down this figure and see that many of Eck's fiddle tunes had been around for some time, and that most of the pop song performances of which he would lead with his dance band were young. Some of those then-new songs survive; many are no longer played.

The next section of this book will concern those of Eck's fiddle tunes that were recorded commercially or during interviews. The closing section is a tune anthology consisting of my transcriptions of all of these, in addition to other versions of many of the tunes—in some cases ancestral versions. However, I also include a handful of fully transcribed contemporary performances. Even though the collectors of Eck's versions of tunes had their own tastes and own goals in mind as they requested specific tunes, repetitions of tune names in the various collections and in the set lists suggest that the array of tunes available for me to transcribe is a reasonably balanced sample—one can generalize about Eck's fiddling and his place in history based on this body of music.

KNOWN IN BRENHAM IN 1900	PLAYED IN 1930s CONTESTS	IN ECK'S REPERTOIRE;
		a date indicates Eck's recording issued that year; F a field recording; and SL presence on one or several set list(s)
		Alexander's Ragtime Band (SL3)
		Amarillo Waltz (1929, F, SL5)
		Apple Blossom (1922, not issued)
Arkansas Traveler	Arkansas Traveller	Arkansas Traveller (1922, SL2)
		Barnyard Blues (SL2)
		Be Nobody's Darling But Mine (SL3)
	Beaumont Rag (SS)	Beaumont Rag (F, SL8)
Big Sis		
Billy in the Low Ground		Billy in the Low Ground (1922)
Black Cat's Foot		
Black Jack Grove		
Black-eyed Susie		
Black Satin		
Bonaparte's Retreat		Bonaparte's Retreat (F)
Bonnie Blue Flag		
		Borger Bounce/Wiggle (F, SL3)
Brannigan's Pup		
		Brilliancy Medley (SL3)
Brindle Steer		
		Brown Kelly Waltz (1929, F, SL5)
Buffalo Girls		
Bull Frog's Eye		
		Cacklin' Hen (F, SL)

Figure 23. Comparison of lists of fiddle tunes.

KNOWN IN BRENHAM IN 1900	PLAYED IN 1930s CONTESTS	IN ECK'S REPERTOIRE;
Cake All Dough		
Campbells Are Coming		
Catfish and Minnow		
	Cattle in the Cane Break (+SS)	
		Cattle in the Cane (F)
		Chadwick (F)
Cheatem		Bill Cheatum (SL)
Chicken in the Bread Tray		
	Chicken Reel (SS)	
Cinda, Fare You Well		Cindy (F*)
	Clarinet Tickler (SS)	
Clear the Track		
College Hornpipe		College Hornpipe (F, SL2)
	Coming Around the Mountain (SS)	
Coonie on the Ground		
Cotton Eyed Joe	Cotton-Eyed Joe	
		Cubianola Rag/Glide (SL2)
		Dark Town Strutter's Ball (SL3)
Devilish Mary		
Devil's Dream		Big Devil Medley (F, SL2)
		Dill Pickles Rag (SL3)
Dixie Land		
Dominion Hornpipe (not issued, F, SL)		
		Done Gone (1922, F, SL2)
		Down Yonder (SL2)
Drunken Hiccoughs	Drunkard's Hiccups	Lady's Fancy? (F)
		[Dry and Dusty] (F)
		Durang's Hornpipe (F)
		Dusty Miller (F, SL)
Eighth of January		
Faulky [Forked] Deer		
Farewell, Whiskey		
Ficher's [Fisher's] Hornpipe	Fisher's Hornpipe	Fisher's Hornpipe (F, SL2)
Fine Times at Our House		
		The Flower Song (F*)
Forked Ear [Forked Deer]	Forked Deer (+SS)	Forked Deer (F)
		Fox Chase (F)
Fuss in the Family		
Gal on the Log		
	Georgia Blues (SS)	
		General Logan's Reel (not issued)
Get Up in the Cool		Get Up in the Cool (F)

KNOWN IN BRENHAM IN 1900	PLAYED IN 1930s CONTESTS	IN ECK'S REPERTOIRE;
Getting Upstire [Getting Upstairs]		
Give the Fiddler a Drain [Dram]		
		Goodnight Waltz (SL2)
		Great Big Taters (1929, F)
Green Brier		
		Grey Eagle (F, SL)
		Grigsby's Hornpipe (F)
	Haste to the Wedding (SS)	
		Hawk Got the Chicken (F)
		Hell Among the Yearlings (F)
	Hell in Georgia (SS)	
Hog-Eyed Man		
		Home on the Range (SL4)
Hop Light, Ladies		
[I] Want to Go to Meeting, But Got No Shoes		
	If I Had a Girl Like You (SS)	
		It's a Sin to Tell a Lie (SL3)
Irish Washwoman	Irish Washerwoman	Irish Washerwoman (F)
		The Island Unknown (1929)
		Jenny Nettle
Jenny on the Railroad		
Jenny Put the Kettle On		
John's Got a New House		
		Just Because (SL3)
		Kansas City Rag (F, SL3)
Killy Cranky [Killie Krankie]		
Kitty is the Gal for Me		
Leather Britches	Leather Britches (F)	
		The Lime Rock (F*)
		Little Brown Jug (F*)
Little More Cider		
Liza Jane		
	The Lone Star Trail	
		Lost Goose (F)
Lost Indian	Lost Indian (F, SL2)	
		Makes No Difference Now (SL2)
Massa in the Cold, Cold Ground		
	McCloud's Reel (SS)	
	Medley Hornpipe	
Methodist Preacher		
		Mexican Rose in F (SL2)
		Mexicana Rose (SL2)

KNOWN IN BRENHAM IN 1900	PLAYED IN 1930s CONTESTS	IN ECK'S REPERTOIRE;
Miss[issippi] Sawyer	Mississippi Sawyer (F)	
Money Musk		
	My Blue Heaven (SS)	
		My Experience on the Ranch (skit with Dueron, (SL3)
		My Frog Ain't No Bullfrog (SL2)
Nancy Rowland		
Natchez Under the Hill		
N_____ in the Woodpile		
		Nightengale Song (F*)
	Nobody's Business (SS)	
Off to Georgia		
		O Johnie (SL2)
[Old] Dan Tucker		
Old Gray Goose		
Old Hen Cackle		
		Old Lime Rock (F)
[Old] Molly Hare		
Old Muse and Pups		
Old Uncle Ned		
Old Straw Bonnet		
		Ole Faithful (SL6)
		The One Rose (SL2)
One-Eyed Riley		
		Over the Waves (F)
Pop Goes the Weasel	Pop Goes the Weasel (SL7)	
Pretty Polly Ann	Pretty Polly Ann	
	Rag Time Annie (SS)	Ragtime Annie (1922, SL)
		Rancho Grandi (SL2)
Rareback [Bareback?] Davy		
		Rhubarb (F)
Ricker's [Rickett's?] Hornpipe		
Ringtail Coon		
Rocky Road to Dublin		
	Rosebud Waltz (SS)	
		Rubber Dollie (SL2)
		Run, Boy, Run (1929)
Rye Straw		
		Rye Whiskey (F, SL2)
Saddle Old Spike		
Sally Gooden	Sally Goodin	Sallie Gooden (1922, F, SL4)
Sally Hamilton		
Sally Johnson	Sally Johnson (1922)	

KNOWN IN BRENHAM IN 1900	PLAYED IN 1930s CONTESTS	IN ECK'S REPERTOIRE;
		San Antonio Rose (SL2)
Sandy Land		
		Satisfide (SL2)
		Say Old Man . . . (F, SL3)
		Schottische in F (F*)
Shoo Fly		
	Sidewalks of New York (SS)	
		Snow Bird in the Ash Bank (F)
Soapsuds Over the Fence		
Soldier's Joy	Soldier's Joy (SS)	Soldier's Joy (F)
		South of the Border (SL2)
	Springtime in the Rockies (SS)	
	Stay All Night, then Stay a Little Longer	
Stump Tail Deer		
		Stumptown Stomp (F)
Sugar in the Coffee		
Sugar in the Gourd		
Suwannee River		
	Sweet Jenny Reel (SS)	
Tailor in the Loft		
		Tears [Waltz] (SL2)
		Ten Cent Cotton (F)
		Theme Song [from Radio Show] (F)
		There's a Gold Mine in the Skies (SL 5)
		There's a Brown Skin Girl Down the Road (1929, SL2)
		There's an Empty Cot in the Bunkhouse (SL2)
	Tight Like That (SS)	
	Tinner's Hornpipe (SS)	
Tom and Jerry	Tom and Jerry	Tom and Jerry (F)
		Turkey in the Straw (1922)
Two-Eyed Jane		
Wagoner	Wagoner (SS)	Texas Wagoner (1929, SL3)
		Wagoner's Hornpipe (F)
Walk Along, Jawbone		
Walk Along, John		
	Walk the Georgia Road (SS)	
Walls of Jericho		
	Waltz in F; Waltz (SS)	
	Wedding Bells Waltz (SS)	
		When I Grow Too Old to Dream (SL2)

KNOWN IN BRENHAM IN 1900	PLAYED IN 1930s CONTESTS	IN ECK'S REPERTOIRE;
		When Its Lamp-Lighting Time [in the Valley] (SL2)
	Where Are You Going My Pretty Gal	
		The Waltz You Saved for Me (SL4)
		When You and I Were Young, Maggie (SL3)
		Whispering (SL3)
		Wind that Shakes the Barley (F*)
Young Gal So Deceiving		

— Chapter 4 —

"ARKANSAS TRAVELLER"

Eck's Musical Inheritances from Minstrelsy and from Fiddling Traditions of the Eastern and Southeastern United States

Eck Robertson's enduring fame centers on his critical role in the development of Texas fiddling and thus of national contest fiddling, which in terms of hours of performance is the dominant stream in American fiddling today. But his own repertoire remained diverse in both sources of tunes and styles of performance. He played tunes that had been made popular in blackface minstrelsy, and he also drew tunes from even further back in history, from older parts of originally British repertoires. In addition, he played an overlapping miscellany of inherited tunes that were already being funneled into the mainstream of Texas fiddling when he gathered them into his repertoire. Last, he drew on bodies of tunes new in his day, but that fit traditional conventions for fiddle tunes, young melodies that could join the fiddle mainstream immediately. In this anthology I explore each corner of his eclectic repertoire, and present both my transcriptions of his playing and a handful of other transcriptions, in most cases of printed or recorded versions of those same tunes.

How did this welter of Eck's melodies and performance techniques point him and other Texas fiddlers of his day in the direction of modern

Figure 24. Side B of Victor 18956, recorded June 30, 1922, the 78 rpm disc representing Henry Gilliland and Eck Robertson's first recording session at the Victor studio in New York.

contest fiddling? How did certain older factors persist in the mainstream of fiddlers' public activities, or assume designated significant smaller roles, or just turn up here and there? We can start to answer these questions by looking at which tunes Eck played, and how he played them. There is no simple way to organize the tunes for discussion. Eck's own groupings of pairs or handfuls of tunes in his own performances were inspired by his affection for certain tunes and by his desire to put on an entertaining show. These last three chapters will introduce an anthology of tunes ordered to reflect some ways that tunes near each other share important qualities, although I am certain that every reader will feel strongly that changing parts of the ordering of tunes could make more sense. In the first, longest group in the anthology, I placed old tunes that were minimally transformed by Eck. The other, much smaller groups include "Sally Goodin" and a few allies, then inherited tunes, "improved" as part of codifying Texas fiddling, and finally tunes that were young in Eck's day.

When Eck and Henry Gilliland went to New York in June 1922 to seek opportunities in the young recording industry, theirs was a relationship that joined generations. Eck was the junior partner; he may have been the driving force behind the trip, but the older and more seasoned Gilliland had the connections to get the duo into the Victor studio. He already knew Martin W. Littleton, a lawyer who did work for Victor, and this must have opened the door there.

The first tune played by Gilliland and his friend Eck for the Victor executives was indeed "Arkansas Traveler," a melody often coupled with a skit in performance. Both text and music were well known before the Civil War, and have remained unflaggingly popular [see the massive entry concerning this tune in Kuntz, *Traditional Tune Archive*, at https://tunearch.org/wiki/Annotation:Arkansas_Traveler_(1)]. When Eck and Gilliland played this melody for the New York Victor personnel in 1922, they were choosing to launch their presentation with what may well have been the best-known fiddle tune in America. "Arkansas Traveler" was certainly the fiddle tune mentioned most in the Texas press during the early twentieth century, and was second only to "Sallie Gooden" in terms of being cited in Panhandle newspapers in connection with Eck. For instance, Eck was invited to perform within a very long program to take place in Amarillo's Municipal Auditorium in 1929, an apparently marathon event during which twelve fiddlers would each play several pieces. "Sally Goodin" is part of Eck's slice of the program, of course, but he listed "Arkansas Traveller" as played by the whole Robertson family band as the first number in a "snappy program" of thirteen tunes that his family would present (*Amarillo Daily News*, March 22, 1929, 3).

Most readers of this book will be acquainted with both the melody of "Arkansas Traveller" and at least the outline of the associated skit. The tune entered print in the 1840s, but the performers and/or publishers already

THE ARKANSAS TRAVELLER

The Sheet Music of this Song can be had of H. J. WEHMAN, Song Publisher, No. 50 Chatham St., New York, or will be sent to any address, post-paid, on receipt of 40 cents in postage stamps.

This piece is intended to represent an Eastern man's experience among the inhabitants of Arkansas, showing their hospitality and the mode of obtaining it. Several years since, he was travelling the state to Little Rock, the capital. In those days, railroads had not been heard of, and the stage-lines were limited; so, under the circumstances, he was obliged to travel the distance on foot. One evening, about dusk, he came across a small log house, standing fifteen or twenty yards from the road, and enclosed by a low rail fence of the most primitive description. In the doorway sat a man, playing a violin; the tune was the then most popular air in that region—namely, "The Arkansas Traveller." He kept repeating the first part of the tune over and over again, as he could not play the second part. At the time the traveller reached the house, it was raining very hard, and he was anxious to obtain shelter from the storm. The house looked like anything but a shelter, as it was covered with clapboards, and the rain was leaking into every part of it. The old man's daughter Sarah appeared to be getting supper, while a small boy was setting the table, and the old lady sat in the doorway near her husband, admiring the music.

The stranger on coming up, said, "How do you do?" The man merely glanced at him, and, continuing to play, replied, "I do as I please."

STRANGER.—How long have you been living here?
OLD MAN.—D'ye see that mountain thar? Well, that was thar when I come here.
STRANGER.—Can I stay here to-night?
OLD MAN.—No! ye can't stay here.
STRANGER.—How long will it take me to get to the next tavern?
OLD MAN.—Well, you'll not get thar at all, if you stand thar foolin' with me all night! [Plays.]
STRANGER.—Well, how far do you call it to the next tavern?
OLD MAN.—I reckon it's upwards of some distance! [Plays as before.]
STRANGER.—I am very dry—do you keep any spirits in your house?
OLD MAN.—Do you think my house is haunted? They say thar's plenty down in the graveyard. [Plays as before.]
STRANGER.—How do they cross this river ahead?
OLD MAN.—The ducks all swim across. [Plays as before.]
STRANGER.—How far is it to the forks of the road?
OLD MAN.—I've been livin' here nigh on twenty years, and no road ain't forked yit. [Plays as before.]
STRANGER.—Give me some satisfaction, if you please, sir. Where does this road go to?
OLD MAN.—Well, it ain't moved a step since I've been here. [Plays as before.]
STRANGER.—Why don't you cover your house? It leaks.
OLD MAN.—'Cause it's rainin'.
STRANGER.—Then why don't you cover it when it's not raining?
OLD MAN.—'Cause it don't leak. [Plays as before.]
STRANGER.—Why don't you play the second part of that tune?
OLD MAN.—If you're a better player than I am, you can play it yourself. I'll bring the fiddle out to you—I don't want you in here! [Stranger plays the second part of the tune.]
OLD MAN.—Git over the fence, and come in and sit down—I didn't know you could play. You can board here, if you want to. Kick that dog off that stool, and set down and play it over—I want to hear it agin. [Stranger plays the second part again.]
OLD MAN.—Our supper is ready now; won't you have some with us?
STRANGER.—If you please.
OLD MAN.—What will you take, tea or coffee?
STRANGER.—A cup of tea, if you please.
OLD MAN.—Sall, git the grubbin'-hoe, and go dig some sassafras, quick! [Old man plays the first part.]
STRANGER.—(To the little boy.) Bub, give me a knife and fork, if you please.
BOY.—We hain't got no knives and forks, sir.
STRANGER.—Then give me a spoon.
BOY.—We hain't got no spoons neither.
STRANGER.—Well, then, how do you do?
BOY.—Tolerable, thank you; how do you do, sir? (Old man plays the first part again!)

The stranger, finding such poor accommodations, and thinking his condition could be bettered by leaving, soon departed, and at last succeeded in finding a tavern, with better fare. He has never had the courage to visit Arkansas since.

Figure 25. The text of "Arkansas Traveller," as arranged by Mose Case.

had personal opinions about exactly how it went, suggesting that this melody had been flourishing in oral tradition for some time. The same goes for the theatrical routine, though that entered print later, in 1858[?], in a sheet music publication of both words and music as arranged by Mose Case, an albino Black blackface and vaudeville performer best known as a guitarist. Case's shaping of the skit seems to have been considered a tidy, complete, market-ready form, worth appropriating; that exact text was repeated verbatim in several other publications. I give Case's published form of the tune in the middle of figure 36. Figure 25 presents a broadside republication of Case's version of the text (I clipped the top and bottom decorative frame to allow the text to become big enough to read.) If a fiddler had the melody memorized, this broadside could help him perform the skit.

Rather than including an explicitly African American theme, the "Arkansas Traveller" narrative explores minstrelsy as class- rather than race-oriented, shaped as a power reversal ritual (a longtime element of minstrelsy, a theme to be increasingly emphasized while minstrelsy was in the process of becoming vaudeville). In "Arkansas Traveller," the farmer gets to be witty and mocking through most of the story, then becomes friendly and generous near its end (although in a last joke again mocks the visitor). This five minutes of dialogue certainly has staying power. I cannot read Joseph Heller's *Catch-22* without recalling the skit's central joke, which concerns the leaky roof that can't be fixed during rain, but doesn't need to be repaired in good weather. And this brief story could easily be expanded—on one occasion the playlet generated a full-length drama in which the traveler was recast as a villain who abducted the cabin owner's wife and daughter. The wife drowns, but the daughter will eventually be rescued (*Buffalo [New York] Courier*, April 21, 1869).

In Figure 26, I reproduce a flyer for a vaudeville entertainment presented each day for a week starting on October 17, 1881, at the Worcester [Massachusetts] Skating Rink. The program promises considerable variety. However, an evening contained less than one would initially suppose; some acts repeated, and the personnel were recycled creatively. Versatile performer George Milbank seems to have been in charge. He was billed as "The Eccentric Ethiopian Comedian" in connection with his portraying the weary traveler in "The Arkansas Traveller" (which was placed about four-fifths of the way through the program). The other two characters are a surprise, a landlady and "Jocko, the Monkey." We are left to imagine what accretions to the long-lived routine introduced these cast members. Two other brief sketches appear in this 1881 program, "Slim Jim's Ghost"—a rural comedy located near the start of the show—and "The Muldoon's at Home" a skit placed at the end of the evening, one doubtless making fun of the Irish. This program also included acrobatics, dancing, trick instrument performance, virtuoso banjo playing, artistic violin moments (the "Remenyi" in the program must have been Ede Reményi, a Hungarian

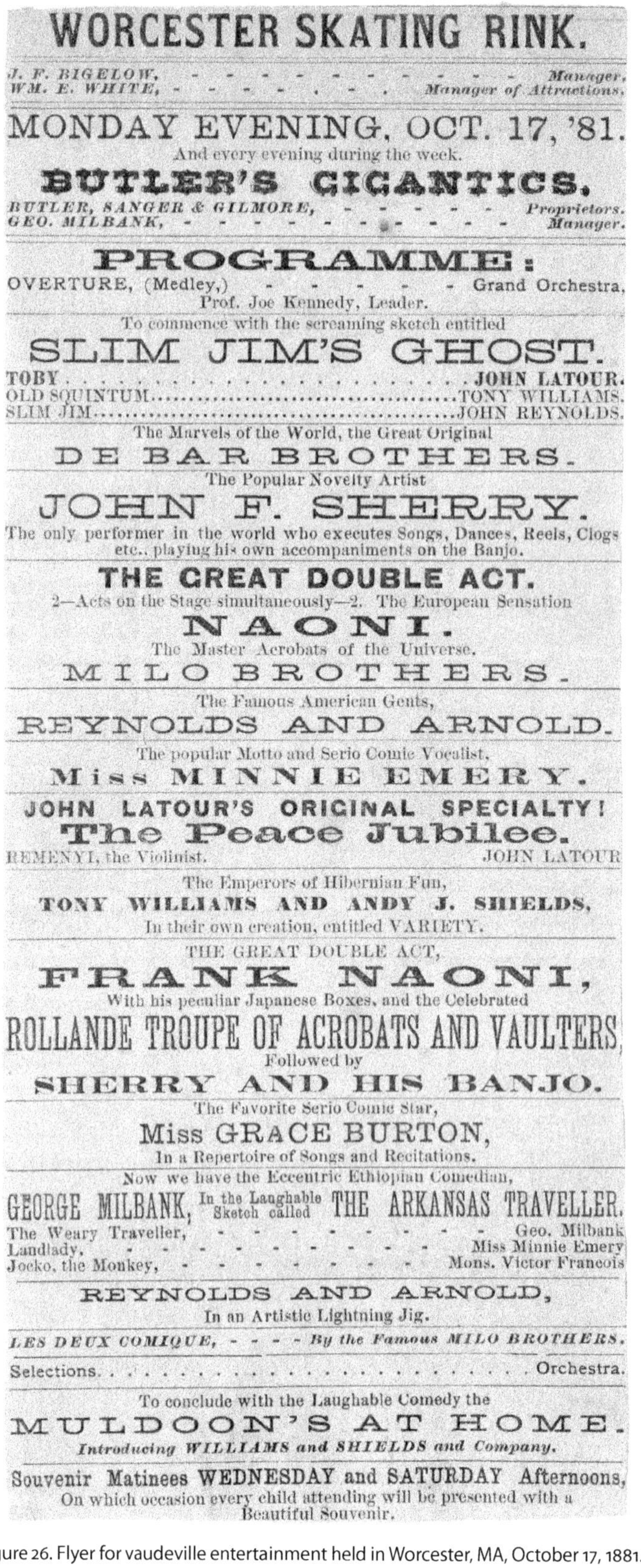

WORCESTER SKATING RINK.

J. F. BIGELOW, - - - - - - - - - - - - - Manager,
WM. E. WHITE, - - - - - - - - Manager of Attractions.

MONDAY EVENING, OCT. 17, '81.

And every evening during the week.

BUTLER'S GIGANTICS.

BUTLER, SANGER & GILMORE, - - - - - - Proprietors.
GEO. MILBANK, - - - - - - - - - - - Manager.

PROGRAMME:

OVERTURE, (Medley,) - - - - - Grand Orchestra,
Prof. Joe Kennedy, Leader.

To commence with the screaming sketch entitled

SLIM JIM'S GHOST.

TOBY . . . . JOHN LATOUR.
OLD SQUINTUM . . . . TONY WILLIAMS.
SLIM JIM . . . . JOHN REYNOLDS.

The Marvels of the World, the Great Original

DE BAR BROTHERS.

The Popular Novelty Artist

JOHN F. SHERRY.

The only performer in the world who executes Songs, Dances, Reels, Clogs etc., playing his own accompaniments on the Banjo.

THE GREAT DOUBLE ACT.

2—Acts on the Stage simultaneously—2. The European Sensation

NAONI.

The Master Acrobats of the Universe.

MILO BROTHERS.

The Famous American Gents,

REYNOLDS AND ARNOLD.

The popular Motto and Serio Comic Vocalist,

Miss MINNIE EMERY.

JOHN LATOUR'S ORIGINAL SPECIALTY!

The Peace Jubilee.

REMENYI, the Violinist. JOHN LATOUR

The Emperors of Hibernian Fun,

TONY WILLIAMS AND ANDY J. SHIELDS,

In their own creation, entitled VARIETY.

THE GREAT DOUBLE ACT,

FRANK NAONI,

With his peculiar Japanese Boxes, and the Celebrated

ROLLANDE TROUPE OF ACROBATS AND VAULTERS,

Followed by

SHERRY AND HIS BANJO.

The Favorite Serio Comic Star,

Miss GRACE BURTON,

In a Repertoire of Songs and Recitations.

Now we have the Eccentric Ethiopian Comedian,

GEORGE MILBANK, In the Laughable Sketch called THE ARKANSAS TRAVELLER.

The Weary Traveller, - - - - - - - - - - Geo. Milbank
Landlady, - - - - - - - - - - - - Miss Minnie Emery
Jocko, the Monkey, - - - - - - - - - Mons. Victor Francois

REYNOLDS AND ARNOLD,

In an Artistic Lightning Jig.

LES DEUX COMIQUE, - - - - By the Famous MILO BROTHERS.

Selections . . . . Orchestra.

To conclude with the Laughable Comedy the

MULDOON'S AT HOME.

Introducing WILLIAMS and SHIELDS and Company.

Souvenir Matinees WEDNESDAY and SATURDAY Afternoons,
On which occasion every child attending will be presented with a Beautiful Souvenir.

Figure 26. Flyer for vaudeville entertainment held in Worcester, MA, October 17, 1881.

violin virtuoso who toured with the young Brahms and who had recently relocated to the United States), songs, ensemble music, and an act mocking the Japanese. Whew.

The Robertson family performance proposed in 1929, while much shorter, was shaped similarly; Eck had crafted a brief but otherwise conventional old-fashioned vaudeville show. Here are the selections in the order Eck listed them, and, to the right of that list, how the individual pieces can be understood to represent the same show ingredients that had

Arkansas Traveller skit,	rural comedy, and ensemble music
Amarillo Waltz	solo violin (meant to be pretty, so I specify "violin")
Barnyard Blues or Cackling Chicken	rural comedy + fiddle skill
Eck, Jr., presenting	a song and banjo solo
Around the World on a Dime.	[a comic song?]
My Experiences on a Ranch	explores a local but disappearing culture; skit with Dueron
Done Gone	banjo and fiddle; introduced in another brief skit?
Kelly Waltz	solo *violin* again
Pop Goes the Weasel	trick fiddling, lots of it
Waggoner	solo fiddle
Novelty Dancing by Miss Marguerite	dancing
Music by the Entire Family	ensemble music

(left-hand column from the *Amarillo Daily News*, March 22, 1929, 3)

been presented in the Worcester Skating Rink vaudeville evening nearly fifty years before:

We must keep in mind that Eck maintained his family band until the family itself dissolved in the late 1930s. Nettie moved out of Borger with the younger children. (The oldest son, Dueron—called "Eck Jr." in the band advertisements—had already graduated from high school and gotten a job that would keep him in Borger.) However, even after the family ensemble was out of the picture, vaudeville tunes and the southeastern melodies peppering vaudeville remained important in Eck's life and career, along with those of his tunes performances of which would feed into and partly shape Texas fiddling.

"Arkansas Traveller" owes its popularity and longevity both to its entertaining narrative and to the independent virtues of the music. The melody is shaped much as are many fiddle tunes. The two strains overlap in musical content but differ in conventional ways. As is typical of fiddle tunes, the strains contrast in tessitura, in the average "lie" of the piece. The primary strain lies relatively low, has a bolder rhythmic profile (that is, it includes notes of different lengths, compellingly ordered), and also hammers home the tonic note of the key—here, we are in D major, so the pitch d is prominent. That first strain ends with a sixteenth-note flourish, which then becomes the source of the melodic sequence dominating the second strain. This subsidiary strain, set overall higher in pitch, continues in rhythmically dense movement that is repetitive, and emphasizes the tonic perceptibly less. While such a broad description holds for many fiddle tunes, the total effect of "Arkansas Traveller" is notably strong and satisfying.

The earliest published version of "Arkansas Traveller" that I have seen is a piano sheet music item by William Cumming published in 1847 (see figure 36, top). It has dotted rhythms notated throughout. Should we hear those rhythms as inheriting the feel of a Scottish dance genre, the strathspey? Or does the dotted notation instead just tell us that the tune should swing? A few other mid-nineteenth-century printed versions are similarly notated, including the arrangement by Mose Case (1858) placed below that of Cumming in figure 36. Most later versions drop the dotting, and look more like headlong reels than leisurely strathspeys (see, for example, Ryan 1883, 26).

In terms of mode, the nineteenth-century printings of "Arkansas Traveller" follow a pattern already common in the great body of fiddle tunes printed in Scotland during the second half of the eighteenth century. Most of those melodies sound more or less in major throughout, but that impression is delicately sabotaged in the tunes' first strains, which lean toward being pentatonic, that is, tending to omit the seventh and especially the fourth degrees of the major scale (except in their cadential measures). Then those same tunes' second strains often include melodic sequences that *do* include the previously "missing" pitches, and so are more fully in major. There is plenty of incidental variation between versions (compare those given in figure 36 with additional nineteenth-century versions anthologized in Goertzen 2020, 126–27). If we juxtapose the versions by Cumming and Case, we notice that the latter version features less pitch contrast, and also loses the melodic turn in its second strain (this specific melodic figure will be preserved in most later versions). In the Case version, the motion is still a sequence, even though a less detailed one. A profusion of such minor differences constitutes good evidence that this tune was in oral tradition. Case was likely primarily interested in the skit anyway. He was a performing blackface minstrel (albeit a guitarist rather than a fiddler).

The version performed by Eck and his much older friend Henry Gilliland, and sold throughout the United States, retains the typical contrast in the ranges of the two strains, though the fact that one fiddler (likely Eck) is playing an octave above the other (probably Gilliland) during the lower strain undercuts that contrast (figure 36, bottom). Their version produces an especially headlong feel by including only a few quarter notes (though there are still more of these in the first strain than in the second one). Their version of the first strain has lost the pentatonic leaning evident in nineteenth-century versions; it is now thoroughly in major. Yes, a few vestigial dodges of the previously expendable scale degrees remain; for example, there is no c♯ in measure 4. However, the push toward a more major-key, more modern feel is clear.

Which fiddler is leading the performance? No testimony survives concerning who is playing the A strain of the tune in its usual range, and who is playing more vigorously an octave higher. My best guess is that Gilliland, whose style reflected that he had fiddled in house parties for decades before fiddle contests came to his part of the country, might have been seemingly "in charge"; he got to play the tune as inherited, in its usual range. Eck could easily double the original line an octave higher; the position work required—rare at the time—was a skill he cultivated. In addition, we see Eck yearning for a filled-out sound, and adding a fair number of open string doubles (in the B strain, the added note being the open string a).

Figure 37 represents a very recent performance of "Arkansas Traveller" by a senior fiddler, Daniel Jasek, who plays in a largely old-time style (although his handful of interpolated triplets represent more recent developments in Texas contest fiddling style). Mr. Jasek, a native Texan of Czech extraction, is a farmer who played for house dances for many years before becoming a regular at fiddle contests. His style reflects the dance environment—it contains just enough incidental variation to add some spark to the performance, but not the sort of building of an overall musical shape that dominates Texas fiddling today. Hallettsville, the site of the Texas State Fiddle Championship, is home to quite a bit of inherited Czech culture—breakfast tidbits sold at the contest include a few tacos but more kolaches. Many parts of Texas received sizeable numbers of German and Eastern European immigrants during the nineteenth century, and it is reasonable to watch for ethnic contributions to Eck's growth as a musician. On the one hand, no obvious musical traces of that part of the old world stick out in his recorded repertoire. On the other hand, a surprising European influence will be discussed in the next chapter of this book.

I will close this section by returning to the nineteenth century to look at uses of this fiddle tune in the genteel side of popular music. Figures 27 and 28 reproduce very different title pages of versions of "The Arkansas Traveller" written for piano. Several northern publishers issued the arrangement by Mose Case, with slightly different drawings, all including sketches of cabin, fiddler, and visitor. This one, from New York publisher S. T. Gordon & Son, even refers to a detail in the narrative by portraying a hole in the roof of the cabin in the illustration. The total effect was rustic and representational. In marked contrast, the cover of the set of variations by Wilhelm Iucho in Figure 28 places the tune in genteel circumstances both through its dedication—to young women studying the piano—and the elegant

Figure 27. Cover of "Arkansas Traveller" published by S. T. Gordon and Sons.

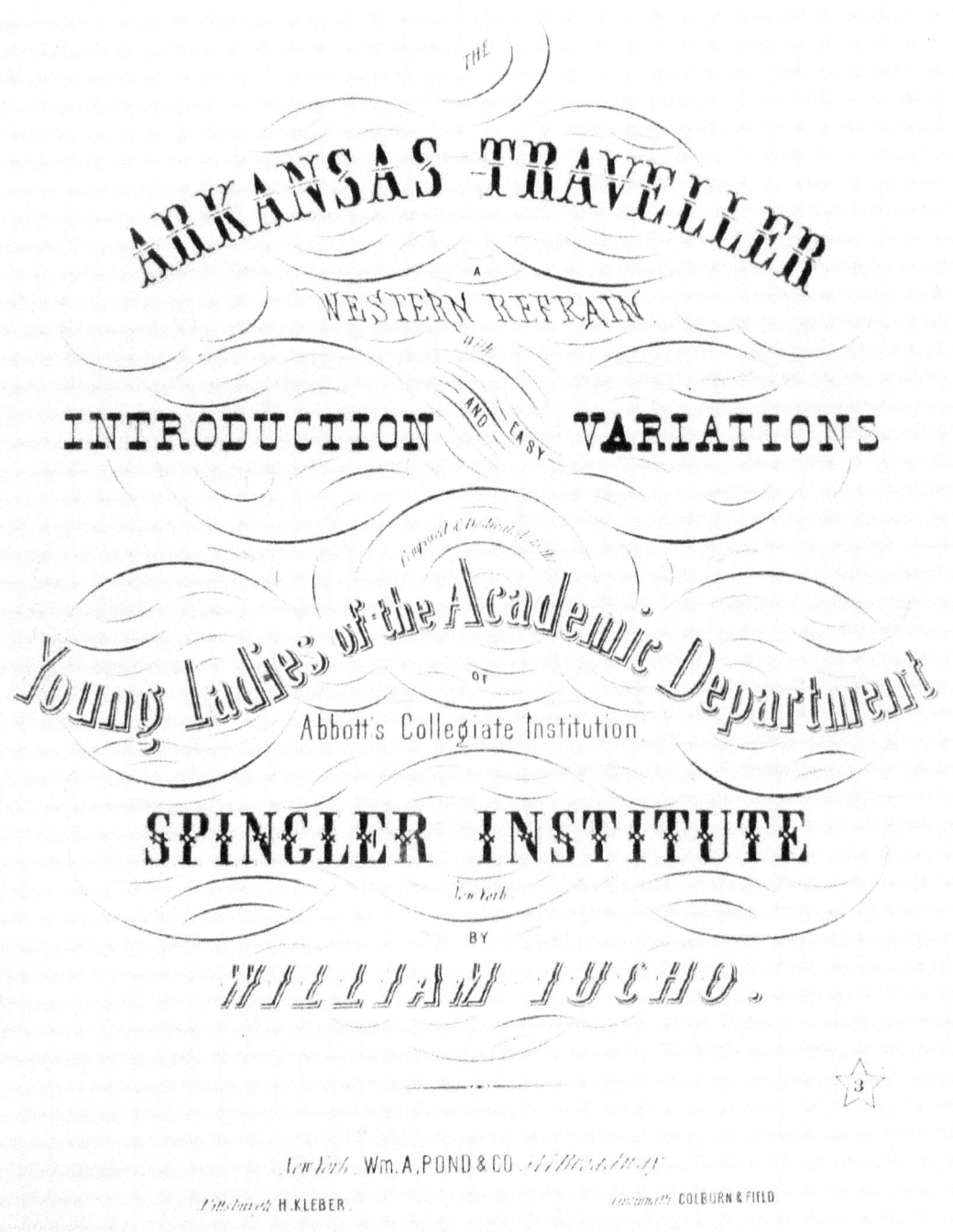

Figure 28. Cover of variation set on tune "Arkansas Traveller" by William Iucho.

swirls on the title page. Iucho, a German immigrant who worked as a multifaceted musician in Pittsburgh, mentions on the title page that "Arkansas Traveller" was a "Western Refrain" (1851; the full score is available as of this writing at https://levysheetmusic.mse.jhu.edu/collection/160/005).

In figure 38 I reproduce the opening section of the Iucho arrangement—the theme, unadorned, then just the beginning of each of the three variations. In the context of piano variation sets for a genteel audience, this is a simple arrangement. But it follows a typical progression: the theme, a variation in duple time (with more notes, now presented in arpeggios, with just a hint of the theme at the start), a denser variation based on triplets, and a character variation (here, the final section is in polka rhythm). Iucho follows this same basic sequence in more elaborate variation sets, just with more steps interpolated. In such Italianate variation sets, each variation maintains the harmonic motion of the theme but otherwise dissolves into an étude answering one or more specific technical challenges. This strategy had long been typical both in art music and in artful arrangements of folk tunes, including in Scottish fiddle collections of the late eighteenth and early nineteenth centuries.

Another approach to expanding the musical content of a given fiddle tune is to insert it into a medley, often a cotillion or quadrille, two terms indicating sets of four to six two-strain dance tunes (normally lacking separate titles) meant to be played in turn without pause, allowing the dancers to extend their stays out on the dance floor. In typical examples, some of the constituent dance melodies will be in 2/4 and others in 6/8. The melodies will not all be in the same key, but their keys will be closely related. Quadrilles/cotillions were in high demand in the middle of the nineteenth century and for some decades into the second half of that century, but in short supply; dance musicians were constantly seeking out new examples of this useful but often musically unexciting genre (see Goertzen 2020, 98–99). Figure 39 shows a form of the well-known "Engagement Quadrille," composed and/or arranged by H. Kleber, a German immigrant who pursued a career performing, teaching, and publishing music in Pittsburgh. This is something of a stunt quadrille. Its unusual aspect is that each section has its own name, with those subtitles indicating stages in courtship. The titles (and their keys and time signatures) are as follows:

1. The Meeting	2/4	C major
2. The Courtship	6/8	G major
3. The Bridal	2/4	G major
4. The Honeymoon	2/4	C major
5. Rackensack Jig or the Arkansas Traveller	2/4	G major

Most of the sections of the "Engagement Quadrille" are musically undistinguished, and solidly set in the specified major keys (that is, with none of the interest-adding hints at pentatonic scales that so often pepper fiddle tunes). This bland effect is typical of quadrilles, and especially unsurprising in a composition by a musician who did not grow up hearing American fiddle tunes. Indeed, the second most striking section, "The Bridal," reminds us that Kleber was from Germany—it sounds much like the ubiquitous German folk song "Muss i denn" (see Holder 1892). A detail: "Rackensack" is a colloquial spelling of "Arkansas." This term, when used as a modifier, was intended to be derogatory or at least quite rustic; early prints of "Arkansas Traveller" often incorporate the word "Rackensack" one way or another. The general lesson of this quadrille is that one way to nourish and expand the musical effect of a fiddle tune is to attach it to other tunes in a medley; the nineteenth-century quadrille offered a formula for doing so.

These versions of "Arkansas Traveller" offer several general lessons. They exemplify the functional versatility of fiddle tunes. The "Engagement Quadrille," although initially published as piano sheet music, I transcribe here as presented by James Buckley as one-line melodies in his all-purpose collection entitled *Buckley's Violin Tunes: A Collection of Beautiful Marches, Waltzes, Quadrilles, Polkas, Scottisches [sic], Operatic Melodies, Hornpipes, Reels, Jigs. Etc. Etc. and Many Other Melodies Never Before Published, Including Buckley's Celebrated Imitations of the Farm-Yard, and Brigg's Power of Music* (1855). That lengthy title is itself an argument for the player of the physical violin to also be competent as a fiddler; fiddle tunes (and some violin melodies) moved freely between social settings. "Arkansas Traveller," initially a reel intended for dramatic use in a minstrel setting (has it become a functional relative of an "operatic melody" at this point?) appears here "domesticated," placed in the cultivated setting of a quadrille. Or should we think of its entry into this quadrille as illustrating the rustic, casually festive flavor capping off the end of many an otherwise formal occasion? The tune and its associated skit seem to have started life in oral tradition, with the tune borrowed for pedagogical purposes in piano settings beginning in the 1850s. It is a lively visitor to a genteel setting in those moments, with these relatively formal moments coexisting with the tune's continued use in blackface minstrelsy. Then the informal entertainment side of the melody's identity returns later, in the publication of tune-with-skit in Mose Case's arrangement, which then reappears both as an independent sheet music item and in anthologies issued by several publishers. It continues to pop up in its guise as an all-purpose reel in numerous collections of fiddle tunes, and continues to flourish in oral tradition at the same time.

Since Eck and Gilliland played "Arkansas Traveller" as a duet for the Victor executives, that is how it reached a broad audience in recorded form. It was not a unison presentation, since Eck chose to add the upper octave. On the one hand, it did not become a fancy arrangement that took careful thought and considerable practice to craft, but rather remained a straightforward hit melody with a conceptually simple reinforcement. On the other hand, adding that upper octave creates a push in the direction of powerful effect that requires virtuosity; this addition requires both duplication of pitches and extensive position work. It is one embodiment of Eck's constant urge to add material to fiddle tunes, an urge toward expansion of musical content and technique that he will pursue along one or another path in every corner of his repertoire.

ECK'S GRAB BAG OF OLDER TUNES

The very oldest segment of Eck's repertoire centers on hornpipes: "College Hornpipe" (also known as "Sailor's Hornpipe," just a century ago returning to mass culture due to its use as the theme of the "Popeye" cartoons), "Fisher's Hornpipe," "Durang's Hornpipe," "Big Devil Medley" (Eck's own arrangement of "Devil's Dream"), and "Dominion Hornpipe," plus equally old non-hornpipes "Soldier's Joy" (perhaps the most-played fiddle tune of the nineteenth and early twentieth centuries, often used as a reel), and the jig "Irish Washerwoman." These tunes share many musical characteristics, and most have a common background—all but "Dominion Hornpipe" have documented histories that reach back at least to the 1780s. "Dominion Hornpipe" is quite rare, though also played later by Benny Thomasson, the revolutionary Texas fiddler of the next generation; we simply don't know how old this tune is. It is similar to but less striking than "Durang's Hornpipe," a comparison that may have doomed it. (Similarly, Eck said that he did not play "Natchez Under the Hill" because he tended to "get it mixed up with "Turkey in the Straw"; Seeger interview, 1963.)

All of these venerable tunes except "Durang's Hornpipe" are rarely played today in either contest fiddling on the Texas model or in urban revivalist fiddling. In short, this is a body of tunes with a much richer past than present. These tunes (again, excepting "Dominion Hornpipe") were all being played frequently in both North and South during Eck's prime, and certainly in Texas. The Brenham contest in 1900 described in chapter 3 included "College Hornpipe," "Fisher's Hornpipe," "Devil's Dream," "Irish Wash[er]woman," and "Soldier's Joy."

Among Eck's recordings, all members of this set of tunes were recorded during the interview with Pat Conte's friend (1970s?). Of these tunes, only "College Hornpipe" was also recorded another time, during the 1959 interview conducted by Vernon Riddle. I would guess that it was Conte's friend rather than Eck who pointed the interview in this particular antique direction. In fact, just before Eck played "Irish Washerwoman," Eck asked this interviewer to confirm that that was the tune's title. Perhaps Conte's friend had prompted Eck with the first few notes of the tune, and Eck dug deep into his memory to find the rest of the melody. However, there is compelling evidence that Eck had played several of these tunes enough times to think about them carefully, and to put his own stamp on them. In particular, four of these performances include the usual two strains in their normal pitch ranges and also one or both strains presented an octave up, requiring Eck to shift into third position. Both "Durang's Hornpipe" and "Soldier's Joy" include versions of the A strain in the upper octave; "College Hornpipe" has the B strain several times in the upper octave; and "Fisher's Hornpipe" starts with the A strain in a high version, and also includes the B strain in third position and above, adding up to a truly difficult version of this common tune.

What musical elements do these specific performances share? First, the melodies are not in the pentatonic mode used in "Sally Goodin" (and in many other of Eck's tunes), but rather are clearly in major—the fourth and seventh degrees of the major scale are not dodged at all. At the same time, all of these tunes have stable, easily recognizable melodic motives, and very stable identities overall. Perhaps these two factors have worked together to shield these tunes somewhat from modern Texas fiddlers' collective stylistic mandate and added personal inclinations to vary strains and to build complex forms as they go through a performance. That is, it may be that *not* omitting the fourth and seventh degrees of the major scale crowds the page, leaving less room for small bits of personalization, for small-scale variety.

Nevertheless, Eck steps a small distance away from the usual printed forms of even these relatively immutable tunes (keeping in mind that these forms are well preserved in dance fiddling in New England and rural New York, where the tunes remain fairly common in oral tradition). In general, hornpipes tend to have more jumps in the melody than reels of the same vintage; they are also a bit more challenging for the right hand, since the fiddler may be asked to switch back and forth between strings more than in other fiddle tune genres, and even more challenging for the left hand. But Eck—perhaps in a sort of historical collusion with the fiddlers from whom he learned these tunes—often replaced some of these disjunct "hornpipe" moments with linear motion, which is more patterned and thus less apt to offer a challenge to the left hand that is specific to a given piece. Please compare Eck's B strains of "Fisher's Hornpipe" and of "College Hornpipe" with those in the versions of those tunes given in Elias Howe's widely distributed publications (see figures 40 and 41).

The jig "Irish Washerwoman" presents a special case. Eck doesn't seem to have a conventional feel for this genre in brisk 6/8 time—he surprises by swinging the tune. "Irish Washerwoman" is old and quite widespread. The first printed version under this name came out in 1792, from the Scottish Gow family ([1792], 31). I place the tune of this version in the middle of figure 46. It's more tonally and rhythmically complex than subsequent versions, with more variety in how the A strain can end, and with the double-tonic element in the third and fourth measures of the B strain (meaning that those measures, rather than remaining in G major, simply move both the melody and the bass down a full step; note also that the bass in those measures is just two f natural pitches per measure). While the history of the tune is tangled, my best guess is that it was indeed originally Scottish, then became much blander when subjected to the English filter, then carried that relatively tame identity to the United States.

I will now shift to the remainder of Eck's older tunes, the venerable melodies that were crafted in the United States, likely during the nineteenth century. A general topic and a concentration within that subject emerge. The larger idea is country life, but with a narrower emphasis under that umbrella: the practice of imitating sounds from the rural environment within tunes named for the producers of those sounds. So, starting with the broad brush of country images, we have "Turkey in the Straw," the second tune that Eck and Gilliland played for the Victor executives in 1922. This tune was then nearly as famous as was "Arkansas Traveller," and may be even more famous today. It was likely descended from the ballad opera song "Rose Tree" (a love song, from the long-lived ballad opera *Poor Soldier* of 1783) by way of "Old Zip Coon," a famous blackface minstrel song. Like those ancestral tunes, "Turkey in the Straw" was initially sung. Perhaps the repeated association with words has kept these various incarnations of this ingratiating melody unusually versatile in the keys in which they have been set; singers like to have versions of tunes to perform that fit their best singing ranges. The tune is unequivocally in major. The key of G major, in which Eck and Gilliland played it, has become the main key, perhaps doing so because singing the melody has largely yielded to playing it (see figure 48).

This duet has some common ground with these fiddlers' "Arkansas Traveller": the fiddlers play in an intended unison much of the time, but Eck takes an upper octave in most passes through the A strain after the first two, and also adds a high flourish in the second half of the B strain. Again, when Eck is playing in the upper octave, it is hard to hear Gilliland. The men seem not to have worked as hard on this tune as they had on "Arkansas Traveller"; moments of imprecise doubling can be heard here and there. Nevertheless, it is still a catchy tune vigorously played, and sold very well for Victor.

Eck also played a version in C major (figure 48, to the right within the figure). It is quite possible that the G-major version is one he learned from his father or uncle or another one of those he called "The Old Masters," and the one in C major represents his own "improvement." Or perhaps both are inherited versions, and he played the G version for recording simply because it was one that Henry Gilliland, his playing partner here, could play readily. In any case, the C version is more interesting. We hear just a bit more variation when strains are repeated, and a bit more position work (the two instances of high c in the G version could be reached by extending the left hand fourth finger, but that note is used more in the C version, gracefully performed with a move to third position). The most interesting difference, however, is the insertion of measures of pizzicato notes toward the end of the C version, likely imitating the turkey pecking; several of Eck's tunes named for birds include similar maneuvers.

The title "Mississippi Sawyer" refers to trees sunk in and loosely anchored in the Mississippi River, with currents pushing part of the tree to the surface now and again in a slow "sawing" motion that causes the rising limbs to pose a surprise danger to boats. This tune, first printed in Virginia ca. 1839 (see Goertzen 2017), spread widely and became very common in much of the United States, but is now rare in Texas, though not entirely absent—Texas Shorty (Jim Chancellor) played it. Eck's version (figure 47) is quite unusual, distinct from typical Upper South practice. He plays both strains in both the original octave and in a lower one. And he varies subtleties of double stopping and of bowing for effect: compare the third and fourth A strains to see varying use of an added harmonizing b, and compare the third and fourth B strains to see him removing slurs to strengthen impact. But the most striking feature is his use of a double tonic, not expected here (we *didn't* hear that in his "Irish Washerwoman," where the oldest versions do include that feature). I have never heard a double tonic section in "Mississippi Sawyer" except in this performance. Eck's version starts out firmly in D major, then surprises in the third measure of B1 with the unsharped c. Here the small melodic figure first presented in the first measure of the strain is being played a step down, and, rather than remaining in the key of D major, the interval of a major third in that melodic gesture is preserved by inserting a c natural. But this is not simply an isolated "double tonic" moment as in the Gow version of "Irish Washerwoman" from the turn of the nineteenth century (figure 46). The note c is always natural throughout the performance; Eck is playing in Mixolydian mode. Eck did not choose to record this melody commercially, and there is no evidence that any of his contemporaries took up his oddly antique version. Was his version experimental, or reproduced faithfully from family or friends? We cannot know.

Eck played another double-tonic tune, the widespread but not ubiquitous "Snowbird on the Ashbank." "Snowbird" is a nickname for the dark-eyed junco, a species of bird often seen during migration seasons hopping on the ground, where it does most of its feeding. Juncos increase their insulating plumage in winter to stay warm—hence the reference to snow. I transcribed Eck's performance and a later one by E. J. Hopkins of this tune (figure 45). Both fiddlers include a closing section that may imitate the hopping around of these birds looking for food on the ground. Eck's version seems antique in several ways, both the double-tonic aspect and his stretching of the cadence of the A section by a beat. Hopkins kept the double-tonic motion—after all, that is the main thing going on in the melody—but brought the cadences into normal configuration, so that the A strain is precisely eight measures long. (In the last chapter, I'll discuss how the long-vs.-normal cadence issue was addressed by Eck in his performances of "Done Gone.")

"Great Big Taters"—its full title is "Great Big Taters in Sandy Land"—is a typical Upper South frolic song, a type derived from blackface minstrelsy. It resembles the more common southeastern tune "Sail Away Ladies," but does have a life of its own based on its own occasionally sung lyrics, which assert that "sandy land" like much of that in the old Southwest is good for growing potatoes, but not corn. J. B. (James Britton Buchanan Boone) Cranfill, Eck's partner in this and one other performance, was a prominent religious figure of the time, in fact the vice-presidential candidate of the small but loud Prohibition party in the election of 1892. Cranfill fiddled as a youth, gave it up for religious reasons for some years, then returned to it—a far-from-rare pattern, the same that Eck's father had followed. He related a mock feud with Eck concerning whose name should go first on the record label, claiming precedence due to his greater weight and age and better looks (*Amarillo Globe Times*, August 20, 1976).

Cranfill and Eck play in fairly faithful unison in this performance (figure 49). "Hawk's Got the Chicken" is the same sort of song, here performed with words, a typical number and flavor of lyrics, a pair of couplets. These are hard to fully make out from the recording. What I hear Eck sing is this: "Run old man and get your gun; hawk's got a chicken and he's gonna run. Flapped his wings and batted his eye; and carried that chicken to the sky."

OLD-TIME TUNES IMITATING NATURE; A MINSTREL INGREDIENT

Is the music of "Hawk's Got the Chicken" pictorial? Are the curving melodic lines meant to imitate the hawk flying? Perhaps, but I doubt it. As in most fiddle tunes, the degree of painting of title or text extends only to generally avoiding having the broad flavor of the music contradict the mood of that title (or, when there is a text, the flavor of those lyrics). Many tunes do feature a section that may imitate sounds from nature, as in the closing section of "Snowbird in the Ashbank." However, a small but conspicuous handful of melodies include sounds suggested by their rustic titles, and the older, specifically American fraction of Eck's repertoire included several of these. His evident affection for these tunes must have been linked to his energetic pursuit of trick fiddling, which was often mentioned in advertisements for his performances; such tunes constituted an important ingredient of his vaudeville shows. He could "make a fiddle talk." In another stunt, when he played "Pop Goes the Weasel," he moved rapidly from holding his fiddle normally to any number of other bodily configurations. On one occasion, he

> was playing the stage, doing that trick fiddling, "Pop Goes the Weasel." Damn, I'd lay down on the damn stage, and just keep playing, and finally kick my heels up like this, you know, and get 'em just way high, and there, still laying there flat on my back playing, directly I just flounced like a damn fish and turned a summersault, [I'd] keep a playin.' Played that sun of a gun and threw my fiddle box plumb across the big stage, and Roden, [with whom he collaborated at this point] caught it. I done that in Oklahoma one time, and everybody said [it] was the most impossible thing they ever saw. Never missed to tune or anything. (Seeger interview, 1963)

And, while Eck never recorded "Listen to the Mockingbird," he played that tune, doubtless imitating any number of bird songs along the way. A newspaper photograph of him performing this piece is not clear enough to reproduce here, but does show him holding the fiddle conventionally, not in any special position adopted for imitating any bird's call (*Lubbock Morning Avalanche*, July 5, 1952, 11).

At today's annual Texas State Championship Fiddler's Frolics, trick fiddling is not part of the main competition; the rules forbid it. However, this gaudy bit of Texas fiddle history is celebrated the night before, in a sub-event called "Anything Goes." This division was renamed "Western Swing" in 2023, but retained the same spirit, with the official description of the category including: "Twin fiddle, bowing tricks, or stand on your head while fiddling. The audience will decide which fiddle player can entertain best with their artistry." The champion in this category in the last few years has been Trustin Baker, a young Missouri fiddler who also either wins or places well every year in the second most competitive actual competition, the bracket called "Gone to Texas" (the competition bracket for Texas-style fiddlers who have the misfortune of residing elsewhere). In the "Anything Goes" ("Western Swing") category, Trustin usually plays the same two tunes, "Orange Blossom Special," part of it played with the fiddle behind his back (see figure 29), and "Listen to the Mockingbird." At the 2021 iteration, the contestants he defeated included one young boy who played while standing on a balance device, and a young girl who played while hula-hooping (figure 30). These two photographs also point out a pair of aspects of the culture around fiddling that has been constant from Eck's day to ours. One is family support for learning and performing traditional music. In figure 29 we also see Trustin Baker's mother and sister, fellow members of the Baker Family Band. Another is the fact that competing fiddlers often support each other as accompanists, as Trustin Baker is doing for McKenna Peterson in Figure 30.

Figure 29. In the 2021 Texas State Championships, Anything Goes division, Trustin Baker performed "Orange Blossom Special" with his fiddle held in a number of surprising positions.

Figure 30. In that same "Anything Goes" division of the 2021 Texas State Championships, young McKenna Peterson incorporated rotating a hula hoop into her otherwise conventional technique. Her accompanist was Trustin Baker.

With "Lost Goose" we move more deeply into an area of the fiddle sonic culture that had been nourished vigorously as part of blackface minstrelsy, that is, playing tunes that announce their rural orientation in a comic way by integrating rural sounds (figure 50, top). Eck (and other fiddlers) imitated the goose honking by employing harmonics, those clear, flute-like tones created by touching a violin string gently at a point that is some integral division of the length of the string. Bowing while touching a string in its middle yields the pitch an octave above the pitch of the string, while touching it a third of the way from either end yields an octave plus a fifth above the fundamental, and so on. Thus, harmonics yield access to a distinctive sound on the pitches in the harmonic series of the pitch of the string (or of a length of it shortened by pressing down the first finger in the normal way).

There's not much to "Lost Goose" other than its harmonics. The goose's identity has been evoked through use of that technical device; that this waterfowl is disoriented is not reflected in musical sound. In fact, Eck (or his interviewers) didn't seem to have been very committed to the "lost" in the title. When he played the tune for Riddle, Riddle named it "Call of the Wild Goose," and Seeger listed it as "Wild Goose Crossing the Ocean" when he anthologized this performance on the *Famous Cowboy Fiddler* LP.

Use of harmonics to represent birds is widespread in the North Atlantic fiddle universe. Below Eck's "Lost Goose" in figure 50, I place the first measures of a Norwegian fiddle tune called "Gammel Gauken," in which harmonics represent the "Old Cuckoo" (the cuckoo being the bird most often portrayed by harmonics in North Atlantic fiddling). Many of the fiddle tunes containing bird imitations follow the same broad formal plan followed in "Lost Goose" and "Gammel Gauken," that is, starting the A strain with harmonics on the tonic and/or dominant of the key of the tune, then proceeding without harmonics in that strain, and not using them in the B strain. Eck may have been more extravagant on occasion: he told Tracy Schwarz that he "used to play 'Red Wing,'" and insert harmonics all the way through it (Seeger interview, 1963).

But while harmonics can evoke several different birds, chickens are not included! Instead, syncopated appearances of high notes, plus occasionally irregular recurrences of such gestures do the job—in Eck's "Cacklin' Hen" (figure 51), see how the figure in the second half of measure 3 returns. As in his "Lost Goose" and in the various Norwegian tunes including harmonics to represent the cuckoo, just one strain features convincing animal imitations; care is taken for the comedy (or other pictorial elements) to be balanced with conventional musically attractive passages. For the most extravagant example of this alternation of tune and direct sonic imitation, think of "Listen to the Mockingbird."

Blackface minstrels employed imitations of animals regularly, especially for comic effect. Several publications intended for minstrel use portray these. Figure 51, which ends with a transcription of Eck's "Cacklin' Hen," begins with photographs of three pages from a book intended for blackface minstrel use (that is, Buckley 1855). The title page shows the same intimacy in minstrel performance between art music (such as "operatic excerpts") and broad comedy illustrated in the 1881 minstrel event program given in figure 26. The second photo shows the middle page of three that list musical mottos associated with animals and other sounds—note the motto for the "hen." The third image is of the third page of "Buckley's Farmyard, or Farmer's Medley," an extravaganza mixing dramatic fiddling (without particular topic) with some of the approximate replications of animal sounds and other outdoor noises illustrated in the second photo. The medley starts with alternations of "Crowing of the Cock" and "Village Bells" (presumably church bells). The page reproduced in Figure 51, showing "Crowing of the Cock" alternating with "Cackling of the Hen," gives us a detailed example of how chickens are represented in minstrel fiddling: the syncopated figure from the roster of mottos is not merely used, but falls in different places in the measure, producing more syncopation. Just as that page ventures outside of birdlife ("The Bleating of a Calf" and "The Braying of an Ass"), the list of musical imitations excerpted on the lower left of the figure ranges from calls of other birds ("Throstle"—an antique term for thrush—"Hen," "Robin," "Duck," and "Guinea Fowl") to "Counterfeit Shilling," "Blacksmith," "Conversation Tone," and "Young Lady Calling" (this musical motto is texted: "Edward! Edward! Edward!"). The next page includes "Children at Play" and "Preacher." Such brief comic caricatures offer a context for another of Eck's tunes, the well-known "Lost Indian" (figure 50, bottom), which dates back in print to the early nineteenth century under the title "Indian Whoop" (in George P. Knauff, 1839 II, #3; see Goertzen 2020, 169).

The last tune I will consider in this section is one that Eck wasn't eager to play. The interview conducted by Roger Abrahams's anthropology students Pat Riggs and Szabi Nagy in 1962 evidently was preceded by some unrecorded discussion of a tune linked to a story about hunting. The interviewers insisted that Eck play it; after considerable complaining, he did so. Here is the relevant section of the interview. In this conversation, Eck referred to a Black servant with the N word, using a matter-of-fact tone; that was apparently the only word he knew describing African Americans.

> That was just . . . you wouldn't notice any difference [between] that and any other tune hardly . . . Governor Alf Taylor of Tennessee told me the story hisself about this tune. It's representing what the [elderly Black servant of Governor Taylor's father] dreamed, you know, and it corresponded: hounds that went out into the woods and jumped a fox and were just circling around him while he was sit down around the roots of a big tree and went to sleep. And he dreamed the tune and went back to the house and got his fiddle down off the wall and played it. That's the way he got the tune . . . He had the tune in his head, you know, but it don't represent too much about the dogs barking or anything thataway . . .

This tune (figure 56) stands out in various ways within Eck's recorded repertoire. It's cast in 6/8, in jig time. The A and C strains both must occur in pairs, since iterations alternate ending on the dominant and on the tonic; the form is a hybrid, melding customary fiddle tune form with an effect more typical of a song. Is the event named—the fox chase—painted in the music? Perhaps. Within the C strain, the high d might represent a hound's howl, especially the high d in the middle of the strain, since that d is approached by a slide, making it sound more like baying. But Eck made a point of saying that that the tune did not "represent too much about the dogs barking or anything thataway." He apparently drew a line between melodies that imitated sounds from outside of music and those that did not. He certainly didn't shy away from tunes referencing animal sounds; perhaps he preferred that this particular tune be associated with the servant's creativity or his act of dreaming rather than the sonic contents of the dream!

While the title of Eck's tune did not come up in this interview, this exact performance was posted on YouTube under the name "Alf Taylor's Fox Chase" (referring to the fiddling Tennessee governor with whom Eck had interacted). The title makes sense, and helps differentiate this tune from today's common southeastern tune "Tennessee Mountain Fox Chase," a 4/4 tune, a headlong reel one strain of which resembles the C strain of Eck's tune in employing a few conspicuous high notes; I transcribed a performance of this widely known old-time tune from the playing of excellent West Virginia–style fiddler Jake Krack (also in figure 56). The one tune I've encountered with the exact title "Alf Taylor's Fox Chase" was recorded in 1925 or 1926 by Al Hopkins and his Buckle Busters (also called The Hill Billies; this was the source of early country music being referred to as hillbilly). This band, formed in Galax, Virginia, was based in Washington, DC. This "Alf Taylor's Fox Chase" is filled with narration accompanied by fiddled sound effects, especially many repetitions of a high lick much like the one that is the most pictorial moment in "Tennessee Mountain Fox Chase." In short, the Buckle Busters' "Alf Taylor's Fox Chase" is a narrated story with recurring music (structured somewhat like the playlet form of "Arkansas Traveller"), while the common tune "Tennessee Mountain Fox Chase" is a reel, a danceable fiddle tune nevertheless peppered with programmatic moments. Eck's tune, connected with a fox servant's dream (during a fox hunt) was one he didn't want to be considered the least bit pictorial, although the C strain recalls the unabashedly imitative gesture prominent in the more headlong tunes with "fox hunt" in their titles.

"Bonaparte's Retreat" has long been a famous and widespread tune in the United States, and remains one of just a handful of novelty tunes that countless fiddlers know. Bayard traces the melody back to an old Irish tune, "The Eagle's Whistle" (1982, 200). When this tune was adapted as a battle-depicting piece, under its new title, "Bonaparte's Retreat," it joined a long tradition of multi-section battle-narrating instrumental pieces—often for piano—popular in both Europe and the United States. One American example, James Hewitt's *The Battle of Trenton*, was published in Philadelphia in 1797. Hewitt's piece consists of a dozen sections of music, including "Drums and Fifes" (actually the already ubiquitous "Yankee Doodle"), "An

Attack" (full of octave leaps and syncopation to evoke the great efforts and frenzied moments of surprise in battle), "Confusion," and "Grief of the Americans for the Loss of Their Comrades Killed in the Engagement," a mournful slow march. The most popular of these battle pieces—both in Europe and North America—was *The Battle of Prague*, by Frantisek Kotzwara (1730–1791), an originally Czech composer whose career was spent in London. Sections from *The Battle of Prague* were regularly excerpted for hand-copied personal anthologies of tunes, in which American youths gathered pieces they knew or intended to learn on flute or fiddle or other treble instrument, with many melodies flourishing in both written and oral tradition. For instance, a copy book signed Hiram Buck and including evidence that the book was compiled in Louisville, Kentucky (in the 1820s, the repertoire it contains suggests), has 109 tunes in it. (The book's accession title in the library of the Center for Popular Music, Middle Tennessee University, is *Manuscript Music Book Belonging to William Egan*, a later owner.) Tune #12 is "March in the Battle of Prague" (15; it is the opening music of Kotzwara's piece), and #85 is "Turkish Music, Battle of Prague" (58; caters to the contemporary vogue for Janissary music, supposedly sounding like that of the bands attached to the Ottoman Empire's Green Berets). Of the tunes included in Eck's recorded repertoire, Mr. Buck included versions of "Fisher's Hornpipe," "College Hornpipe," "Irish Washwoman," and "Lord MacDonald's Reel" (which Eck called "Leather Britches," as was generally customary in the southern United States in his time).

Two of the dozen other war-oriented pieces in Hiram Buck's manuscript copybook are entitled "Buonaparte's March" (#30, 27) and "Gen. Buonaparte's March (#100, 66). These are sturdy marches in G major; neither resembles "Bonaparte's Retreat." Indeed, there are a handful more of pieces with "Buonaparte" (variously spelled) or "Napoleon" in their titles that turn up regularly in early nineteenth-century instrumental collections (some published, some not). None of them is our "Bonaparte's Retreat," but together they offer a context for it. Of course, the broadest of the several musical contexts to which this tune then belonged was that of marches, which have since become the province of bands. "Bonaparte's Retreat" survived as a descriptive piece, like "Cluck Old Hen."

Eck's performance of "Bonaparte's Retreat" doesn't surprise in the pitches he plays, but he embraces the music as a linear narrative of a battle more literally than became usual in the twentieth century (figure 52). He was among the fiddlers who speed up during the piece; he said that he was imitating the guns firing: "That's guns a shootin'. Cannon where they come in that bass. The little strings are the small guns" (Seeger interview, 1963). He played "Bonaparte's Retreat" in an uncommon version of an already uncommon tuning. Both the g string and e string are lowered to d; thus, the g is lowered a fourth and the e just a major second. The result is low D, DAD (a variation on the less rare low D, DAE, the tuning in which this tune is generally played today). He also employed the scordatura low D, DAD for a pair of languid 6/8 tunes whose titles he did not recall (figure 53). One "had something about the nightingale" (Seeger interview, 1963). Dozens—perhaps hundreds—of songs from the nineteenth and early twentieth centuries "had something about the nightingale"; none that I located matched these untitled tunes that Eck hadn't quite forgotten.

During the part of Seeger's interview of Eck in 1963 devoted to pieces in unusual tunings, Eck played two pieces in the truly rare tuning of low E, EAE. It is much like the low D, DAD of the previous two tunes, but with the open string a as a constant between these tunings, the general effect shifts. In low D, DAD, the key of D major is emphasized strongly—there is lots of droning on d, the tonic. In low E, EAE, the pitch a is now the only tonic, with the dominant pitch of e the one constantly reinforced (in A . . . well, not convincingly A *major*, but A nonetheless). The more common of these two tunes, "Say Old May, Can You Play a Fiddle?" belongs to the end of the next chapter (see figure 67); "Get Up in the Cool" belongs with the most obscure of the tunes in the present chapter (figure 54). Eck said of that title: "I think that is the name of it." He stated that he had learned it from his uncle (presumably one of his father's brothers; Seeger interview 1963). The point in playing it at all was to provide a companion piece to "Say Old Man," that is, a second piece in this extremely rare tuning.

What might the title "Get Up in the Cool" mean? A "col" is "the lowest point of a ridge or saddle between two peaks, typically affording a pass from one side of a mountain range to another" (*Cambridge Dictionary*), while the word "coulee" suggested this to Steve Green: "a kind of box canyon or ravine where cows might stray and need to be tracked down—the thinking being that this was somehow connected to life and work of cowboys and ranchers" (email June 23, 2023). This would have been a topic of interest to Eck, given that he presented lantern views of ranch life as an ingredient of some of his shows. As I read "Teddy Blue," Abbott's insider narrative of cowboy life (1955), his meaning of "coulee" is what I grew up calling arroyo, a desert creek bed that is usually but not reliably dry. Steve discovered that the title was part of a song: From the Abilene, Texas, *Taylor County News*, June 28, 1889: "It is a pretty funny sight to see a man on a mule and the mule going backwards. It recalled to my mind an old song which starts off thus:

Old Mr. Rareback,
Get up in the cool,
You'll never get to heaven
A ridin' of a mule.

A bit later Green came across this, in a book, "The Story of Coal and Iron in Alabama":

You ride a gray horse
And I ride a mule
Beat me to Heaven
Have to get up in the cool!

Another citation reads: "Our blacksmith, John Darnell, has to get up in the cool to keep up with his work these days." (*Miami Record-Herald*, April 7, 1905)

Finally, from the *Galveston Daily News*, July 8, 1892:

❊ ❊ ❊

A NIGHT IN A VILLAGE

"Git Up in de Cool" and Other African Melodies.

It was Saturday night—a hot June night, too. An unfortunate representative of the Texas press by the unlucky delay of a railroad train was forced to spend the night in a little one-horse flap-jackery, misnamed "hotel," in a small village in eastern Texas. The said scribe therefore sat in a perturbed state of mind and a hide-bottomed chair in front of the aforesaid hostelry bewailing his sad lot. It had been his misfortune to spend a night in this identical inn only two weeks before, and he had concluded that it would be a good idea for the state of Texas to lease the place as a penal institution, for scarcely anything short of capital punishment could equal the torture of living twenty-four hours in that bug-infested house. He knew that on this sultry night the ravenous insects would be out in full force to perform the operation of phlebotomy upon him. The tavern dog, his only companion, as he sat out upon the moonlit piazza, was disposed to be social, and lying down at the bohemian's feet, he began to scratch vigorously. He evidently wanted to divide fleas with the sad-eyed traveler, but he only received an unkind kick for his liberty, and ran away yelling with pain. As the canine cries died away the strains of a banjo accompanied by a negro's song came floating on the sultry zephyrs from a cabin down in the hollow. The words are certainly appropriate to the weather. They ran about thus:

Ole brudder bull frog live in de pool,
Long wid de tadpoles nice an' cool.
Old sister turkle dove ain't no fool,
She flop 'er wings and sing out, "Git up in de cool."

Wish I was as rich as ole Jay Goul',
I'd smoke fine terbacker and git up in de cool!

You ride the jackass and I ride de mule,
You nebber git to heaben till you git up in de cool.

There were seven or eight more stanzas to this African melody, but the journalist did not catch them all. Each one, however, dwelt upon the importance of "getting up in the cool."

(Thank you, Steve!). Eck did mention that he thought the tune "had words," so linking it to a song does seem valid (Seeger interview, 1963).

Fiddle tune titles can be simple labels, but many instead bear messages: they are very short poetry. For me, these two meanings of "getting up in the cool" both work well, and mix differently each time I think of the title: getting up early in the morning, and getting into any source of cooling water. But Eck—if he actually thought about this title as being more than a memorable identifier of the tune—might well have also thought about the geographic associations of "col" and/or "coulee."

I have no insights about Eck's rare tune "Chadwick" (figure 57), which he played for Vernon Riddle. "Rhubarb" (figure 58), also recorded by Riddle, was sufficiently liked by this fellow fiddler that he learned it and passed it on. "Run Boy Run" (Victor V40205, side A, 1929; renamed by Victor from the more usual "Run N----- Run"), added minister J. B. Cranfill to the Robertson family ensemble. When Eck played with Cranfill, they played in an exuberant intended unison (figure 57).

"Durang's Hornpipe" is the last tune in the first part of the music anthology. It fits equally well among Eck's old inherited tunes and in the remaining half of his repertoire, the part that is for the most part younger, including many melodies that have found secure spots in the contemporary Texas fiddle repertoire. Eck's version serves as a transition between the overall older and little-modified half of his repertoire and the varied group that accepted change gracefully in order to remain part of Texas fiddling. The tune was named for actor and dancer John Durang (b. Lancaster, Pa., 1768–d. Philadelphia, 1821). Like many eighteenth- and nineteenth-century professional musicians active in America, Durang was of German stock. His part of Pennsylvania was full of music—he remembered harvest frolics like this: "during the whole day, the taverns crowded, in every room a fiddle and dancing" (Durang 1966, 5). Durang was exposed to many comic "operas," which included many British tunes in (or about to enter) oral tradition. For instance, he heard the theatrical work called *Poor Soldier* (26) that featured the tune "Rose Tree," which would become in turn "Old Zip Coon" and "Turkey in the Straw" (114). He became embroiled in lively showmanship that did include him dancing many hornpipes—solo male dances, often with Durang in a sailor outfit (17). These were intricate, virtuosic show dances. One recurring trick in which he excelled was dancing a hornpipe on a running horse. Late in his career, around 1790, he noted that he danced "a Hornpipe on thirteen eggs blindfolded without breaking one."

ECK'S MUSICAL INHERITANCES FROM MINSTRELSY AND FIDDLING TRADITIONS

Hornpipe melodies' heightened requirements for adeptness of a fiddler's left hand matched the dancer's need for an agile body.

Durang stated in his memoirs that "Durang's Hornpipe" was composed expressly for him by one "Mr. Hoffmaster, a German dwarf, in New York, 1785," a man who also was one of Durang's fiddle teachers (22) (from Downer's "The Memoir of John Durang, American Actor 1785–1816" [1966]). Hoffmaster's composition came a year after Durang's debut with the company of Lewis Hallam in 1784. Hallam had just returned from a long period in England that encompassed the Revolutionary War (Emmerson, 1972).

Durang transcribed the tune in his *Memoir*; I copied his transcription as figure 59, top. We can't know just how the actual dance went. The melody suggests a recurring short dance figure for the A strain in measures 1, 3, and 5 of the tune, with different physical responses matching the measures between. Then the B is less broken up melodically—it suggests a more extended dance sequence, one a full eight measures long. Flutist and music store owner Edward Riley adjusted this and hundreds of other tunes to be equally suitable for many solo instruments in 1821 (later volumes in later years); his "Durang's Hornpipe" in is G major (figure 59, middle). The policy of arranging published collections to suit different instruments equally well continued into the energetic activity of Bostonian Elias Howe Jr. (1820–1895), publishing gigantic and widely-distributed instrumental collections from 1840 on. Howe's most striking new contribution to "Durang's Hornpipe" was the figuration in measure 4 outlining the A chord (figure 59, bottom).

Checking *American Vernacular Music Manuscripts ca. 1730–1910* for variant versions penned in individuals' manuscript copybooks turns up five examples of this melody. One is very like Durang's own version, but with small changes (the second half of measure 4 is raised an octave, and the B strain has tiny changes in the same position in the strain). Another resembles the Riley example (it is in G, the only one of these five to not be in D), but again, the approaches to cadences go their own way. Two examples match the Howe version precisely; Howe's published collections were very popular. Yet another version is a bit more distinctive than the others. I won't give more details here; this would be a good example for readers especially interested in the early history of American fiddling to get acquainted with *American Vernacular Music Manuscripts ca. 1730–1910*, a wonderful tool. Here is a summary of what Eck and his compatriots inherited with "Durang's Hornpipe": It was composed in 1785, spread quickly and widely, experienced lots of minor variation in oral tradition—this fluid variation then also reflected in written tradition—without losing its essential identity, and remained a mildly flexible tune in parallel oral and written traditions in the early twentieth century.

Eck's version of "Durang's Hornpipe" was recorded by Conte's friend, likely in the 1970s (figure 60). He was interested in Eck's oldest tunes, including this and other hornpipes. But if he was seeking *style* as antiquated as the tune itself, he would have been disappointed. Eck's arrangement is typical for him, well on the road to a modern Texas contest version. It does have Howe's fourth-measure arpeggio on the A chord; that figuration is still fairly standard today. The sequence in the B strain that showed some influence of art music in the use of leaning tones requiring accidentals is gone, unsurprisingly. A version of the A strain appears in the upper octave—no surprise from Eck or from Texas fiddling after him. Eck very tentatively tweaks the beginning of the B strain: we will witness more of that in the last version of the tune anthologized here.

I chose a recent performance of "Durang's Hornpipe" to exemplify excellent modern Texas contest style tune arrangement, one by Jason Andrew (figure 61). Jason was born and still lives in Whitewright, Texas, some sixty miles from Eck's childhood home in Hunt County. Jason learned from his grandfather, the famous Louis Franklin, and his uncle Larry Franklin. He was in the construction industry for some time, but is now a freelance musician, teaching fiddling, judging, competing (he won the Texas State Championship in 2018), and performing. His playing is hard-driving and full of improvisation; his improvising falls into subtle structures. His version of "Durang's Hornpipe" has three strains; he toys with both the A and B strains. Briefly: the C strain reminds us considerably of both the A and B strains. A appears with minor changes (see, for example, how A8v' moves the contour of A8v into the range of A, and how the last A consolidates details of all the previous A strains). The beginning of the B strain varies constantly, alternating between thinning out rhythms and restoring the eighth-note texture. More could be said, but the point here is that the work that Eck initiated in building tidy structures that reach well beyond alternating pairs of A and B strains is easy to see and enjoy in Jason's arrangement of "Durang's Hornpipe."

— Chapter 5 —

"SALLY GOODIN" AND THE TEXAS FIDDLE REVOLUTION

"Sally Goodin" (another tune title spelled variously) was the first tune associated with Eck Robertson in print, in the 1918 ad in the *Vernon Weekly Record* that began with the words "Of Course You're Coming" (figure 14). That ad continued with the declaration that "A. C. (Eck) Robertson . . . challenges any man in the United States to a contest playing 'Sally Gooden' . . ." (January 22, 1918, 12). This tune would be the first he recorded as a solo effort (in 1922), and would remain the melody with which he would be most closely associated, both in his own testimony and in countless newspaper articles. It is still the tune—in his distinctive and well-known recorded performance—that Texas fiddlers cite as his most important contribution to the development of contest fiddle variation technique. That belief is true on a general level: the bumper crop of variation in Eck's performance has stimulated Texas fiddlers to try to match him in enthusiasm and thoroughness. But while some aspects of how he assembled his extraordinarily influential "Sally Goodin" endure in a straightforward, transparent way in modern contest fiddling, other

Figure 31. Side A of Victor 18956, recorded July 1, 1922, Eck Robertson's first solo recording, made at the Victor studio in New York.

specific aspects of his innovative compositional technique were startling at the time, remain enigmatic, and are less thoroughly incorporated into modern variation technique. Eck's widely distributed recorded performance of this tune merits a very close look.

The fiddle tune—and sometimes song—"Sally Goodin" was well-known throughout the South while Eck was growing up. It was performed frequently in every setting where fiddles were heard, including contests. For instance, its name popped up in 1903 in a short article in a smalltown paper in Kentucky, the *Cloverport Breckenridge News*:

> **Your Uncle Fuller Coming**
>
> Glendeane, Ky., Oct. 14—1903. Editor of the Breckinridge News:—Dear Sir,
>
> I see the Old Fiddlers' Contest comes off Oct. 29. You can bet your last dollar I will be there dead or alive. This man who played while the insects entered Noah's Ark don't have any effect on me, and he will tell you all so after it is over. I go away back and bring up the old pieces that Adam and Eve played in the garden, the oldest music on record. All I ask is a fair show and if I don't get the prize I will make some man scratch his head where it don't itch. I don't need any snake oil and I am the old snake himself and you will hear me rattle on the 29. I know that I can win if I don't have to play over twenty four hours. I am good for that long and never play the same old tune the second time. So you can look for Uncle Fuller.
>
> I mean all I say and more and if they want a step or two of old-fashioned dancing I can hit a lick or two now. I want such men as old Noah for our judges, and I am safe.
>
> Here are the names of some more old tunes, three quarters 'round: Old Sallie Gooden, Brickyard Joe, Grey Eagle, Buttermilk and Cider and Charlie is a Lady's Man. And I will play the test when I come, so look out for your Uncle Fuller.
>
> Yours,
> Louis Ashley (October 21, 1903, 16)

This paragraph appeared in a lengthy description of a community celebration held in Keowee, South Carolina:

> W. G. Russell is nearing four score years, and is still brisk and lively—loves the old tunes played on the violin, and would have me play all of them from old Sallie Gooden on down to the Fall of Paris ["The Downfall of Paris" was a common alternative title for the tune best known as "Mississippi Sawyer"]. Mrs. Russell is a fine entertainer, and a noble Christian woman. I played for her "In the Sweet Bye and Bye," and all liked it. (*Keowee Courier Newspaper Archives*, September 3, 1913, 6).

Earlier in its long life, "Sally Goodin"/"Sallie Gooden" was often texted. A fiddler might intersperse short pairs of lines in no particular order, homespun couplets expressing affection for Sally. Indeed, whether or not a fiddler chose to sing as part of a performance, both musician and audience had heard various forms of the lyrics many times; the text stayed part of the effect of the tune whether or not heard. Both Hank Williams and Woody Guthrie sang versions with unusually long texts; Fiddlin' John Carson's recorded version is more typical in the length of the lyrics. It begins like this: "Blackberry pie and raspberry puddin'; Give it all away just to see Sally Goodin." (I am tempted to believe that the legendary Sally acquired the last name Goodin *because* it rhymed with "puddin'"; all three men's versions are readily available on YouTube and/or other obvious locations on the internet.) Most early twentieth-century fiddlers who sang while performing this tune just inserted a single verse like Carson's once or twice. But more fiddlers played the tune without singing along, like Eck. Today that remains the most common option, certainly holding for Texas-style fiddlers. But fiddlers still know the gist of the lyrics. Eck related the story behind the tune as follows, according to Oklahoma fiddler Byron Berline:

> There was a girl named Sally who had two boyfriends. The two boys were both fiddle players, and one of the boys had the last name of 'Goodin.' Sally couldn't decide which one to marry, so she thought a fiddle contest between the two would be a good way to make her selection. Of course, the fellow Goodin won the contest, and Sally became Sally Goodin. They were very happy and had a productive life with 14 children, so I'm going to play 'Sally Goodin' 14 different ways. (Kuntz, *Fiddlers Companion*, entry for "Sally Goodin")

The music is based on remarkably simple ingredients. Regarding its key: Like many American fiddle tunes, "Sally Goodin" gives an immediate impression of being in a major key (almost always A major, though some older versions were instead in G; again, see the excellent entry in Kuntz, *Fiddler's Companion*). However, the actual mode is either close to or fully in the common pentatonic subset of major—the notes constituting major but lacking the fourth and seventh degrees. That is, in what looks on the printed page to be A major at first glance, the notes d̲ and g♯̲ are omitted or at least deemphasized (by having those two scale degrees appear just in weak spots in passing passages, likely briefly and off the beat). This mostly pentatonic vocabulary does not surprise us, since so many of our fiddle tunes have this same modal flavor. It is the same general effect that I described for "Arkansas Traveller." However, the details of this approach to mode—starting with the balance of major and pentatonic—differ from fiddle tune to fiddle tune, from performer to performer. In "Sally Goodin," the dodging of the pitch g♯ at the cadence of most phrases sticks out; this major scale's customary "leading tone" has been supplanted by f♯, which is following by a syncopated, early-arriving a, the tonic of the key. The f♯ follows two iterations of e, the fifth pitch (dominant) of the scale, perhaps with other pitches filling in after each e, creating a memorable figure. The total formula—e, down to c♯, up to e, up to a, down to f♯, up to a (an a that arrives off the beat and lasts long)—gains a high profile due its distinctiveness and frequency of use at cadences (figure 62). Forms of the "Sally Goodin" cadence have come to be used in many other tunes.

Concerning its form: "Sally Goodin" as played in old-time music generally follows convention in both the relationship of strains and in its form. Its two strains overlap in contents, but the beginnings of those strains contrast in range. The A strain energetically circles around the tonic a in a narrow range. The melody twirls closely above the a in the first two measures, then approaches closely from below in the next two measures, with those four measures repeating to fill out the eight-measure strain. The B strain travels just a few pitches higher, to the e that is the fifth degree in the scale. This strain's first half adopts the cadence used twice within the A strain, but the strain's second half can rise to the a on the e string. While these intricate but undramatic melodic gestures continue, there is near-constant droning going on, either on a or on e, that is, the open e string or the note a whether on that open string or fingered on the g string, if the fiddle is tuned GDAE. Managing that requires some dexterity, regardless of whether the fiddle is tuned AEAE (the traditional tuning for melodies in A major or in its pentatonic subset in old-time fiddling in the Southeast United States) or the "normal" violin tuning of GDAE, which dominates more fully in Texas. When the tune is played in the AEAE tuning, the drone on a is performed by having the left hand third finger pressed down on the lower e string; the fourth finger does that job when the fiddle is tuned GDAE. Eck could play this melody in either tuning; for the 1922 recording he tuned his fiddle to AEAE. Modern practice in Texas fiddling rarely employs such cross-tunings (called scordatura by art violinists); GDAE is used for nearly all melodies, including for "Sally Goodin." Late in life, Eck had also shifted to normal tuning for this tune (Spielman 1972, 183). Regardless of the tuning, it's a bit of a challenge to hold down one finger of the left hand while the other fingers rapidly trace intricate patterns. Performances of "Sally Goodin" still include the highest percentage of double-stopped moments among all of the frequently played contest fiddle standards.

To imagine the general flavor of the many versions of "Sally Goodin" heard in Texas before Eck revolutionized the shape of performances of the tune, we can visit contemporary but quite traditional old-time performances from the Upper South. I transcribed two such performances in figure 64. First, consider the version by farmer Richard Bowman (b. 1953), whose playing I consider the gold standard for styles centered geographically where Virginia, Tennessee, and North Carolina meet. Bowman's playing is clean, loud, rhythmically strong, and contains little or no variation. He loves to play for dancers, and the manner in which he plays at contests simply duplicates how he plays at dances.

In contrast, another old-time dance-oriented fiddler from western North Carolina, farmer (and laborer in a variety of other professions) Marcus Martin (1881–1974), favored pervasive variation. For clarity, I presented all of the strains of his performance of "Sally Goodin" aligned in the transcription—eight measures on every staff. Some minor variation of each strain appears immediately. Then, this low level of incidental variation continues throughout the piece; after a while, nearly every measure replicates a measure from earlier in the piece. As a result, I could then abbreviate the notating process, simply placing a Roman numeral and perhaps a measure number in a recurring measure rather than writing out all of the pitches. So, in the second B strain (staff V), the last four measures are identical to those measures in the first B strain (staff II). The third A strain (staff VI) is a mixture of the A strains transcribed on lines I and III, and so the transcription of the pitches in that third A stain can be abbreviated as a series of "I" and "III." This species of variation—a texture of pervasive but unsystematic series of tiny surprises—yields an effect that is sparkling but undramatic. It produces a texture rather than a form, perfect for dances, since it could end whenever it was convenient for the dancers to stop, just as could Bowman's version and countless other old-time performances of the tune.

ECK ARRANGES "SALLY GOODIN"

Eck shaped his arrangement of "Sally Goodin" carefully, and then left it alone. He looked down on fiddlers who had the temerity to revise it further. In his words, "Sally Goodin":

> . . . never was changed to speak of since I've learned it and that's been way back in them days when they was lots of the old master fiddlers playing all over the country . . . and they played it like the song goes. You know, there ain't but two parts to it, as far as the song goes—the voice of the song, you know. But when you play the tune like I play it and like I've heard others play it—as I call it, the old masters, why they've got position playing in it, and their execution is much better than just playing two parts in it. But still, I don't get away from "Sallie Gooden." It's still like the two parts, but I use different positions on it. [The new parts are] just an improvement, like most of fiddlers do, as the time rolls along. . . . Well, the high part is a little different . . . when you go on to the fine [high] strains. Then there's droning comes in there, like I play it, and the different things, different notes in the high tone part. It's still all "Sallie Gooden." . . . Any part I play

it, it still sounds like "Sallie Gooden." That's why it's called the old master way of playing it. But there is guys trying to play parts in . . . notes that don't belong there. Even makes it odd sounding. They are part of some other tune, something like that. Young boys are messing it up!

Eck did add considerably and *systematically* to the raw material of the tune (the basic two strains). Reshaping "Sally Goodin" can't push much in the direction of accumulating more rhythmic density—the tune's twisting path is already tightly packed with short notes. But rhythmically *thinned* strains are an option, and these abound in Eck's re-creation, often with this thinning combined with exploring an upper range. Eck's new high strains require lots of shifting to and from third position (in which the left hand first finger is placed where the third finger normally stays). There is considerable variety in how these added strains are constructed. Eck placed them in sets of three or four strains, each of which accumulates melodic momentum within the set. I will call these sets of strains "patches."

I believe that most of the apparently new material added by Eck was derived from the original A strain by him. There are twenty-six strains, twenty-six sets of eight measures each. Four are the basic A strain, played unchanged (starting respectively in measures 1, 65, 153, and 176). This "home" A strain starts the piece, ends it, and serves to mark big sections within the performance. Why didn't Eck play the basic A strain in pairs, as is normal in his (and most) fiddling? Perhaps the fact that this strain divides into identical halves constituted enough of an impression of repetition. That is, once through the strain sounded like twice (most later and current performers do play the basic, "home" A strain in pairs, at least to start the piece). Eck's B strain, however, does appear in full-length pairs, with modest but important progress in its identity. The first B strain (the second eight-measure strain played) is quite traditional in its shape (compare Eck's version with the versions of Bowman and Martin). The second B strain (starting in measure 17) ends differently, with additions that serve to introduce new musical ideas. This transitional section (measures 21–24) holds its opening pitches for three beats, then for the next two beats. These relatively long notes introduce the topic of stretching, which creates suspense. Also, the line ascends to the a on the e string for the first time, doing so twice, suggesting that the upper limit in pitch explored by the tune has become flexible. This lessens the surprise of the high c♯ placed at the start of measure 25.

The subsequent iterations of the B strain might not be immediately recognized as versions of the original B strain. However, there are important links from the start: see the use of the notes c♯ and e to begin measure 49, echoing that emphasis in measure 9. But is this really a version of the B strain? Measures 53–56 make this clear—these replicate measures 21–24, the ending of the second version of the original B strain. The new form of the B strain returns unchanged during the rest of the performance, constituting strains #7–8, 14–15, and 20–21.

However, the biggest surprises and most important new factors in Eck's "Sally Goodin" occur in the many strains not yet discussed. There are four extended "patches" of new strains, all full of rhythmically thinned (or rhythmically repacked) forms of the A strain, strains #4–6, 10–13, 16–19 (these three sets share how they are built) plus the final inner patch, strains #23–24. The first patch is the simplest. I invite the reader to compare measures 25, 33, and 41. Measure 25 features the high c♯ an octave up from the c♯ so important in measure 1; measures 26–28 confirm that this strain is a form of the basic A strain, but up an octave and with its beginning thinned. Then, comparing strain beginnings, measure 33 is a bit more active than was measure 25, and measure 41 breaks that activity into short notes. After a two-B-strain interruption in this kind of activity, we encounter a second "internally growing" patch of strains. The second patch consists of the strains #10, 11, 12, and 13, beginning with measures 73, 81, 89, and 97. Strain #10 takes us to the range of the original A strain (and thus back to first position for the fiddler's left hand). We hear a held c♯ over a, much as in measure 25, but enlivened through syncopation. Then this becomes denser and more dramatic in the subsequent strain beginnings. In the third patch—strains 16–19—measures include more notes, but little changes increasing excitement slowly and systematically work just as steadily. We hear a busy f♯ falling to e figure in measure 121, then a bigger stretch of a to e in measure 129, then that pair of strains repeats, both sections made yet denser.

In short, in the series ("patches") of strains 4–6, 10–13, and 16–19, Eck has made tiny, meticulously measured incremental changes within each patch, always adding power at a steady pace. This process is the most striking aspect of his performance, and, as far as I can tell, was without clear precedent in American fiddling. The final group of new strains, #23, 24, and 25, is innovative in another way. I'm not sure what to make of strain 23, a recurrence of AP2.4. Perhaps it should be heard as a general reference to the strain patches. But strains 24 and 25 (which are identical) break new ground. They refer in a clever way to the end of the cadence that is first heard in measure 4, then recurs throughout the piece, the movement from the note f♯ to a to end phrases. Once again, Eck emphasizes a melodic relationship by holding an important pitch a long time, that pitch now being the penultimate pitch in so many phrases, the f♯. He further emphasizes that f♯ by adding its own dominant in a double stop, that is, adding c♯ (which had also been the most important note other than the tonic a at the beginning of the piece, in measure 25, and in many other locations). That prominent, stretched-out f♯/c♯ double stop turns the focus on the recurring quick cadence of f♯ to a; it becomes a kind of mega-cadential figure for the whole piece.

What could be the background for this remarkable arsenal of melodic and formal devices marshalled by Eck in "Sally Goodin"? His arrangement is even more startling than delightful. If Eck believed that he had learned this way of putting a performance together from another fiddler, he had plenty of opportunities to have said so; he was careful to award credit to the fiddlers who influenced him, and was meticulous in acknowledging those from whom he learned specific pieces. None of that is in the record for "Sally Goodin"; he considered this arrangement very much his own. But I see several possible sources for aspects of the arrangement. One possible path of influence was from the Hooker clan, a family of fiddlers who lived nearby in Hunt County while Eck was a kid learning to fiddle. When young Eck slipped out of the Robertson dog-trot cabin to play dances, he was traveling and performing with his older brother Quince and with a boy named Pat Hooker, both of whom Eck later would name as primary influences (Spielman 1972, 182). When Eck played the tune "Grigsby's Hornpipe" for Mike Seeger, he stated that he was the only one that played that tune, and that he had learned it from "Brother Walker Hooker, Old Man Walker Hooker," who was Pat Hooker's father. That tune includes formal procedures that could have influenced Eck's "Sally Goodin."

I invite the reader to listen to Eck's performance of "Grigsby's Hornpipe" on YouTube, and to consult my transcription in figure 66. Strains #2 through 4 show very simple, very obvious incremental change: Strain #2 starts on the note e, Strain #3 up a step to $f\sharp$, then Strain 4 up to a, with those three strains otherwise very similar—these strains comprise a section clearly developing in the direction of adding intensity. Strains #6, 8, and 9 proceed similarly, in this case by making the opening gesture progressively more complex. These two series of strains seem to me to be parallel in effect to the three "patches" of strains in "Sally Goodin," Strains #4–6, 10–13, and 16–19.

If only we had a performance of "Grigsby's Hornpipe" by "Brother" Hooker to compare with Eck's playing of the tune! If Eck replicated Hooker's version with little or no change, the similarities between Hooker's "Grigsby's Hornpipe" and "Sally Goodin" would offer compelling evidence arguing for significant influence of the elder Hooker on Eck's masterpiece "Sally Goodin." But it's also possible that Hooker's version of "Grigsby's Hornpipe" was more elementary, and Eck built upon it. If so, his arranging of "Grigsby's Hornpipe" may have been a musical experiment in which he tried out techniques that he would employ in a more systematic and dramatic manner in "Sally Goodin."

The tune name "Grigsby's Hornpipe" probably referred to "Grigsby's Cowboys," a military unit that was created when Eck was a child. The group's name may have intrigued Eck; remember that he presented a window on ranch life during some of his shows. Melvin Grigsby, attorney general of South Dakota in 1898, decided that cowboys from the western

United States would make good cavalrymen in the war with Spain. He arranged an amendment to the Volunteer Army Bill to authorize creating such a regiment, which he then commanded. But few of the troops made it to Cuba and combat. Most were stuck in camp in Georgia, and many succumbed to typhoid there (Cohen 1997, 136). From a newspaper article, we learn something about the bright side of their life in camp: "Grigsby's Cowboys had defeated all opponents in baseball, foot races, wrestling and boxing, stated the Sioux Falls *Argus-Leader*'s special correspondent with Grigsby's Cowboys. The cowboys had also kept the peace when a regiment from Wisconsin wanted to disrupt a Salvation Army meeting" (*Black Hills Pioneer*, November 4, 2013, quoted by the South Dakota Historical Society Foundation).

A more plausible suggestion concerning influences on the building of Eck's "Sally Goodin" issues from what at first may seem an unlikely source. In the late 1980s, when I made my first attempt to transcribe Eck's daunting performance, I was living in Norway. Although I was researching the music of Norway's "regular" fiddle (*vanlig fele*), I also heard plenty of fiddling on the *hardingfele* (Hardanger fiddle), the eight-string fiddle native to Norway's western mountains. Although this type of fiddle, like the *vanlig fele* in Norway, plays in quite a number of local styles, some aspects of variation techniques bridge several hardingfele styles. I heard multiple styles of continual variation in much fiddling on the hardingfele, including one very specific sort of variation. In this type, a small but conspicuous change right at the beginning of a phrase or section strikes the ear boldly, then builds in repetitions of that passage, adding energy that will culminate in shifting to a different melodic ingredient (see Hopkins 1968). This was deliberate, carefully crafted change that remained stable from performance to performance. That contrasts with modern American contest fiddle variation, in which numerous details of melody vary regularly *during* the courses of repeating individual strains, not just at the beginning. The exact type of variation marking quite a few hardingfele pieces reminded me instead of precisely what Eck had done in crafting the "patches" in "Sally Goodin."

I will demonstrate how this hardingfele variation technique works through a close look at a typical performance of what may be the most famous hardingfele piece, a *halling* called "Fanitullen." The halling is a solo male dance in which modest physical motions—beginning with just walking stylishly—build to an explosive climax in which the dancer leaps high to kick a hat suspended on a stick held sideways 6 to 8 feet in the air. Having the music of the hardingfele accompaniment also accumulate power during this dance—one in which physical motions are ordered to build momentum and suspense—makes sense.

I transcribed about half of a performance of "Fanitullen," and marked the score to show how this kind of melodic tiering takes place (figure 65). The fiddler was a genial and skilled hardingfele master from the Norwegian area of Sogn named Haakon Solaas (now deceased); this performance is available on YouTube as of this writing. Solaas is not making up the variations on the spot; his version is a careful cumulative act of construction kept the same in his various performances, and crafted in much the same way by most players of this common piece. Here is how it works: Each section of "Fanitullen" starts with a two-measure gesture, which is repeated. The third iteration of the gesture is changed through new articulations or new rhythmic factors. Then the ante is upped once more in the fourth iteration, and we've built up enough energy to push up to a new melodic idea, to the next section. Thus, each of these sections of "Fanitullen"—each section is named with a letter on the transcription—is like a brief form of what I call a patch in "Sally Goodin." Some sections are subtle in their internal changes, some are not: for an especially clear example, compare the "F" section at the bottom of the transcription of "Fanitullen" with the first patch in "Sally Goodin."

I should explain why I transcribed "Fanitullen" in A major, and employed the tuning of AEAC♯. The hardingfele is a bit smaller than a violin. It is tuned in many different configurations, but the pitch levels of the four bowed strings rest on the average about a major second higher than those of a violin/fiddle. (That holds whether the violin/fiddle is tuned GDAE, or to the normal A-major tuning of AEAE, or the rarer option of AEAC♯, typical for pieces incorporating left hand pizzicato.) I chose the tuning of AEAC♯ for my transcription for two related reasons. First, that specific tuning puts the pitches of the strings in the interrelationships typical for hardingfele for this piece, but at the right tension for the violin (that is, parallel to but lower than the tuning of the hardingfele). Second, there is a good chance that Dr. Howard's eight-stringed purchase described in chapter 2 was not fully a hardingfele but rather a hybrid, a violin body modified for hardingfele type tuning and resonance. My suspicion is based on the shape so vaguely traced by the old photograph reproduced in figure 16; those contours look right for a conventional violin. If I am right, AEAC♯ is exactly the right tuning for this transcription! In any case, the tuning of AEAC♯ encourages modern fiddler/violinists to play this fun tune.

Norwegian scholars have been less interested in this sort of analysis than in the exhaustive collecting and transcribing of complete regional repertoires and in the fascinating complexity of meter in hardingfele performance (see, for example, Johansson 2017). The main American scholar of the hardingfele, Pandora Hopkins, did very little transcribing for her book on the hardingfele. However, among her handful of fascinating transcriptions, she wrote out a halling displaying exactly the sort of incremental variation that I described (a West Coast halling in the manner of Finn Vabø; 1986, 107).

But how likely is it that Eck could have heard a hardingfele played, and not just toyed with in passing, but rather played enough for him to understand and incorporate the technique of constructing melodies characteristic of the Norwegian dance called the halling? Remember that Eck's main home in the late 1910s into the 1920s was in Vernon, where he was fiddling with the Vernon Fiddlers, a group which included him, an older fiddler named Lewis (or "Lefty") Franklin, and the administrative leader of the trio, eccentric doctor and oil millionaire A. P. Howard. The good doctor seems not to have been a great fiddler, but he had charisma, a form of eloquence (that is, no hint of restraint when bragging), and plenty of money. Remember that in the fall of 1919, when he paid for the Vernon Fiddlers and other Texas musicians to travel to Atlanta for a Confederate Reunion, Dr. Howard loudly challenged Georgian fiddlers led by Fiddlin' John Carson. Who was better? This didn't result in an actual confrontation, but aroused newspaper interest, and a published colloquy. We learned from the extended newspaper coverage that Howard had brought several violins on the trip. I repeat a salient portion of the newspaper article: in one interview, "Dr. Howard . . . told of the $25,000 instrument he has brought with him to [Atlanta], a genuine 'Strad.' This violin is very old, and was found several years ago in the attic of an old Norway barn, where it was roughly wrapped in a ragged bundle." What? A Strad salvaged in an "old Norway barn?" How could that claim not have aroused skepticism?

Let us return to pictures of Dr. Howard's collection of violins from 1922 given in Figure 16. These photographs tell a layered story. In the article, Howard emphasized the supposed value of the instruments, the $25,000 Strad, plus an Amati and a "Cordovora"—a made-up name—each worth $20,000, he boasted. The supposed Amati is the dark violin on the upper left, then the averred Stradivarius is the decorated one next to it. Finally, below, we see the eight-string "Cordovora," set up as a hardingfele, with eight strings—four sympathetic and four to be bowed.

My best guess is that the Stradivarius and the "Cordovora" (likely the Amati, too) were sold to Dr. Howard by Ole Evensen, the Norwegian immigrant mentioned in chapter 2. Evensen farmed in Oklahoma just twenty-five miles north of Vernon, quite near Altus. He claimed to not only farm as his sole profession but also to be a prestigious luthier. He said he had worked for the Norwegian court—and that he still did so!—and had adjusted Ole Bull's and Ole Theobaldi's violins. We can't know how much of that was true, but we do know that Mr. Evensen convinced Dr. Howard and a reporter for the *Vernon Record* of his credentials' validity (April 2, 1918, 1). Lastly, the Victor catalog portrait of Altus resident Henry Gilliland, Eck's partner in the 1929 trip to New York, shows Gilliland holding a fiddle with hardingfele-type decorations, doubtless also Evensen's work.

Let us look more closely at the census records of Evensen and of his wife. Evensen had left Norway in 1876 as a teenager with his family, and farmed with his father and brothers in southern Minnesota for a few years. He married Lena, a girl seven years younger, who had been born in northern Iowa but whose parents were born in Norway. Ole and Lena (!) did not remain in the Upper Midwest. They got in on the aftershocks of the Oklahoma land rush, acquiring a farm in the settlement of Olustee, twelve miles southeast of Altus, which is twenty-five miles due north of Vernon (via a much-traveled route, what had been the Great Western Cattle Trail). They owned this farm; they were not renters like the various Robertson families. Evensen was classified in the census as a "general" farmer; the Evensens were not sharecroppers of any kind (1920 United States Federal Census OK-Jackson-Olustee-district 0119; formerly district 0146). To end the Evensens' personal story: By 1930, Lena was a widow, and had moved to nearby Altus, where she was a landlady for two young men, one being Thomas Fergerson, identified as her nephew. Then, by 1940, she and Fergerson were back at the farm outside of town, in Olustee.

Ole Evensen had entered Eck's story by 1919. While staying at Dr. Howard's house in Vernon, Evensen offered to assess and fix local residents' violins (in an interview for the local paper, the *Vernon Record*, April 2, 1918, 1). When he sold Dr. Howard the hardingfele (or violin equipped to play as a hardingfele), he must have demonstrated the instrument as part of his sales pitch. He probably also played it during the regular jamming that took place on Dr. Howard's porch. And Eck could have had plenty of additional contact with Evensen—remember that Eck's piano tuning ads printed ca. 1920 gave one phone number in Vernon, Texas, and another in Altus, Oklahoma, the substantial town closest to Evensen's farm in Olustee.

In any case, the hardingfele (or adapted violin) *was* taken along on the big trip to Atlanta. It was by that time said to be owned by the third Vernon Fiddler, Lefty Franklin, while the Strad was now acknowledged to have been "partly made by a Norwegian," doubtless Evenson. In sum, I am close to certain that Evenson demonstrated hardingfele tunes for the Vernon Fiddlers in connection with bilking Dr. Howard, and probably regularly just for fun. Living so near Vernon, he must have become an adjunct member of Vernon's intimate community of enthusiastic fiddlers, a group led by Eck's and Lefty Franklin's fiddles and Dr. Howard's wallet.

This might not be the beginning of the story of Eck's exposure to Norwegian fiddling. There were very few people of foreign birth living near him until late in his life, when he lived in Amarillo. But back when he was a teenager living on the south edge of Hunt County, ENE of Dallas, his eldest brother lived about fifteen miles south in Wills Point, near to Grand Saline, which was a shopping destination for a small Norwegian immigrant settlement located another twenty miles south, at Four Mile (see Russell 2006). Other opportunities for Eck to have heard hardingfele music can be imagined: For instance, there could have been a few Norwegian fiddlers among the countless cowboys passing through the Vernon area without leaving census entries or other evidence, cowboys who really did sing while herding cattle at night—this pleasant layer of sound could cover unavoidable potentially alarming sudden sounds that might trigger stampedes (see Abbott 1955, last chapter).

The overall picture is clear: Yes, in our Upper Midwest and Pacific Northwest, where most Norwegian immigrants settled, Norwegian hardingfele repertoires coexisted with Anglo-American fiddle repertoires, and these fiddlers heard each other frequently (see, for example, Shaw 2020 and Ellestad 2014). In comparison with this, interaction between Norwegian and Anglo-ancestry fiddlers in Texas was rare and could easily *not* result in transfer of music. For instance, an immigrant farmer brought a hardingfele to Bosque County (west of Waco) late in the nineteenth century, but it was converted to use as a violin, with a violin's bridge and without sympathetic strings (Lawshae 2011, 10–13). However, if I am right in believing that "Sally Goodin's" intimate architecture came out of Eck's hardingfele experience in the Texas Panhandle, and that Ole Evenson was the hardingfele-playing contact, that particular little bit of exposure really mattered; it was enough to explode into the revolutionary formal structure of Eck Robertson's "Sally Goodin." Again: the contact with Evenson was nothing like the broad cultural artistic interaction that we know took place between fiddle communities in Minnesota; this was just a couple of guys jamming now and again on Dr. Howard's porch. Nevertheless, this one instance of musical contact in Texas bore powerful fruit, profoundly influencing the mainstream of American folk fiddling. Why did this nano-scale cultural collision catch fire? It resulted from luck, from continued contact between Eck and one or more Norwegians, and, above all, Eck's energy and ambition. He spoke very insistently about being absolutely faithful to those whom he called "The Old Masters"; he learned melodies with faithful precision. But he also matter-of-factly stated that he had "improved" every one of his tunes. The word "improved" could mean as little as playing a strain both at its original pitch level and up an octave, as in the cases of many of the melodies in the first part of the tune anthology. "Sally Goodin" was at the other end of a continuum; its "improvement" was radical. Is my hearing a connection between hardingfele tune development during performance and Eck's arrangement of "Sally Goodin" unassailable? Eck's own independent creativity was certainly involved, but the odds are excellent that the contact with Ole Evenson was a critical contributing factor, and his much earlier interactions with senior fiddlers in Hunt County may have had a role too. It's how these ingredients balanced in his creative process that we cannot know.

"SALLY GOODIN" TODAY

How has Eck's "Sally Goodin" fared since its national exposure when Victor distributed his recording in 1923? Eck continued to play this arrangement as long as he was performing. Indeed, he seems to have played it most of the times that he performed publicly. His version and other fiddlers' personalized takes on it never left center stage in Texas or in the ever-expanding territory of contest-style fiddling. Marty Elmore, longtime competitor and judge in Texas fiddling, said this about the tune as he entered the stage to compete at the 2020 Gatesville, Texas, fiddle contest: "I know we talked about [encouraging] playing different tunes, but I've never in my life—I've been going to contests for over forty years—been to a contest where 'Sally Goodin' was not played. I'm playing 'Sally Goodin'" (observed on a YouTube record of this event).

At the 2023 Texas State Championship, the competition included about 200 judged performances, about a third of which were of tunes that had been recorded by Eck decades earlier (either in commercial recordings or in interviews). Of the half of his repertoire reflecting inherited southeastern performance, just "Soldier's Joy," "Arkansas Traveller," and "Fisher's Hornpipe" were played at the contest—once each, by kids, most likely as a result of tutelage involving books. Of Eck's early, uncommon SE oral tradition tunes, "Lost Indian" was aired once. In contrast, many of the tunes of Eck's that I placed in the second half of the anthology in this book popped up in the main competition brackets, many repeatedly: "Beaumont Rag," "Billy in the Low Grounds" (thrice), "Brilliancy," "[Brown] Kelly Waltz," "Brown-Skinned Gal," "Durang's Hornpipe" (6x), "Dusty Miller" (10x), "Forked Deer" (2x), "Grey Eagle" (3x), "Hell Amongst the Yearlings," "Lime Rock," "Ragtime Annie," "Sally Johnson" (11x), "Say Old Man" (2x) "Tom and Jerry" (13x; an unusually big day for this tune!), and "Wagoner's Hornpipe" (2x). We heard "Sally Goodin" nine times. It was played by the winners of the Freshman Division (fiddlers aged fifteen or less; Luke Eggert won), the Gone to Texas Division (won by Dennis Ludiker of Spokane, Washington), and in the climax of the contest, the Texas State Championship, where Carl Hopkins triumphed for the sixth time.

I transcribed for this book recent performances of "Sally Goodin" by perennial champions Carl Hopkins and Alita Stoneking Weisgerber. Why do I gravitate to contest winners for contemporary performances of tunes Eck played? The judges are themselves past champions and thoughtful and knowledgeable evaluators, and audiences almost always back the judges' official verdicts with their applause and with comments among themselves; the winners at this prestigious contest really do express the repertoires and techniques that this fiddle culture values most. The champions' performances are genuinely representative.

Carl Hopkins, a recently retired welder living in Porter, Texas, learned much about fiddling from his father, E. J. Hopkins, but even more through lifelong friendships with other fiddlers about his own age, especially Wes Westmoreland III. Carl is a convivial and exciting performer; when he is playing at the center of a jam, crowds gather instantly as if succumbing to an irresistible gravitational force. He barks out a laugh when he surprises himself while improvising—when that happens, if I don't notice the little positive detail of melody or error that pushed the laugh into the air, I check my recording later: there's always a reward. Fiddling brought Carl his wife, Tonya Rast Hopkins, a member of one of Idaho's top fiddle families. He has won the Texas State Championship and other prestigious contests many times, and been asked to judge this and other contests frequently. He is a valued insider in Texas fiddle culture.

Alita Stoneking Weisgerber, a top fiddler from Missouri, lives in Minnesota as of this writing. Her father, grandfather, and many others of the Stoneking clan filled their lives with traditional music in local styles. Lee Stoneking, her grandfather, a farmer in Johnson County, "caught tunes at house parties, picnics, and dances and to listening to records and at fiddle contests" (Marshall 2022, 266). Full and quite entertaining anecdotes ranging from matters of fiddle to detailed descriptions of farming appear in the words of his son Fred, both fiddler and skilled "family historian and raconteur" (Marshall 2022, 269); in his testimony, we witness the tug of war between local tradition and the broader identity of old-time music, and how this dynamic meshes with change. Fred's daughter Alita cherishes the old tunes (and the playing styles they exemplify), but has become a star in the national contest style that stems from Texas fiddling. I hear her most years at the Texas State Championship; she and her husband, native Minnesotan Tom Weisgerber, have each placed first in the "Gone to Texas" division of the contest, the bracket in which fine Texas-style fiddlers living elsewhere compete. Her transcribed performance is from 2014, a year that she won that division.

Carl's and Alita's versions of "Sally Goodin" show deep respect for Eck Robertson and his iconic version of the tune, plus equally keen awareness of their own responsibility to temper and enrich tradition with their personal creativity. They and most skilled fiddlers who play and personalize "Sally Goodin" play more notes per measure than did Eck, but his more rapid pace (M. M. = about 140, rather than their ca. 115) makes the impression of density comparable. But intimate differences between modern versions and Eck's original composition abound. If one is familiar with Eck's "Sally Goodin," a new opening gesture strikes the ear—The 3–3–2 feel of the opening; the little bits of leaning tones, the added emphases on figuration right before cadences.

Both Carl and Alita pay close attention to the overall form of Eck's "Sally Goodin," and modify that form about the same amount, but in very different ways. I placed my short descriptions of form (done through labeling strains with alphabet designations) between Eck and Carl's versions, on the second page of figure 62. The inner A strains that are built together to comprise sections, the three "patches," are named to correspond to those of Eck's strains that they replicate or at least closely resemble. I attempted

Figure 32. The first measures of the "patch" ingredients of Eck Robertson's 1922 recording of "Sallie Gooden," compared with the parallel parts of recent performances of "Sally Goodin" by Carl Hopkins and Alita Stoneking Weisgerber.

to line up the three versions' diagrams vertically as much as possible to show the similarities, pushing the lower two diagrams a bit to the side to make sure all remained on the page. Comparing the relatively long alphabet diagrams of Eck's and Carl's versions of "Sally Goodin," we see that Carl was following Eck's progress for much of the piece, but near the end was in a bit of a hurry—his first patch is short a strain, and the B area between patches is also short, twice. His third patch is also curtailed, but he then launched into a new idea that fits well there, playing the basic A strain up an octave. Eck didn't do that in his "Sally Goodin," but incorporating a strain lifted up an octave in a performance was one of his routine maneuvers, so Carl's doing that seems endorsed by history. Carl then continued his performance, which from that point forward became fuller than Eck's in term of both number of strains played and dramatic moments. To summarize: Carl spent two-thirds of his arrangement following Eck closely, then added his own eloquent musical commentary towards the end.

Alita did something quite different. Her arrangement was paced like Carl's—note how well her letter diagram fits below his for much of the pair of performances. But Carl's choice of "patch" ingredients fits within what Eck did, while Alita has rearranged the order in which the different "A patch" strains appear. I tried to clarify how this produces a different musical narrative in figure 32. In that figure, I align the three A patches of the three performers, putting just the first measure of each patch strain in the transcription. Carl meddled a little with Eck's order of ideas; he started late within the first patch, and cut off the third patch early in order to jump to his version of the basic A strain taken up an octave. But Alita departed further from Eck's model. She had observed that the first patch of Eck's was the most powerful, and surmised that if that patch's gestures could be shifted to the middle of the piece (instead of in their position in Eck's composition, in which they initiated the innovative business of crafting the strain patches) this would create more of an arch effect, moving the highest-sounding music to the center of the performance. Her revision worked quite well. Both contemporary fiddlers' approaches to form were successful, and, coupled with the playing strengths of Carl (his flamboyant insertion of lots of short notes, especially triplets) and of Alita (with the most solid command of the bow and thus of both tone and subtle accents in the contest fiddle world) both master fiddlers create fine modern versions of "Sally Goodin."

A surprising footnote to Eck's own playing of "Sally Goodin" came up in the Seeger interview: Eck sometimes interrupted the progress of a performance of this tune with trick fiddling (1963). He noted that on those occasions:

> I'd say "I'm going to play the whole Gooden family, all the different parts representing the different ones of the family, or something like that . . . down to the last baby of three years old." . . . When I'd pull that stunt, I'd also tell the audience "I'm going to actually make this violin talk, speak the words, so many child in the house five years old or older can understand it, much less grown people." . . . When I'd play the thing all the way through, then I'd stop. I'd say "Here goes 'Sallie Gooden' to call in to milk the cows." She starts off yodeling like the famous Jimmie Rodgers did, and everybody knew him. I'd imitate him, yodeling on the violin. Then I stopped, when I'd imitate him, you know. I'd say "now she calls the calves . . . hollerin' 'Sook, sook, sook, calvie, sook, calvie'" just as plain as could be; couldn't be spoken any plainer that I could make it say it on the violin. And that just raised the doggonest laugh. . . . I'd just stop and give them

time to laugh, and then start again. And say "About that time, a baby woke up, and I'd represent the baby callin' for his Momma." And I'd say "Momma, Momma, Momma—I just want my Momma." Well that'd just take the house down. . . .

How did Eck's virtuosic arrangement of "Sally Goodin" influence his fiddling of other tunes? We hear him use the rhythm of the regularly recurring cadence of that tune in plenty of cadences within his arrangements of other tunes. The general idea of building a performance by packing it with variations certainly became part of his playing; I'll explore that topic in the rest of the analytical part of this book. But just one common tune seems to come directly out of the techniques of "patch" building that dominated "Sally Goodin" and the rare "Grigsby's Hornpipe." That is Eck's "Say Old Man, Can You Play a Fiddle" (figure 67).

The first characteristic of "Say Old Man" that makes a big impression is its modal flavor. It's on the pitch a, a common choice. However, it is set in an unusual tuning that emphasizes e, the dominant of a: low E, EAE (that is, E on the G string tuned down, E on the D string, then the A and E strings unmodified, as in the very rare "Get Up in the Cool"). At first hearing, the melody's A strain sounds as if it is in minor and the B strain as if it is in major. But the modes are actually more exotic than that. The A strain, with which the performance starts, features the pitch g natural immediately and c natural prominently too, but includes neither the pitch f natural nor f♯ (with a tiny exception, an f natural in an ornament played twice in strain A′ ′). To me, this part of the tune sounds in a hexatonic gapped dorian mode. Then the B strain features the note c♯ but leaves the g as natural and again omits f and f♯; it's in a hexatonic gapped mixolydian mode. Yes, most listeners won't be familiar with those modes either as academically described or as heard, and will simply hear minor versus major, but they still may sense a whiff of the unusual, that impression increased by optional double stopping on the very low e (in the performance Eck did for Seeger, not the transcribed one done for Riddle) and certainly the sympathetic resonance of that low e. The exact nature of the exotic modepair isn't vitally important, but its exoticism is. Did Eck think through this contrast? It is tempting to ascribe the c♯ in the B strain as inspired by finger convenience—Eck is in third position (with his index finger on a, when on the e string), but he inserts the high e several times. Rather than shifting his left hand position up to catch that pitch, he likely just reached up with his fourth finger, as remains common today. It is much easier, when reaching up like that with the fourth finger, to finger a c♯ rather than a c natural with the third finger. Whatever the reason for switching to using c♯ in that strain, the modal contrast between strains is striking and attractive. The transcription is of a performance not in the unusual tuning. Eck played the tune for Seeger in that tuning, but the performance was interrupted by a tape change. I worked instead with a performance in GDAE, doing so partly because the tune is now played in GDAE at contests.

The direct influence on this tune created by Eck's experience composing "Sally Goodin" is primarily in the *form* of "Say Old Man, Can You Play a Fiddle." The performance begins normally enough, with the A strain played twice (the second time with a mild stretch in measure 1). But the rest of the performance consists of precisely the kinds of "patches" so important in Eck's "Sally Goodin," that is, three to five versions of a strain with small changes at the very beginning of each, those small changes adding systematically and cumulatively to forward momentum. The sets (patches) of B strains are especially transparent in that way: the basic B strain includes the note high c♯ twice, strain B′ adds a high e, then strain B′′ traces a loop of c♯, e, c♯. In the patches of A strains, Eck instead toys with stretching the note a in various ways. This piece is exceptional in this way, giving the impression of an experiment, one resembling the play with patches in "Grigsby's Hornpipe" and especially "Sally Goodin." Eck played it regularly.

— Chapter 6 —

"SALLY JOHNSON," "DONE GONE," AND THE CONSOLIDATION OF THE TEXAS FIDDLE REPERTOIRE AND STYLE

How did the variation within the "patches" in "Sally Goodin" affect how Eck Robertson put together other tunes of his that would also become Texas fiddle standards? I will look first and longest at "Sally Johnson," which is a useful special case. We have two rather different recordings of Eck playing "Sally Johnson," and so can witness him weighing compositional alternatives. Also, contemporary contest versions present enough additional variety to demonstrate what modern fiddlers believe are the essential ingredients of this popular breakdown.

"Sally Johnson," already common throughout the South in Eck's day, was played under this name and another, "Katy Hill" (it continues to thrive in the bluegrass sphere under the latter title). This tune possesses especially powerful forward motion. It has some affinity with "Sally Goodin" in the character of the initial twisting melodic gesture and in the transferred cadential figure. But the central characteristic of "Sally Johnson" is the tight matrix of resemblances between its various sections. Its B strain both

Figure 33. Side A of Victor 19372, recorded July 1, 1922, at the Victor studio in New York.

resembles and complements its A strain. It has the same rhythmic texture, with lots of eighth-note runs alternating with figures of a dotted quarter note followed by more running eighths. The dotted quarter is expanded in strain "As" (As means A stretched, that is, the "s" means that it includes some long notes in prominent locations), and also in the C strain, which resembles the A strain in rhythmic texture and contours, but is "stretched" even further, and placed in the lower range. The general point here is that "Sally Johnson" is made of attractive, impetus-building music, but we do not hear a dramatic contrast between distinctive strains. The nature of the tune is less a clearcut alternation of moods, A strain versus B strain, than simply hurtling ahead.

Eck's approach to shaping this raw material changed over time. In his 1922 commercial recording of the tune (Victor 19372, Side A), he played a short version of "Sally Johnson" and went directly into a short version of "Billy in the Low Grounds," creating a medley (see figure 68). Why did he combine these particular two tunes? Perhaps this occurred to him because both melodies contain some conspicuous spots emphasizing the six chord, what music theorists call the submediant—the minor chord sharing two pitches with the tonic major chord. In G major, the key of "Sally Johnson," that chord is E minor; see how the pitch e is emphasized in the fourth measure in each B strain. These days, accompanists generally go to an E-minor chord there (Eck couldn't ask for that in his commercial recording in the 1920s, instead having to accept whatever harmonization the Victor studio accompanist chose to play). In each of Eck's complete renderings of "Sally Johnson" in interviews (that is, where the tune is presented as a complete piece, not as a companion of "Billy in the Low Grounds"), he does two things. He adds pairs of A, B, and C strains to make a performance of normal duration, and he adds emphasis to the note e in the location discussed above. He does this by performing the e as a double stop on that pitch—the left hand third or fourth finger scoops up on the a string to e, while the bow is tipped to also play the open E string. Most modern performances incorporate this gesture.

The corresponding attention to the submediant—the six—chord in "Billy in the Low Grounds" fills parts of every strain. That tune is played in the key of C major; the submediant is A minor. The note a sticks out in measures 3 and 7 of each strain. In early recordings, that a is generally harmonized with an F chord; in recent decades it is A minor. In sum, "Sally Johnson" and "Billy in the Low Grounds" although in different keys and made up of differently contoured main strains, have a parallel harmonic factor that creates a degree of compatibility between the two tunes. That makes combining the tunes in a medley seem like a reasonable choice.

So, creating a medley was Eck's first solution to the question of how he could add content to "Sally Johnson." He put together other medleys, notably "Big Devil Medley" and "Brilliancy Medley." But his preferred method of enriching performances of an inherited tune was to reduce internal redundancy, which is how he approached later performances of "Sally Johnson." In his original version, the basic strains contained the same high amount of internal repetition as do most fiddle tunes published in the early nineteenth century. In the A strain, the gesture filling the first two measures returns to start the second phrase (in the fifth-to-sixth measures). Also, the wrapping up of the A strain, in the seventh and eighth measures, will return to end the B strain . . . which has its own high redundancy quotient (compare the odd-numbered measures). The oldest published tunes Eck played, not just "Arkansas Traveler" but also the even older body of hornpipes, contain about the same generous quotients of internal repetition.

By the 1960s, Eck had loosened up such patterns. Compare the early measures of his "Sally Johnson" played for Vernon Riddle in 1959 with that part of the 1922 recording. In the version played for Riddle, the first and fifth measures no longer quite match, nor do the second and sixth measures, and so on. But then comparing this version with any of the modern versions reveals a much greater level of variety in the modern performances, and does so in three ways. The parallel measures (1 and 5, and so on) are more different from each other. There are now more bits of syncopation, including quite a few measures in which eight eighth notes are grouped as 3–3–2 (see Wes Westmoreland's first measure, figure 69), and repetitions of strains are generally varied to incorporate more contrast and drama than Eck regularly employed. Eck said that his "improvements" of tunes never obscured the original melodies, while younger fiddlers did add too much variety, obscuring those melodies (Seeger interview, 1963). We can see that Eck's performances from the 1960s sit about halfway on a continuum reaching from the oldest published fiddle tunes to modern contest style in terms of quotients of internal variety.

Contemporary versions of "Sally Johnson" share strategies to make this piece carry enough interest to stay at the center of contest fiddling. I will explore four modern performances, looking most closely at a fine performance by Wes Westmoreland III, who has won the Texas State Championship more times than anyone else, and who is respected throughout the contest fiddle world. Wes grew up in a family including strong fiddlers, and interacted often with other youngsters within the fiddle contest environment (particularly Carl Hopkins). He worked for ten years in Mel Tillis' Country Western Band in Branson, Missouri. He returned to school after that, and as of this writing is a pharmacist who still plays fiddle as much as he can. In his "Sally Johnson" (figure 69) he offers a double clinic, one in how to polish a melodic surface through refining details, and the other, functioning on a broader level, in how to arrange substantial fiddle performances to create subtle but powerful musical architecture. Listing his more intimate refinements would take pages; I'll mention just a few. We see two kinds of variation coexisting from the very beginning of the performance. Comparing the first measure of each of the first four A strains, we see Wes adding emphasis through stretching the first note—an eighth note the first time, the next time a quarter note (with added slide to both members of a double stop), then a half-plus-eighth (measures 1, 9, and 17), then a return to an eighth. This resembles how Eck constructed his "patches" (although here with smaller gestures, and not offering an extended cluster of A strains, but rather the normal alternation of strain pairs). At the same time, Wes varies other parts of the same strains with less system, more as in western swing (compare, for example, these measures occupying the same position in many of the A strains: measures 2, 10, 34, 74, and 114); Eck seldom varied performances in this way. The first small variations (mm. 1, 9, and 17) join the fabric of these later ones. Wes is not recreating the drama of Eck's patches, I believe, but Eck's example—both directly and as filtered through intervening generations of fiddlers—lurks behind Wes's variation techniques, helping reinforce the overall effect.

Concerning form: While I give a simple letter diagram of Wes's performance at the end of figure 69, I will amplify that diagram here to highlight important structures:

Group 1	2	3	4	5	6	7
A As B! B	As! A Cs C	As A As!! As!!	B B A A	Ar Br A! A′	A′′ ′A′ Cs C	As A Bs B
X	Y	Z	simplest?	Z	Y	X

Yes, I have refined my letter designations of strains here. In addition to adding an s to letters naming strains that start with a stretched first note (remember, As means an A strain starting with a lengthened note), I add an r for strains in which the opening figure has been replaced with a rhythm-dominated figure. Last, I add an exclamation point when some aspect of a strain really hammers the listener's ear (measure 17 exemplifies this: adding the double stops outlining a G-major chord is a great way to create immediate contrast between strains A and B). Some broad points emerge from the diagram. First, Wes is still working in four-strain sets, this time seven such sets, in each case with two fairly orthodox forms of the A strain joined with a pair of strains that contrast with the tamest A strain. Second, in their general effect, the strain groups go from fairly simple to complex, then the reverse, with a simpler basic set in the very middle—the broad aural impression becomes a mirror or palindrome (also, compare the two sets labeled X, and also the two sets labeled Y). Third, notice the placement of especially dramatic moments, such as the rhythmic stretch followed by a rhythmic crowd in mm. 81–82, and the chromatic outburst in mm. 116–17. Last, notice how the air is let out of this energetic performance during the last four strains. These are the tamest strains as a group, and also relax within the group: compare mm. 193 and 201, and mm. 209 and 217.

This is masterful musical architecture. Each of Wes's other performances of "Sally Johnson" traces a similar but unique form (see Goertzen 2012).

The next version of "Sally Johnson" comes from retired welder Carl Hopkins, a close friend of Wes, and accorded as much respect by knowledgeable fans of Texas fiddling (figure 70). Carl takes the B strain as central, beginning and ending with it to create his own mirror form. As in Wes's version, the core of the performance includes wild areas of rhythmic contrasts and chromatic adventure, here mm. 49–65. Overall, Carl's version is more ornate within less space; he is a thoroughgoing energizer, a romantic in comparison to Wes's more restrained, classical approach. These two versions show how different excellent performances can be, even right at the center of the Texas fiddle world.

The remaining two versions of "Sally Johnson" illustrate how Texas contest style has differentiated into regional substyles. The version performed by Tristan Clarridge shows his playing at the National Oldtime Fiddlers' Contest and Festival, a large contest held in Weiser, Idaho. This contest does have a national reach, but remains strongly focused on the Northwest. Clarridge received lessons early in life on both art violin (his teacher specialized in Baroque performance) and fiddle. He and his sister Tashina, both professional musicians, are recurring champions at the "national" event. Their playing styles—and those of the other Northwestern stars that dominate this contest—do add art music values and techniques to their Texas-derived contest fiddling. This recast style has been nurtured in Weiser in tandem with that contest's rules requiring short, concentrated performances. In order to march briskly through performances of literally hundreds of contestants, strict time limits have been in place for decades. Under the rules in force as of this writing, each player must air short versions of three tunes—a breakdown (like "Sally Goodin," or "Sally Johnson"), a waltz, and "tune of choice" (such as a rag, polka, or other) within a total of four minutes (five minutes at the upper reaches of the contest brackets, that is, in the top "Grand Champion" bracket, or six minutes in the final face-off). Tristan's contest performance of "Sally Goodin" that I transcribed for this book (the second tune within Figure 70) occupied a minute and 33 seconds within his Grand Champion's time allotment of five minutes. In this and the other top performances in Weiser, there is simply not enough time to build a carefully shaped performance like Wes's or Carl's; chromaticism and exquisite virtuosity instead flow generously from start to end. Note how Tristan enjoyed churning through piles of triplets in mm. 14–15, before the first A strain has even been aired, and note the frantic but fun complexities appearing as early as mm. 33–48.

The last performance of "Sally Johnson" I transcribed for this book is from the Southeast. Daniel Carwile is from northern Alabama, and has won the Tennessee Valley Old-Time Fiddlers convention (in Athens, Alabama) seven times, as well as the US Grand Master Convention and other contests. He has a degree in music education from Vanderbilt University, has classical violin training, and is also at home in bluegrass and Celtic musical environments. He and his wife Amy operate the well-regarded Carwile String Studio in Lexington, Kentucky. I cannot count the number of times I have seen Daniel on stage in Athens, sometimes competing but more frequently accompanying his students or his friends on guitar or tenor guitar. His "Sally Johnson," recorded at a jam session in California, features eclectic Texas-style contest fiddling as modified in the Southeast (figure 71). He develops each of the usual components of contest-style performances of the tune fully. His mid-performance explosion of chromaticism (mm. 81–96) is a slide-fest for the first finger on the a string—lots of b♭s going to and from b natural). He has a certain relaxed feel to form that I associate with the Southeast—note how the double-stop arpeggiated sweep on the G-major chord does appear well after the start of the piece (in m. 33), and also quite late (m. 129), in a tidy version of the "backing off" of intensity typical for this piece. The hundreds of hours that Wes and Carl have spent playing western swing and Tristan many kinds of music were lived in bluegrass by Daniel, which left him and the other bluegrass-accustomed virtuoso fiddlers leaning toward incorporating lots of different strains. Bluegrass rhythms—lots of instances of a measure full of eighth notes falling into various combinations of two groups of three plus one group of two, like bluegrass banjo "rolls"—tend to be invoked especially generously.

Chromaticism can appear early (see m. 5) and remain more a part of the picture during a performance in the Southeast than is usual in Texas. Thus, positioning such features in a way to shape musical drama receives less attention than in orthodox Texas style. I have the impression that fiddlers experienced in bluegrass think less about these questions of form; after all, when they are performing as members of bluegrass bands, their solo portions are brief, and overall shaping of form comes largely from alternating soloists—giving turns to banjoists and mandolinists, and perhaps even guitarists.

Analyses similar to that of "Sally Johnson" could be done for many of the other current Texas fiddle hits that Eck had played: for "Durang's Hornpipe" and for the tunes in the part of the anthology between "Sally Johnson" and "Done Gone." This group of tunes constitutes a sizeable share of the meat-and-potatoes fraction of Texas fiddling (as do many in the next section, starting with "Done Gone"). "Billy in the Low Grounds," coupled in a medley with "Sally Johnson" in Eck's 1922 recording, illustrates Eck experimenting with small-scale variation both within his first recording of it and over the decades (figure 72a). First, he added to the standard inherited two strains of this very old piece, creating a stretched-note additional A strain, nicely poised between being obviously a version of A and something new and dramatic; the last B strain does this more gently. He also indulged in a fair amount of incidental variation. Just the first measure varies between the first two A strains, and also between the first two B strains. Also note the small differences between his recorded forms of the tune from the interviews with Seeger and with Conte's friend.

Nearly all of Eck's tunes have some special attractive feature, perhaps part of the long-term identity of the tune, perhaps something he himself contributed. But he persisted in playing a few melodies whose appeal is hard to recognize. For example, he recorded versions of "Apple Blossom" with Gilliland in 1922 and with Cranfill in 1929, but Victor did not deem those cuts worth issuing. He played that piece at a coffee house called the Golden Vanity in Los Angeles, where he was taking part in a folk festival in 1964 (figure 72b). It was an unexciting moment in a generally fun evening! While "Billy in the Low Grounds" is a top-twenty choice among the more frequently played Texas tunes, "Apple Blossom" is rarely heard.

"DONE GONE": NEW TUNES THAT ECK PLAYED

This section of the tune anthology contains the youngest handful of the tunes that Eck frequently played, which present considerable variety at the same time that they fit gracefully into his broader repertoire. Nevertheless, we must keep in mind that he always played more old tunes than new. Over and over, he studied pieces played by the "old masters" he respected so much, and revised those tunes to incorporate his own taste and great skills; he worked hard and effectively to transfer melodies many decades old into his more listening-oriented age without losing their essential traditionality. But a fair number of what became his own standard pieces had not been around long enough to have been polished by his father or his uncles or the other older fiddlers he revered. These tunes were fairly new creations, often in new forms.

Figure 34. Side B of Victor 19372, recorded July 1, 1922, at the Victor studio in New York.

Many among Eck's newer tunes started with the modernized harmonic schemes characteristic of ragtime, with more than the formerly typical ration of two strains, and with direct reference to rapidly changing culture. I will look especially closely at two of his own favorite tunes, "Done Gone" and "Beaumont Rag." In "Sally Johnson," Eck took veteran music as raw material for more modern fiddling. Whoever composed "Beaumont Rag" wrote something new, but positioned this novelty to incorporate tradition. However, I will commence this final section with what was then a brand new tune with a poignant message, "Done Gone."

Eck told the story of Matt Brown composing "Done Gone." The setting was dramatic:

> Brown [was] coming from Dalhart to Amarillo here, way back in the early days, afoot [Dalhart is about eighty-five miles NNW of Amarillo]. The medicine show he was with went broke in Dalhart . . . Matt Brown took his fiddle and suitcase and started for Amarillo afoot. And it was hot weather—even dead cattle on the road, starved to death, no grass. All the feed was burned up, all the grass burned up, just a bunch of mesquite bushes all along the road, you know, and things like that, and all it was long dead. And he's starving to death hisself. Water: wasn't a house along the road nowhere, them days—way back in the early days—and there wasn't nobody had any car; wasn't anybody had any car, just once in a while somebody'd have a car . . ." (Seeger 1963)

And the action of the story was simple but compelling:

> He got about fourteen mile to Amarillo here—walked all the way from Dalhart. And [when] he'd gotten about fourteen miles [from] Amarillo, and he looked back in the north, he saw the dust rising. Just a bank of dust coming toward him—it looked like red-lookin' dust, you know, in the air. And just swarming. He . . . saw it was a car coming toward him. He thought he'd get to ride the rest of the way in to Amarillo; he'd done walked—he'd give out, starvin' to death for water; wasn't a windmill along the road nowhere where you could stop to get a drink without walkin' five mile off of the road . . . the sun just boiling down, just hot as the dickens . . . He thought sure he'd get to ride into town; he just stepped to the side of the road and waved his fiddle across the road after he set his suitcase down; he waved his fiddle across the road tryin' to stop that guy.
>
>   . . . That man just shot the gas in the car and went by him like a cyclone. [Brown] took his fiddle case, the fiddle out of the case, and composed that tune, and called it "Done Gone." That's where it got its name and the way it got its name, as he watched that car go by him; as it zipped by him, and he watched the dust melt away in the distance as it left him. (Seeger 1963)

After this recounting of what seems to have been an oft-repeated and well-polished story, Eck stepped back and reflected on his own learning and revision of the tune: "I learned it from him—the tune just like he played it. And I made a little bit of change in it after I made the record, though. I thought of a certain few notes that he made, the stroke he made with the bow, that represented that car as it zipped by him" (all three quotes from Seeger interview 1963).

Matt Brown's "Done Gone" and its prefatory anecdote reflect their time and place—the first decade of the 1900s, when only a few Fords had made it to the rural Panhandle. The music of "Done Gone" starts unremarkably (see figure 80). If we look just at the first two strains, we see a fiddle tune in all ways typical of early twentieth-century Texas fiddling. The A strain sits a little lower than B in its early measures, and, after an opening arpeggio, traverses a full two octaves in just over a measure and a half. If one compares this to the opening gestures of tunes with long histories and broad geographic sweep like "Billy in the Low Grounds," it becomes clear that relatively recent and relatively western versions of given tunes have larger opening gestures. "Done Gone" possessed such a bold curve from its birth— it entered the world at the point in evolution of melodic style that "Billy in the Low Grounds" attained over many decades. The content of B overlaps considerably with that of A, reminding us of the high level of internal redundancy of many an older fiddle tune's older versions. The B strain does start higher, and doesn't venture into the A strain's lower reaches. This is all typical. Even the key—B♭ major—seems a bit old-fashioned, more typical of the late eighteenth century than the nineteenth century. In short, "Done Gone," in its first two strains, is an attractive tune but not the least bit surprising.

Attaching the C strain transforms the tune. The melody reminds us of the A strain, but now constricted in range and insistent on the new tonic of g (the strain is in the relative minor of B♭, G minor); it's the morose sibling of the A strain in terms of mood. At the same time, it also joins that substantial array of tunes that can be heard as literally representational—in measures 21–22 (and again in measures 30–31) the rule-breaking extra measures let us see that car in the distance twice, or have the hitchhiker's hope flicker twice. That results in the C strain (and C′) being nine measures long. According to Eck, "a violinist" pointed out that Eck's echoing Matt Brown's compositional choice in this instance was incorrect (meaning an error in phrase construction): "I shouldn't have repeated that individual part on the record. . . . [I] always did think that the man I learned it from was wrong—I played it just like the man I learned it from . . . Matt Brown" (Seeger interview 1963). At the bottom of figure 80, I show how Eck's revision of "Done Gone" worked. When Eck played this tune for Riddle, Seeger, and Conte's friend—it was evidently one of his favorite tunes—he removed the "extra" measures. But he instead toyed with the immediately previous measures, adding an obtrusive staccato articulation to some notes, and making the ornaments a bit more prominent. I believe he made these changes to illustrate hope and frustration in a different way than Brown had done or than he himself had done in his commercially recorded version of 1929. In any case, Brown's composing that distinctive scene-painting third strain matters—it makes the tune work musically and fit the times. The third strain matters more than, for instance, the third strain in "Ragtime Annie," which Eck (and some modern players) include in their performances, but other fiddlers omit (then and especially now). In "Ragtime Annie," adding a third strain in the subdominant underlines the pedigree of the melody as a rag, but doesn't seem needed if the tune is approached as an average fiddle tune, not as a rag.

"Beaumont Rag" shows Eck again working with a young tune to make it his own, but reshaping this one much more drastically (figure 83). Samuel Peacock and Smith's Garage Fiddle Band first recorded this tune (Brunswick DAL 736, October 26, 1928; figure 82). Peacock, a prosperous barber living in Cleburne—his shop had a dozen seats!—led "Smith's Garage Fiddle Band," which consisted of Peacock, two of his brothers, and another musician. The name of the band celebrated their patron Sheriff Smith's business in nearby Corsicana (these two cities, about an hour's drive apart today, are both just a bit south of Dallas). Peacock was skilled, widely appreciated, and made a dozen recordings with the Brunswick company in 1928–29. He died soon after that; had he lived longer, he surely would have contributed more to the development of Texas fiddling.

In a description of Beaumont and the oil field culture of the early years of the twentieth century, physician George Parker wrote: "At first the dances were held in a large tent, but later a hall over a store was rented for such entertainment. I was always a guest at these dances in the hall, but in order to be present and still care for my practice, I used to keep my horse saddled and my emergency bag tied to it. I had my reputation for speediness in answering calls to maintain. The story became popular that I could get to a case in a saloon, gambling house, place of ill repute, or my office, dress the bruised and beaten person, and get back to a dance in time for the next number!" (1948, 67). Those must have been rowdy affairs, but at least some of the music will have been the same as at tamer dances: "In spite of the danger, violence, and hardship at Spindletop, many families managed to succeed in making good lives for themselves. Rising above their circumstances, the settlers created their own sedate entertainments as alternatives to [what went on in] saloons, gambling halls, and bordellos. In Batson [about forty-five miles from the Spindletop oilfields by very muddy track], they held dances on wooden platforms, serving ice cream, soda pop, and lemonade. They did the waltz, the two-step, and the schottische, while a five piece band (cornet, two guitars, and two violins) played the 'Beaumont Rag' and other favorites" (an oft-repeated narrative quoted, for example, in Linsley et al. 2002, 182).

Samuel Peacock's "Beaumont Rag" (figure 82) is definitely a rag in character, with strains of either twelve or sixteen measures, pervasive syncopation, a newly expanded harmonic vocabulary, and more than two strains (the third emphasizing the subdominant key, although cadencing in the tonic). This performance works with pairs of strains, and has a ration of incidental variation differentiating the two journeys through the A strain, which Peacock treats as primary (as do most subsequent fiddlers, although not Eck). Strains A and C contrast nicely; B derives in a simple way from C; D lets players show off who are comfortable playing in fifth position.

Eck made Strain B his primary material (see figure 83). He apparently enjoyed that strain because of its complex bowing and the syncopated melody emerging from that right-hand virtuosity, and offered that strain in three versions that explore different approaches to the rhythmic texture. His performances (the ones for Seeger and that for Riggs and Nagy are virtually identical to this one) present three groups of four strains each, in all cases including two passes through some form of the B strain. Rather than a rounded form, it's cumulative—all three strains make it into the final grouping. Wes Westmoreland's virtuosic performance (figure 84) synthesizes earlier approaches, with a dominant A strain—the strain going first and last, and being infused with the most variation. Other modern performances resemble his in terms of using Samuel Peacock's A strain as the primary one, and also in level of complexity and general character, although the strains are often ordered somewhat differently.

Eck's six rags comprise a sizeable fraction of his repertoire. Yes, he played only a cursory form of "Kansas City Rag" in his interview with members of the New Lost City Ramblers (1962; figure 81, bottom); playing it was probably not his idea. Kansas City, a transportation hub, nurtured the same sort of mix of frontier chaos and respectable town as did oil towns like Beaumont and Borger, and apparently was therefore as deserving of having lively music named for it. Kansas City was an "ill-kempt metropolis known far and wide as the "Pittsburgh of the West," with parts "as teeming with humanity and vice as any unruly seaport." "A smutty and religious town," the writer Edward Dahlberg recalled his childhood home, whose inhabitants—numbering some 160,000 by the time author Haskell arrived—were "wild about Christian Science, vice and lots of penance." It was "A frontier town that boasted more than twice as many saloons and gaming houses as churches, where Jesse James's farmhouse was a local landmark and the proud citizenry took the outlaw's orphaned son to its bosom" (2007, 1–3). But Eck didn't work on this tune, did not "improve" it, instead he just played this short form.

Although Eck was not very comfortable with waltzes, he worked hard to command a few, writing one ("Amarillo Waltz," figure 91), and making an extra effort to arrange another ("Brown Kelly Waltz," figure 90). Waltzes have a complicated and prominent history in American popular music.

In the parade over time of fashionable dances—at least one young dance genre looming large and nudging its immediate predecessors out of the limelight in American mass culture for each generation throughout United States history—the waltz appears twice. Rather simple two-strain waltzes burst into the picture in the late 1810s to 1820s; quite a few appear in *Riley's Flute Melodies*, volume 3, from the late 1820s or the 1830s (available online). These range from crowds of little, forgettable pieces to ones borrowed from art music, such as one labeled simply "Freischutz," drawn from the Weber opera *Der Freischütz*; this and other well-liked operas would be subjected repeatedly to such plundering.

But the Strauss-style leisurely, longer waltz made a bigger and more lasting impact, starting in the 1870s, an impact enormously amplified in the waltz song craze of the turn of the twentieth century. Legions of traditional fiddlers adopted at least a few waltzes into their repertoires. We don't know how the enormous hit "Over the Waves" ("Sobre las Osas," Juventino Rosas [1868–1894], 1888) came to be part of Conte's friend's interview of Eck (1970s?; figure 87). Eck's announcement of it on this recording is simply: "Over the Waves Waltz." Eck placed plenty of grace note ornaments in his arrangement, and ventured up the neck as far as fifth position (measures 85–90). That required an unusual level of skill and some advance planning! But his use of double stops remains cautious. Most are of the easiest type, in which one or both pitches are open strings, or, if both notes are fingered, one of them is left over from immediately before the double stop (for example, mm. 49 and 50). But there are some moments when he must place both fingers at once (generally the first and second finger; this is fairly easy in G major, the key of each of his waltzes), and there are other tricky moments—see m. 42, second beat, where he must place the first and third finger simultaneously, then slide the formation up to third position seamlessly. We can hear tiny hesitations: he is conscious of the difficulty. All of this adds up to a much more wooden performance than that of West Virginia's Clark Kessinger (figure 88; recording on YouTube).

Eck's "Brown Kelly Waltz" filled both sides of Victor V40334 (1929; Figure 89). The "Brown" in the title refers to the tune's prolific composer, Matt Brown, who also wrote "Lime Rock" and likely "Ragtime Annie." We don't know the identity of "Kelly" (but see Kuntz in *The Fiddlers' Companion* on "Keller's Waltz"). Here, to get a full sound, Eck recruited another fiddler to double the tune at various intervals, including the lower octave. The faithful, extraordinarily well-practiced blend suggests that his assistant in this recorded performance was his multi-instrumentalist son Dueron. Eck was especially interested in the A strain, presenting it in various guises, and ending with a version of that strain that seems cumulative and is certainly lovely. This long arrangement was well-liked.

I also transcribed a modern performance to show how much these fiddled waltzes have come to be saturated with difficult double stopping, done to enrich sound, to open the door wider to individual creativity, and simply to demonstrate virtuosity in this sphere (figure 90). The fiddler here, Tom Weisgerber, is a pillar of Texas fiddling in Minnesota, and husband to Alita Stoneking Weisgerber (see figure 63). Tom plays "Kelly Waltz" frequently ("Brown" is now often omitted from the title); his is a wonderful version, displaying impressive technique, including lots of fine position work coupled with intricate, varied, and creatively chosen double stops. The form Tom has crafted works well: an initial 32-bar A strain full of double stops precedes a 16-bar B in which filigree replaces the double stops, then a 32-bar A the first half of which inverts many of the doubles—making a high strain that transforms A—then returning to the first A. That suffices to fill out a delicate, lovely waltz, and Tom stopped his performance of "Kelly Waltz" right there during the 2023 Texas State Championship. But in his 2021 contest performance (the one transcribed in figure 90), he added a sixteen-bar C strain showcasing a trick element—left-hand pizzicato—and a closing, peaceful sixteen-bar D strain. All of this shines. I follow that transcription with two other fiddlers' versions of the very beginning of the piece in order to show how much personal creative space the use of so many double stops allows.

The last waltz in the anthology is Eck's own "Amarillo Waltz," recorded commercially in 1929 (Victor V40298; figure 91). All three of the tunes for which he claimed authorship were named for cities he knew well, presumably to curry favor with the audiences in those cities. "Borger Wiggle," "Stumptown Stomp in Grand Saline"—both breakdowns (figure 92)—and "Amarillo Waltz" are all serviceable pieces played by just a few of Eck's friends or avid fans in later generations. Vernon Riddle, one of Eck's interviewers, competed in some of same contests as the senior fiddler, and passed on these and others of Eck's tunes after his own post-retirement move to his original home, South Carolina.

None of Eck's few original compositions for fiddle garnered a sizeable or secure place in the Texas fiddle repertoire. Similarly, "The Island Unknown," a generic broadside ballad, did not catch other musicians' attention (figure 93). The story explores familiar territory. A young man goes to sea, leaving behind his parents and sweetheart. The ship founders. The protagonist survives the wreck. Up to this point, we are in a version of the "Robinson Crusoe" story. A number of both old and young ballads involve fatal aquatic experiences; our narrator is fated to die on the "unknown" island. Neither these lyrics nor the melody surprise. However, the vocal harmony and violin part represent interesting compromises between pop music procedures and traditional ones. Eck sings the melody. Nettie's part goes smoothly from a unison with the melody to simple parallel thirds or other elementary options and back again to unison, offering a model for ballad harmonization that seeks out a genteel border between pop music and oral tradition but doesn't cross the line into becoming saccharine. The fiddle part strikes a similar compromise, first offering a lightly ornamented pass through the melody as a prelude. When the voice enters, the fiddler shifts to playing a harmony part containing only the simplest double stops. For the last phrase of every verse, the fiddler reverts to the ornamented version of the melody that had been aired at the end of the prelude. The motivation for this ballad remains a bit of a puzzle. There is no evidence that Eck performed it often—why did he arrange and record it?

ROADBLOCKS, COMPLAINTS, AND AN ENDURING LEGACY: A "COWBOY" FIDDLER AT THE CROSSROADS

The Texas of Eck's childhood and young adulthood gathered up immigrants from far and wide, but especially from throughout the South, and so juxtaposed various southern fiddle styles and repertoires. As Texas acquired its distinctive culture, with its own forces massaging the myriad of arriving oral traditions, it became less of a melting pot for fiddle styles than a combination of filter with site of transformation, a vibrant crossroads for change. Today, Texas has become a wellspring, the locus and source of the contest styles that dominate in much of the South and West, especially in a sociological sense—the styles favored by many of the most direct inheritors of fiddling in terms of both family traditions and socioeconomic status: working-class participants. Of course, the American Upper South as a haven for players in a complex of old-time styles—and the Ozarks as its own old-time world—stand apart from the Texas-centered fiddle contest world, as do urban revivalists of the old-time styles, wherever they live. But even these contrasting styles, these examples of persisting difference, have been shaped to some degree by the nature of Texas fiddling. Many players in old-time styles, particularly the revivalists, self-consciously orient their repertoires and practices *away* from the Texas and Texas-flavored fiddle contest world; they define their styles partly through opposition.

When we listen to early Texas fiddlers other than Eck, we do generally hear traces of styles more common elsewhere in the South, styles that were not destined to thrive in Texas (see *Old Time Texas Strings Bands* 2001a and 2001b). There were exceptions—for instance, Samuel Peacock, head fiddler in Smith's Garage Fiddle Band, deserves a closer look than there is room for in this book. And a few contemporary fiddlers in Texas have made a point of seeking out and learning from older fiddlers in alternative styles; Howard Raines stands out among those modern Texan fiddler/researchers (see Raines 2013). Eck's choices were not the only path leading to modern Texas style, of course, but his influence was truly remarkable and is widely acknowledged. Fiddlers I ardently wish had been recorded, but were not, include those who mentored Eck such as Polk Harris and Matt Brown, and of course Eck's father and uncles. All of these "old masters" must have left marks on Eck's repertoire and technique and on the playing of other Texas fiddlers. We can't measure those traces nearly as much as we would like to, but we can celebrate the contributions they made to Texas fiddling both in general and through their collective influence on Eck.

Eck Robertson was every bit as ambitious as he was talented and hard-working, yet in the end nearly as frustrated as he was ambitious. Charles Wolfe narrated Eck's recording history and business dealings in exhaustive detail in his book *The Devil's Box: Masters of Southern Fiddling* (1997, 12–29). Wolfe summarized Eck's fate: "He had all the skills, versatility, commercial appeal and personality to become a major recording figure in the 1920s and 1930s, but he did not" (1997, 28–29). I believe that both Eck's remarkable accomplishments and his deep disappointments can be tied as much to character as to circumstance. T. R. Fehrenbach, in his sprawling *Lone Star: A History of Texas and the Texans*, characterized his fellow Texans as embodying what he believed to be the psychology of the frontier: touchy and independent, determinedly self-reliant—indeed, in many cases, self-important (2000, 256–57). These are essentially the same traits that "Teddy Blue" Abbott ascribed to his fellow cowboys in his *We Pointed Them North: Recollections of a Cowpuncher*: "independent, proud, sensitive" (1939/1955, 212–13). Of course, quite a few Texans don't fit this description, but Eck did, and I have known quite a few contemporary Texans who do. Eck's not attaining the success he desired was a result of the interaction of unkind circumstance and his Texas-style obdurate character.

The Panhandle's days as a true frontier were fresh in memory when Eck arrived around 1907, and his dizzying hopscotch of relocations within the Panhandle through about 1940 seemed designed to keep him on the edge of frontier life; he kept shifting to small, young towns, to less developed locations. There were still cowboys working on ranches in the 1910s, but there were now plenty of barbed-wire fences, too; the cowboys' way of life was changing as rapidly as were the lives of all other Texans. Eck attempted to explore and take advantage of this cultural juncture. His and Nettie's making of lantern slides of ranch life to incorporate into their stage shows, followed by their furnishing of live music for silent western movies, constituted their continually evolving strategy to profit from the feverish transfer and transformation of living history into marketable nostalgia. It is hard to imagine that when Eck seized this moment, the moment didn't seize him right back. He adopted the type of cowboy formal clothes he would wear to his first recording session in New York—he claimed to have been the first western-garbed musician—and also was happy to adopt the stage sobriquet "Famous Cowboy Fiddler." It's a shame that the studio recording of his skit "My Experiences on the Ranch" was not issued; perhaps we could have witnessed some kind of digest of his transformation! In any case, it matters that Eck had really visited ranches. He took both his eyes and his fiddle along—he saw, he listened, he took part.

Larry McMurtry, a Texan author deeply ambivalent about Texas history and culture, noted: "Most of us, without particularly meaning to, have by now accumulated—from commercials, from ads in magazines, from picture books, from movies—a mental archive of images from the West, a personal West-in-the-mind's-eye in which we see an eternal pastoral very beautiful but usually unpeopled, except for the Marlboro Man. These potent images, pelting us decade after decade, finally implant notions about how the West is that are as unrealistic as are those of the dime novelists. If, on the other hand, we go to photography for information, rather than fantasy, we can learn a great deal about what life was like for people who actually lived in the West . . ." (2001, 20).

In Eck's day, the western dime novel was still a youthful genre; it was indeed dime novelists who had recently and thoroughly cultivated the images of the West that would be drawn upon by the movie industry. Dozens of both American and European authors cranked out formulaic prose western after formulaic prose western. American Zane Grey (1872–1939), with his seventy-eight books, certainly was industrious and influential. But the size of his contribution pales when compared with that of Norwegian author Rudolph Muus (1862–1935), who wrote 500 westerns, according to McMurtry (2001, 4). Ole Evensen, the Norwegian immigrant who interacted with Eck and the other fiddlers in Vernon, was of an age to have been acquainted with Muus's widely disseminated output. Reading western dime novels written and published in Norwegian might have inspired the young Evensen to take the unusual step of abandoning the cultural comfort of the Scandinavian immigrant enclaves of the upper Midwest and relocating to Olustee, Oklahoma, so near to Eck's home in the 1920s.

Actual cowboys came from all over North America and Mexico, with a broad racial mix and a sprinkling of Europeans thrown in. During the work day, their variety in background was submerged in the patterns of rigorous labor of their collective profession. But in the evening, bits of cultural eclecticism could surface. Eck must have witnessed and even contributed to this; "My Experiences on the Ranch" featured *him* fiddling. His belief that his participation suited the setting may have been self-serving—it was for-profit entertainment, after all—but enough cowboys shared enough of his background for his fiddling to fit into cowboys' evenings.

Under what circumstances did Eck begin to visit ranches? He noted that he was asked to come, to fiddle for parties (Seeger interview 1963). Also, by the early 1900s, many ranches in the Panhandle were established properties owned by affluent families. Children in these prosperous families needed teachers, and so it became common to have at least one live on the ranch. Raising and educating daughters often meant owning a piano, and therefore needing to arrange periodic visits from piano tuners and repairmen such as Eck. But the state legislature passed laws that favored small farms (in order to make more profits from land sales). The cattle drives were over, and cowboy culture was fading quickly. Why did Eck and Nettie start their project documenting ranch life? If this was primarily a show business maneuver from the start, how did it occur to them? Was it personal curiosity at first, then the realization that their visits presented a mercantile opportunity to profit from nostalgia? I believe that one important psychological ingredient had to do with character, with how Eck's attitudes meshed with those of the cowboys and therefore with those of many male Texans (both Texans of that day and today). If I am right, then Eck felt at home in what was left of ranch life, and taking on the persona of "famous cowboy fiddler" felt natural.

The window on cowboy life Eck then promulgated in Texas started with the medium McMurtry recommended—actual photographs—which then were assembled to become parts of several kinds of shows, which then connected well with Eck and Nettie's adding live music to silent Western movies that were playing in their part of Texas. In the interview with Seeger in 1963, we learn that Eck finally headed to California in 1937, and tried to enter the film music profession. Of course, Eck carried his personal and documented memories of cowboy life to Hollywood. He certainly would have drawn carefully on his knowledge to advance his professional hopes, but he equally certainly remained more allied to lived experience than were the dime novelists or were established musicians in the young movie industry. His firsthand knowledge—and his own touchy independence—may not have helped him in Hollywood, instead interfering with his getting a foothold in the film world!

In the end, it seems unlikely that Eck ever had much of a chance to enter the Hollywood pop music business on his own terms. He reported that he didn't get along with a particular individual already established in this music business; he was outraged that this person (unnamed) was "robbing his ensemble." He further complained that that this same person "just played songs. That guy played Hawaiian-style guitar, and couldn't accompany breakdowns" (Seeger interview 1963). His verbal formulation "couldn't accompany breakdowns" is an important one. Eck may or may not have read dime novels. When he had furnished music on the spot for silent movies—especially westerns—he made his own creative choices. I believe that he expected that his acquaintance with both cowboy myth and actual ranch life would result in him having a say in deciding which music would become integral parts of the new Westerns that were being crafted with sound as an ingredient. Further, he surely felt that his repertoire of fiddle breakdowns would function well in that aesthetic environment. Soon, alienated from some members of the Hollywood western movie community, and disabused of his expectation that the film community would welcome his distinctive contribution to their knowledge and craft, he returned home.

This was not the only time that Eck had a rough experience with procedures in the production and consumption of popular culture. He bragged that theater owners who were required to confine their bookings to acts that were sent out on a contracted rotation that was codified in New York would, when he showed local theater managers in person what he could do, slip him into the parade of contracted acts for several nights. That sounds gratifying, but has a flip side: we have learned through that anecdote that most entertainment in those theaters was indeed arranged in a rule-bound sequence that he could only rarely crack. Finally, Eck wrote to the RCA Manufacturing Company in 1940, asking if they would like to record his playing again. The company had forgotten him; the answer was a double-pronged "no." That letter, dated October 24, 1940 (addressed to Eck in Dallas; could he have been living there again briefly?), was signed by Stephen H. Sholes, head of Recording and Record Sales at RCA: "We appreciate very much your interest in suggesting that we make some recordings of your fiddle playing. However, just at this moment, we are not in need of this type of music nor do we plan a recording expedition to Dallas before next spring. As you undoubtably know, it is now impossible to make phonograph records by any instrumental musician who does not belong to the American Federation of Musicians." Eck kept this letter—it remains among his small cache of papers on deposit at the library of the Country Music Foundation.

The dismissive note from Sholes raised two issues. To be allowed to work as a professional instrumentalist, Eck would have needed to join a union. There is no evidence that he ever attempted to do that, perhaps partly because of Sholes's additional offhand remark that RCA was "not in need of this kind of music." Fashion had moved on. Fiddle music and other "hillbilly" music had yielded up its small rivulet within pop music; it had been largely replaced in popular taste by the very country music that it had spawned. This concerned both the money from sales of recordings and employment at dances. The main public venue for fiddling became special events, mostly fiddle contests. Eck knew that environment well, and thrived in it. But this activity could at best yield occasional prizes and associated busking opportunities, not steady or substantial wages. Fiddling in Texas (and in much of the country) had come to a crossroads in function that changed musical needs and shrunk fiddlers' incomes.

Nostalgia has always involved change, both filtering and exaggeration. Nostalgia fueled by changes in life in the Texas Panhandle had enough psychological strength and momentum to support fiddle contests to some degree. Enough money could be allocated to purchase prizes for competitors and thereby to create weekend pleasures for small but not tiny audiences, ones like the several hundred people who still attend the Texas State Championship annually. Contests of Eck's day did not yield enough money to support him as a professional fiddler, and his band the Sleep

Disturbers seems not to have been a success. Of course, that made him no worse off than then were and still are plenty of fine performers in all branches of the arts. There are always many more talented and hard-working musicians than available full-time jobs as performers. But this was a tough crossroads for Eck to face.

Eck's certainty that his ways of selecting and shaping tunes were superior hurt him professionally, that is, likely interfered with his hope to enter the movie business, but his musical predilections *would* fit the newly dominant performing situation. At contests, audiences devoted more energy to listening carefully, and so increasingly elaborate fiddling was rewarded. Eck's physical and mental virtuosity helped him win many a contest during his younger days, and then triumph in senior competition brackets later in life.

Eck claimed that his mentors—"the old masters"—were as skilled as he had become, and that he was their direct heir. Here is a passage from the 1963 interview with Seeger:

> What do you mean, "the old masters"?
>
> Well, I mean the old masters . . . the older men that played the fiddle back in my boyhood days, young days, you know. They was some of the greatest fiddlers living in the country, you know, different [places] I've lived in. I met a lot of what I call the old masters just like the genuine old time fiddlers that was up in . . . [they] had the execution, you know, the art and so on, different from just a common jack-leg fiddlers. They were . . . the only fiddlers them days that really played the tunes right, and still, the same, when you meet up with one of them today, he's got the tune more right, and if there's any of them living. . . . I'm about as old as any of them now, that's living, and that's why people write me from all over the world. They still remember hearing their father or their grandfather play tunes, you see, and I came nearer playing like them than anybody else.
>
> What is the difference between the "old master" and the, as you say, the "jack leg"? . . .
>
> Well, the average jack leg fiddlers plays . . . in other words, he's not got the execution or the tune either. He only plays usually a two part tune, and it's just the same thing over and over.

But Eck also felt that the adding of content had to be calibrated so that it did not obscure a tune. His last brief description of the ideal balance between faithfulness and creativity was this: "not skipping anything," but also "not putting in parts that don't belong" (Spielman interview 1972, 187). He claimed that he played many a tune just like the "old masters" had played them, but he was just as insistent that he, like all fiddlers, sought to "improve" tunes. So how did he balance these contradictory claims?

Eck clearly had an enormous repertoire of both common and rare tunes, and of tunes from all parts of the South, and from all eras of fiddle history, reaching back in some cases to the late eighteenth century. Some of these bore other names in their earlier history. "Billy in the Low Grounds" was originally "The Braes of Auchtertyre" in late eighteenth-century Scotland, "Leather Britches" was "Lord MacDonald's Reel," and so on. Other tunes of this vintage have long had the same names, for instance "Irish Washwoman" and many of the hornpipes in this book's Tune Anthology. Yet others of his tunes are rare enough that their histories remain obscure (for example, "Chadwick," "Rhubarb," and "Dominion Hornpipe"). The very best contemporary fiddlers have similarly large repertoires. This allowed Eck and now allows the champions of today to oscillate their tune choices, balancing offering the comfort of shared recollection with the excitement of the unfamiliar.

One way to add punctuation to a performance of a series of tunes is to intersperse melodies that feature special effects. Eck's "Lost Goose" included harmonics, his "Hawk's Got the Chicken" a few sung couplets, his "Lost Indian" a nonlexical vocal effect that we were meant to believe imitated a howl. His "Rye Whiskey" included some left-hand pizzicato and, like many tunes, took advantage of a given unusual tuning to feature lots of drones and unusual full sonorities; "Get Up in the Cool" is an especially striking example of this. Other tunes add melodic moments that imitate sounds from outside of music, perhaps allowing a story to emerge, for example "Cacklin' Hen" and of course "Bonaparte's Retreat." Eck's frequent use of these effects reflected his own history in minstrel ensembles as a teenager and the mixed fiddle history of Texas during his life. These factors don't survive at contests except as rare bits of fun during breaks from the formal competition, though most fiddlers do know a few such tunes. Trick fiddling and fiddling illustrating or creating narratives show no signs of disappearing—think of "Orange Blossom Special"—but it's not nearly as big a part of the picture as during Eck's day.

Eck generally played slightly (or very) unusual forms of tunes, even when those tunes were ubiquitous. For instance, compare his form of "Fisher's Hornpipe" with the widely distributed "brand name" version published dozens of times by Elias Howe, and compare Eck's "Arkansas Traveller" with earlier printed forms. In the most concrete demonstration of this principle, compare the relatively standard form of "Turkey in the Straw" that he recorded with Henry Gilliland with his personal version, which is in a different key and contains all sorts of interesting touches. Eck rarely varied strains when repeating them immediately—that will become customary for later Texas fiddlers—but he did so in this performance of this common tune. On the other hand, in an age during which unusual-length strains were fairly common—sometimes as awkward extensions but other times creating and then resolving tension in that sphere (see Old-Time Texas String Bands 2001a and b; Raines 2013)—Eck normally employed strains of conventional lengths.

In dozens of tunes, Eck played a strain several times at the usual pitch level, then later transposed that strain up an octave. This constitutes a very elementary way to add variety—sticking with same strain, comfortably familiar, but in a higher range, so somewhat different and certainly exciting and exhibiting impressive skill. In an even simpler effect, duets could be of a melody in its original and raised forms simultaneously throughout a performance, as in the duets in Eck's commercial recordings of "Arkansas Traveller" and "Brown Kelly Waltz." Playing in positions was nothing new. Among his specific "old masters," Polk Harris and Matt Brown commanded this skill. A sizeable minority of fiddlers from at least as early as the Civil War regularly exploited third position (see Goertzen 2020, 112–33) and even fifth position, including one S. L. Pfeiffer of Alabama (Goertzen 2020, 118–19).

Eck employed many other kinds of variation. He might change just a few notes when repeating a strain. This did not illustrate any habit of improvising, but rather created bits of mosaic that reappeared several times in a piece. For a good example of this, compare the B and B′ strains of his "College Hornpipe." In quite a few cases, he would thin out the rhythm in a part of a strain, stretching a pitch or series of pitches, and often incorporating a bit of syncopation; see his "Snowbird in the Ashbank." And of course repetitions of material at the upper octave could often be conjoined with these more immediate batteries of types of variation—see his "Soldier's Joy" and his "Mississippi Sawyer."

Eck explored several ways of expanding the traditional two-strain fiddle tune construction. The most conceptually simple enlargement of that structure is the medley. His experiments in this area had mixed results. Eck's "Big Devil Medley" was not played by other fiddlers, as far as I know, and Eck's medley of "Sally Johnson" and "Billy in the Low Grounds" did not inspire imitation. However, his "Brilliancy" is still in the Texas fiddle standard repertoire. A handful of tunes he played were written with integral third strains, such as "Ragtime Annie" (with a third strain sometimes played today but often omitted) and "Done Gone," in which the third strain portrays part of the linked narrative, and is always played. Many others of Eck's tunes were granted "extra" strains by him (perhaps echoing his "old masters"). A tendency to favor tunes with "more parts to them" is typical in modern contest fiddling (as Carl Hopkins expressed to me in 2015). The overall shift from common practice before and after Eck's persuasive participation included these factors: Fiddlers went from playing in a dance style—the left hand planted firmly in root position, in a situation in which the main desirable qualities were good cheer, steady tempo and dynamics, and sheer endurance—to virtuosity including plenty of position work, and to performances with graceful and extended dramatic shapes. Tuning went from multiple cross-tunings to uniform use of violin tuning, GDAE. Trick fiddling went from a meat-and-potatoes ingredient of many a multi-piece performance to isolated moments, or to between-the-brackets entertainment.

What do Eck's fiddling preferences add up to? He lived amidst a number of superimposed, related types of crossroads. In terms of general culture, the broad theme of rural versus increasingly urban life had its subtopics, notably the rapid-fire growth and then complicated receding of cowboy culture (with the profession declining but bits of psychology enduring, often in caricature). In terms of music, the national cycle of changes in dominant dance genres interacted with local needs; for fiddling, all kinds of repertoires and styles imported from elsewhere in the South were channeled into the virtuosic stream of contest fiddling, with Eck's influence strong, consistently powerful for many decades. "Sally Goodin" was certainly a game changer, but, at least as significantly, facing Eck in contest after contest and jamming with him at those events chipped away inexorably at individual fiddlers' inherited differences in style.

Negotiating the various types of crossroads on which fiddling was poised in Eck's day resulted in major choices being made. Fiddling went from being a main secular music genre to a niche role connected with nostalgia. Multiracial participation went to almost completely white fiddling for that reason: Many Anglo fiddlers were nostalgic for an era that most Blacks were glad was at least partly in the rear-view mirror. Overall, the audience per capita for fiddling shrank, but the institution of the contest, supported by increased leisure time and easier transportation, helped keep fiddling vital. Eck enjoyed winning at these competitions. He was happy to be advertised as being a *champion*. Calling a fiddler a champion is not the same as characterizing them as excellent or inspiring or convivial or endearing. It can include those qualities but is not driven by them—competition is the alpha ingredient, the musical rodeo at the center of a general good time.

Eck insisted that his view of fiddling was absolutely correct. He was very skilled, and even more sure that he was right. This held him back professionally; prosaic success as a pop musician would pass him by. But that same stubborn vision strengthened his effect on traditional-yet-transformed Texas fiddling, on pushing music that already had a broad reach and a distinguished history in a direction that would guarantee it an enduring niche in American culture.

❋ ❋ ❋

Eck's last years were spent in a rest home in Borger; a letter dated May 15, 1972, was addressed to him at Magic Plains Nursing Home, 200 Tyler St., Borger. His eldest daughter and her husband, Odessa and Caleb Owenby, must still have been living a dozen miles north of Borger in Stinnett, which was and remains a much smaller city than Borger, despite its being the county seat of Hutchinson County. The Owenbys placed Eck where they could keep an eye on him and on his professional caregivers. Eck had his fiddle with him, and kept it close even when he no longer could play it.

Figure 35. Distant and close views of Eck's grave in Westlawn Memorial Park, Fritch Texas (a dozen miles west of his home in Borger during the 1930s).

Eck's parents and most of his siblings are together in the capacious family plot in Eastview Memorial Cemetery, just east of Vernon, the city where Eck lived for much of the 1920s. That is a cemetery of considerable age, still moderately tidy but certainly not manicured, featuring bare patches in the lawn, fire ant hills, sporadic shade, and young windmills in the distance. There was certainly room for Eck in the Robertson plot, but he instead was buried just west of Borger, in Fritch's Westlawn Memorial Park, a more modern, geometrically tame and carefully groomed facility about eight miles west of the nursing home. Even though the large extended family is buried some two hundred miles away, the flowers on Eck's grave the day we visited suggest that some of Odessa's descendants might still live nearby (Odessa and her husband are not themselves buried in Hutchinson County). Figure 35 shows his grave in the regimented rows of the cemetery (on the lower left in the photograph) plus a closeup of the stone. The day that we visited (in July 2021), lovely silk flowers set it apart within the rows of standard-sized gravestones, as did the tiny violin depicted below the center—with the words "In Loving Memory" chiseled beneath—and especially the motto "World's Champion Fiddler."

TUNE ANTHOLOGY

Transcribing slows down experience, allowing close study of music; transcriptions serve as tools aiding analysis despite the dangers of selective focus, that is, of overemphasizing the elements of music susceptible of being translated into graphics. Transcription can also be a tool for transmission, a nonaural aid in a process of transmission that is essentially aural. This is not really a new factor, since fiddlers have often been music literate to one or another degree throughout history. Some fiddlers read pitches laboriously, others do this easily, but few fiddlers devote much energy to deciphering rhythms. Fluent or not, most fiddlers who read music use the printed page as a source of reminders or as a skeletal introduction to a piece, to be treated freely.

The bowings I include are guesses based on audible accents. All players should draw on their own expertise in bowing, approaching my suggestions as just that. The better contemporary contest fiddlers point out that their mandate to improvise—and joy in doing this—limits how representative a transcription of a given performance can be. But keep in mind that Eck was a meticulous arranger, not an improvisor. When we have recordings of several of his performances of a given tune, they are usually near-exact duplicates. My transcriptions of his playing are relatively reliable representations of sound. His body of tunes and performances, when coupled with a close look at his life in historical context, offers a grand opportunity to better understand how American contest fiddling took on its current shape.

TUNE ANTHOLOGY

The Arkansas Traveller and Rackinsac Waltz

Cumming 1847; for piano, right hand of first tune

The Arkansas Traveller

Mose Case, 1858. For piano. Only RH copied.

Arkansas Traveler (Country Dance)

Henry C. Gilliland and Eck Robertson, Victor 18956, 1922

Continues; total form: AABB AABB AABB AABB AABBA. Gilliland is especially hard to hear. I regard my transcriptions of both Eck's playing (the upper part, I believe) and especially that of Gilliland as friendly guesswork.

Figure 36. Eck Robertson and Henry C. Gilliland's performance of "Arkansas Traveler," with earlier printed versions.

Arkansas Traveller

Daniel Jasek, 2021, Goertzen

Figure 37. "Arkansas Traveller," played by nonagenarian fiddler Daniel Jasek at the Texas State Championship in 2021. Jasek owns a farm near the contest site.

Figure 38. Digest of late nineteenth-century theme and variations arrangement of "Arkansas Traveller" made by W[ilhelm] Iucho.

Figure 39. "The Engagement Quadrille," a dance suite that ends with "Arkansas Traveller." The composer-arranger Henry Kleber wrote this piece for piano (he was a German immigrant, a teacher of Stephen Foster). This reduction of what had become a genteel piece is here returned to a rough-and-ready status in [James] *Buckley's Violin Tunes* (1855), a collection intended for the use of blackface minstrels, the cover of which is shown in figure 51.

Fisher's Hornpipe

Howe, Musician's Companion, I, 1844, p. 50

Fisher's Hornpipe

Figure 40. "Fisher's Hornpipe" as widely distributed in the ubiquitous collections of Elias Howe and this tune as performed by Eck.

TUNE ANTHOLOGY

College Hornpipe
Howe, Musician's Omnibus, 1862, p. 45

Nine tunes all run across one crowded page in the contradance section of Elias Howe's Musician's Omnibus, each with dance instructions beneath the single line of music. Below "College Hornpipe," we read: "First lady balance to 3d gent, turn the 2d gent; 1st gent balance to 3d lady, turn with 2d lady;1st couple down the centre, back and cast off, right and left."

College Hornpipe
Eck Robertson, 1959, Riddle

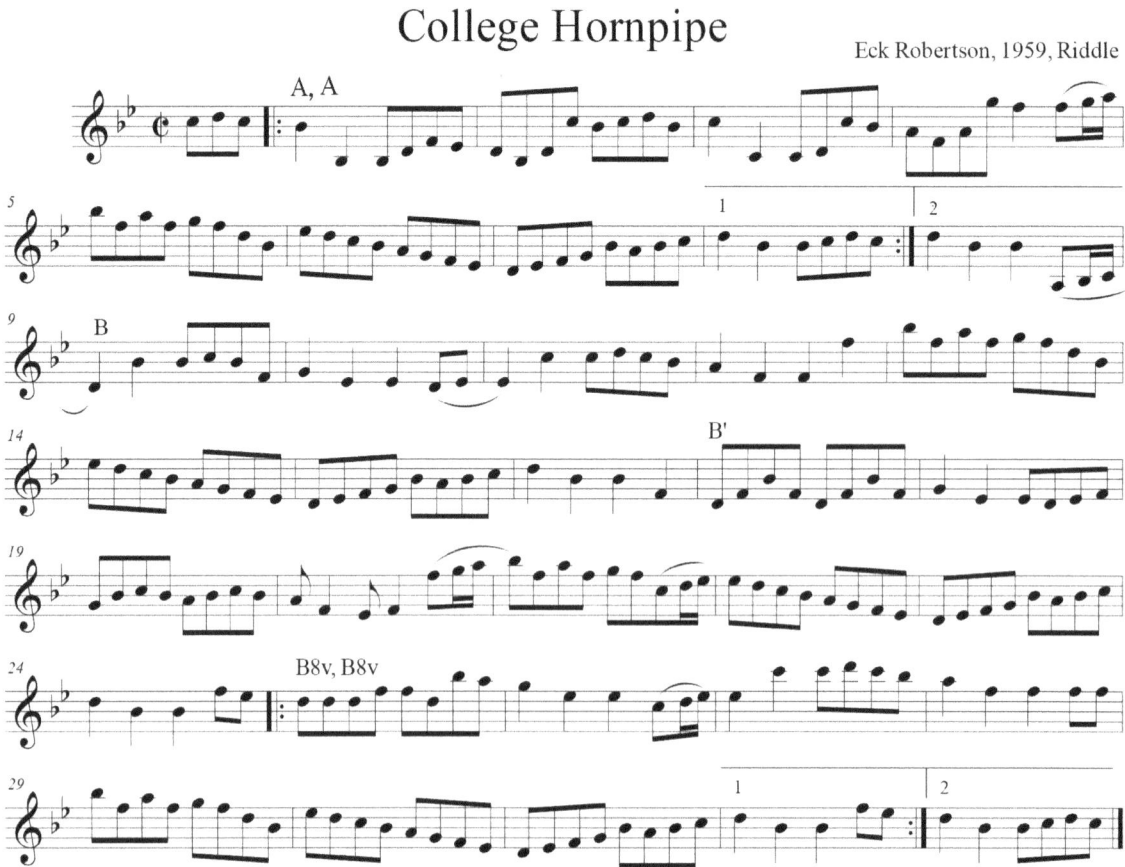

Complete form: A A B B' B8v B8v   A A B B' B' B8v B8v   B' B A A B B' B8v B8v; ends with "shave and a haircut" tag.

Figure 41. "College Hornpipe" as widely distributed in the ubiquitous collections of Elias Howe (in this case, with dance figures) and this tune as performed by Eck.

TUNE ANTHOLOGY

The Devil's Dream

Howe, Musician's Omnibus, 1862, p. 41

Big Devil Medley

Eck Robertson, Conte's friend, 1970s?

Continues in an unusual ordering of strains; total form: A A B B A' A C C   A' A C C (ending with held a).

Figure 42. "The Devil's Dream" as widely distributed in the ubiquitous collections of Elias Howe and this tune as performed by Eck as the first tune in a medley that he had arranged.

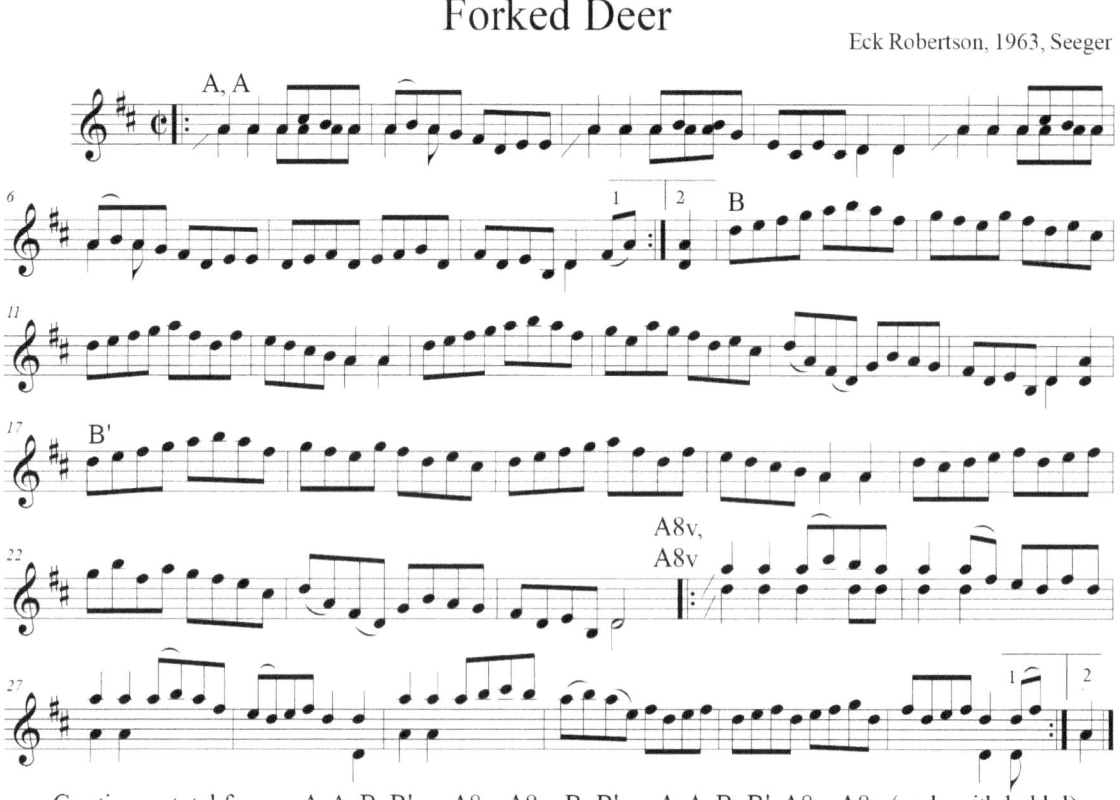

Figure 43. Two older tunes in Eck's repertoire. "Dominion Hornpipe" is likely of the same vintage as the other turn-of-the-nineteenth-century hornpipes; "Forked Deer" is among the older fiddle tunes probably created in America.

Hell Among the Yearlings [Cattle in the Cane]

Eck Robertson, 1963, Seeger

Total form: A A B B'   A' A' B B'   A A B B' A'.

Soldier's Joy

Eck Robertson, Conte's friend, 1970s?

Continues; complete form: B B A A   A8v A8v A A   A8v A8v A, with the last A strain ending with a held d.

Figure 44. Two more older tunes in Eck's repertoire.

Snowbird in the Ashbank

Eck Robertson, 1959, Riddle

Snowbird on the Ashbank

E. J. Hopkins, 1974. On LP E. J. Hopkins, Contest Fiddlin', B3.

Figure 45. "Snowbird in the Ashbank" performed by Eck and by E. J. Hopkins. This modal tune is played more frequently by old-time fiddlers than by contest-style performers.

TUNE ANTHOLOGY

Irish Washwoman

Form: AABB AABB.

The Irish Washerwoman

Irish Washwoman

Figure 46. "Irish Washerwoman" in late eighteenth-century Scotland, mid-nineteenth-century America, and by Eck.

TUNE ANTHOLOGY

Mississippi Sawyer

Eck Robertson, Conte's friend, 1970s?

Figure 47. Eck's version of "Mississippi Sawyer"—an old American tune—is unusual in its use of a "double tonic," a figure played and then repeated a step lower; compare how this is done in the first, oldest version of "Irish Washerwoman."

TUNE ANTHOLOGY

Old Zip Coon

Howe, Musician's Omnibus, 1862, p. 41

Turkey in the Straw

Henry Gilliland and Eck Robertson, Victor 19149, side A, 1922

Continues; the complete form is: A A B B' A' A" B B' A' A" B B' A' A" B B' A' A". Gilliland and Robertson play in unison for much of the performance. But in strain B', Eck plays what I transcribed, although Gilliland seems to be playing B in its original form--his part is hard to make out.

Turkey in the Straw

Eck Robertson, 1963, Seeger

Continues, yielding this total form: A A' B B'   A" A" B" B'"   A" B"" B""" A"   A" B" B" A".

Figure 48. A blackface minstrel tune, "Old Zip Coon," from Howe, this tune renamed "Turkey in the Straw," as played by Eck and Gilliland in this tune's most common key, G, and finally a version in C that Eck also knew and performed for Seeger.

TUNE ANTHOLOGY

Great Big Taters in Sandy Land

Eck Robertson, 1963, Seeger

Continues; complete form: A A' B A A' B A A' B A A' B A A' B A A' B A A'.

Hawk's Got the Chicken

Eck Robertson, 1963; on Famous Cowboy Fiddler

Continues, so that the total form is A B A C   A B B A*   B* C A B. The last strain ends with the above swept G chord. During the first four measures of the A* strain, Eck sings "Run old man to get your gun; the hawk's got a chicken and he'd going on the run." Then, during the first four measures of the next strain, B*, he sings this once "He cocked his wings and he batted his eyes; and he carried that chicken to the sky."

Figure 49. Two tunes to which fiddlers often attach a verse or two of text. Eck doesn't happen to sing along with "Great Big Taters in Sandy Land," but does attach two couplets to "Hawk's Got the Chicken."

TUNE ANTHOLOGY

Lost Goose

Eck Robertson, 1959, Riddle

Continues, so that the total form is: A A B C A A B C.

Gammal Gauken [Old Cuckoo]

Kristen Odde, 1988, from Lom, Norway; Goertzen

Continues, with two paired strains. Harmonics appear only in the first strain (see Goertzen 1997, 203).

Lost Indian

Eck Robertson, 1959, Riddle

Continues, so that the complete performance is: A B A C B A C B A C B (the second C section omits the voice).
Also, what may be heard as an unmetered C section precedes the performance. Are we to imagine hearing a distant cry?

Figure 50. Special effects tunes, featuring harmonics in "Lost Goose" and "Old Cuckoo," and a special tuning and vocal call in "Lost Indian."

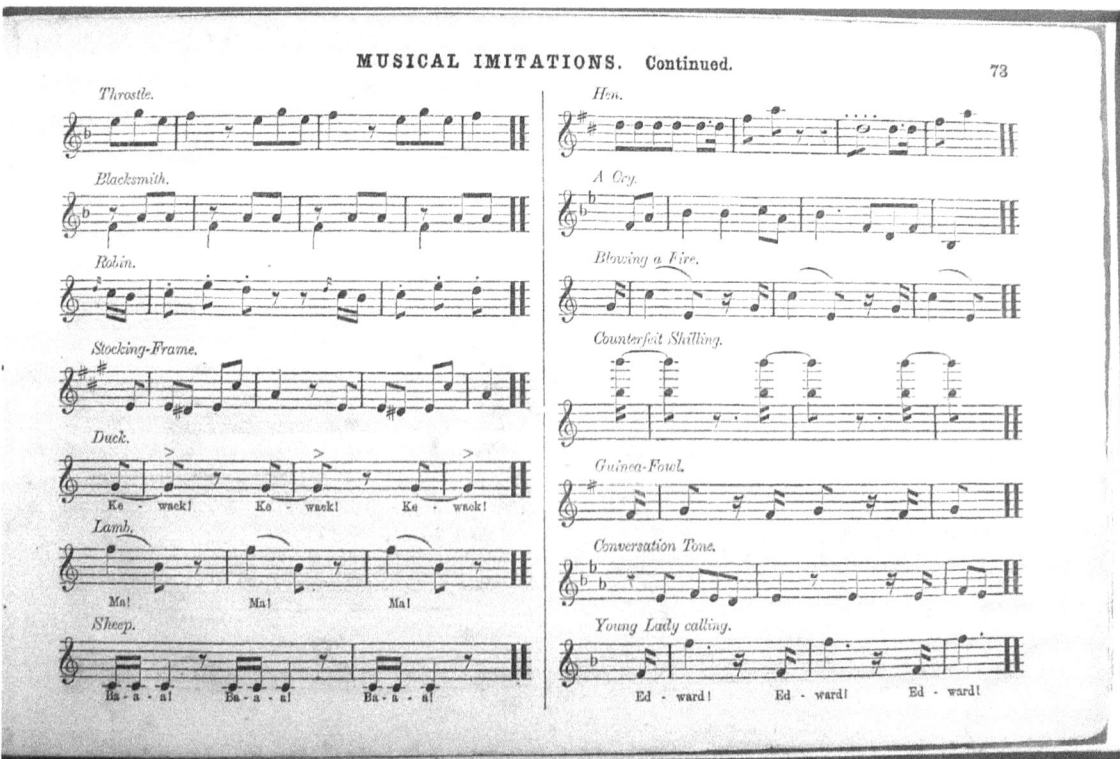

Figure 51. An animal imitation adopted from minstrelsy. I include the title page of [James] *Buckley's Violin Tunes* [1955], a page from that collection of miscellaneous bird imitations, an excerpt of a skit including hens—note how Buckley inserts surprising rhythms—and Eck's own version of a very common tune, "Cacklin' Hen."

Bonaparte's Retreat

Eck Robertson, 1963, Seeger

Closes with C and D, so that the total form is this: A A B B   A A C D   A D' A C' C D.

TUNE ANTHOLOGY

Bonaparte's Retreat

Benny Thomasson, from Benny Thomasson, Legendary Texas Fiddler: Recordings from 1966-1969, CO-CD-2737, cut 4.

Continues; total form: A A B B C C' B' A A C C B".
The final B (form B") is recast as follows, starting midway in the last measure of the preceding C strain:

Figure 52. "Bonaparte's Retreat" as performed by Eck and a contrasting version played by Benny Thomasson, the most important innovative contest fiddler of the next generation.

- 183 -

TUNE ANTHOLOGY

[Titles forgotten]

Eck, 6/6/1966, Seeger

"What the hell did he[his father's brother] call that tune? And there's another one he played like this:"

Both tunes played tentatively, with pauses; both forms probably AABBAABB etc.

Figure 53. Two tunes Eck played in the same unusual tuning as is typical for "Bonaparte's Retreat"; he didn't remember the names of these tunes.

Figure 54. Another tune in a related, even more unusual tuning, "Get Up in the Cool."

TUNE ANTHOLOGY

Rye Whiskey

Eck Robertson, 1963, Seeger

Tuning: AEAC#

(All pizzicato is left hand).

A repeats, followed by:

Continues, total form: ABAC ABAC AB.

Figure 55. The tuning for "Rye Whiskey," while distant from normal tuning, is the favorite one for inserting special effects, especially left-hand pizzicato.

TUNE ANTHOLOGY

[Alf Taylor's Fox Chase]

Eck Robertson, 1962, Riggs/Nagy

Tuning: ADAE?

Continues. If we treat strains as 16 measures each, the complete form is this:
A B A C   A C A B   A C A, with the last A strain ending on a held d.

Tennessee Mountain Fox Chase

Jake Krack, 2014, Goertzen

Continues; complete form: A B C C' A B C C' A B C C' A B C C'.

B strains after the first each contain a different modification of the second half. For instance, that part of the second B strain starts like this:

And this gesture (a hound call?) occurs more times in each successive C strain.

Figure 56. Eck's rare tune depicting a dream of a fox hunt, and a common old-time tune with the same plot.

TUNE ANTHOLOGY

Chadwick

Eck Robertson, 1959, Riddle

Continues; complete form: A A B B   A A B B   A A B B.

Run Boy, Run [usually Run N...., Run]

Eck Robertson and family, plus J. B. Cranfill.
Victor V40205, side A, 1929

Form: A B A B A B A B A B A B A B A B A B A (this last A just four measures long; ends on f#/d double stop).

Figure 57. Two miscellaneous tunes that Eck seldom played.

TUNE ANTHOLOGY

Rhubarb

Eck Robertson, Conte's friend, 1970s?

Continues, with total form: A A B B   A A B B A.

Rhubarb

Josh Johnson, after Vernon Riddle. Youtube, n. d.

Total form: A A B B   A A B B.

Figure 58. Eck's rare "Rhubarb" and a version transmitted in South Carolina by his fan, fellow fiddler Vernon Riddle

TUNE ANTHOLOGY

Durang's Hornpipe
Hofmeister, in Durang's Memoirs, 1785

Durang's Hornpipe
Riley's Flute Melodies, 1821, p. 91

Durang's Hornpipe
Howe, Musician's Omnibus, 1862, p. 43

Figure 59. "Durang's Hornpipe" in the late eighteenth century, early nineteenth century, and mid-nineteenth century.

TUNE ANTHOLOGY

Durang's Hornpipe

Eck Robertson, Conte's friend, 1970s?

Continues, creating this complete form: A A B B'   A8v A8v B" B   A' A' A8v A8v   B" B A' A'.

Figure 60. "Durang's Hornpipe," a synthesis performed by Eck.

TUNE ANTHOLOGY

Durang's Hornpipe

Jason Andrew, 2023, Goertzen

Total form: A A B B C C   A A B' B' A8v A8v   B" B" A8v' A C C.

Figure 61. Jason Andrew, a modern skilled player, interprets "Durang's Hornpipe."

TUNE ANTHOLOGY

Sallie Gooden

Eck Robertson, Victor 18956, Side A, 1922

Figure 62. "Sally Goodin" played by champion Texas fiddlers in 1922 and 2023.

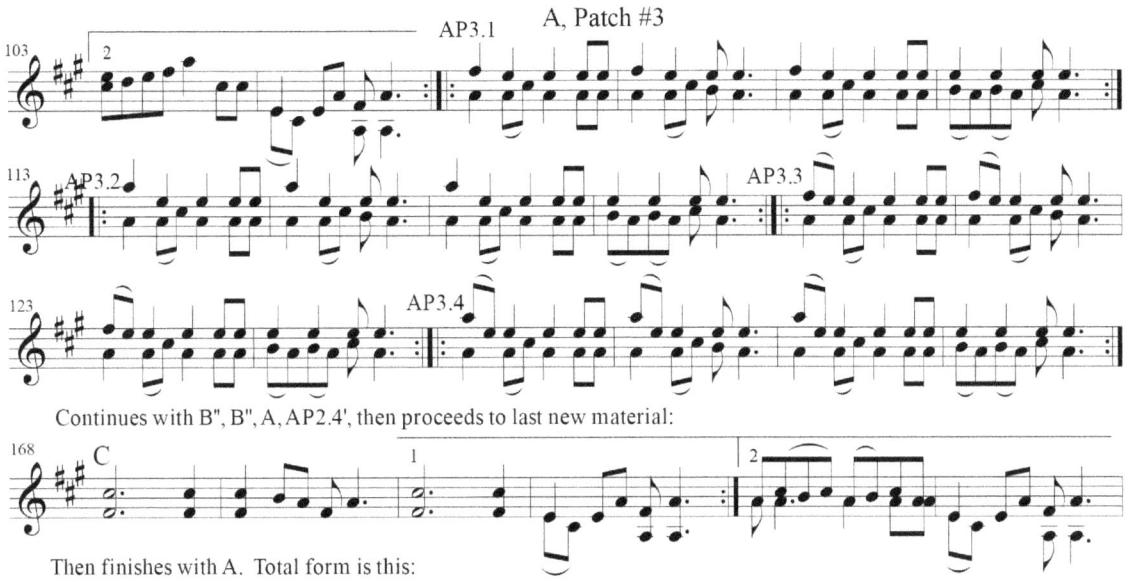

Continues with B", B", A, AP2.4', then proceeds to last new material:

Then finishes with A. Total form is this:

A B B'   A1.1 A1.2 A1.3   B" B" A   A2.1 A2.2 A2.3 A2.4   B" B"   A3.1 A3.2 A3.3 A3.4   B" B" A2.4   C C A

In contrast, the total form of the 2023 performance by Carl Hopkins is:

A A B B'   A1.2 A1.3   B"   A2.1 A2.2 A2.3 A2.4   B'''   A3.1 A3.2 A8v A8v   B' A2.1 A B B'   A/C C C A A

And the total form of the 2014 performance by Alita Stoneking Weisgerber is:

A A' B B' A3.1 A3.2   B"   A1.2 A1.1 A1.3 A1.3'   B'''   A2.1 A2.4   C C A2.4 A

Sally Goodin

Tuning: GDAE

Carl Hopkins, 2023, Goertzen

- 195 -

TUNE ANTHOLOGY

Sally Goodin

Alita Stoneking Weisgerber, 2014, Goertzen

Figure 63. "Sally Goodin" travels: a performance by Alita Stoneking Weisgerber, a Texas-style fiddler from Missouri living in Minnesota.

Sally Goodin

Richard Bowman, 2001, Goertzen

Total form: A B A' B A' B A' B A' B A' B A' B A' B A' B tag (could continue much longer at a dance).

Sally Goodin

Marcus Martin, When I Get My New House Done, 2007

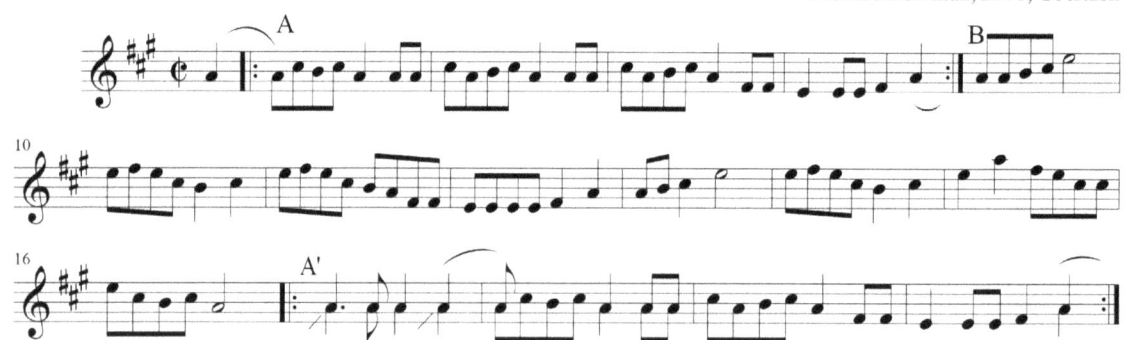

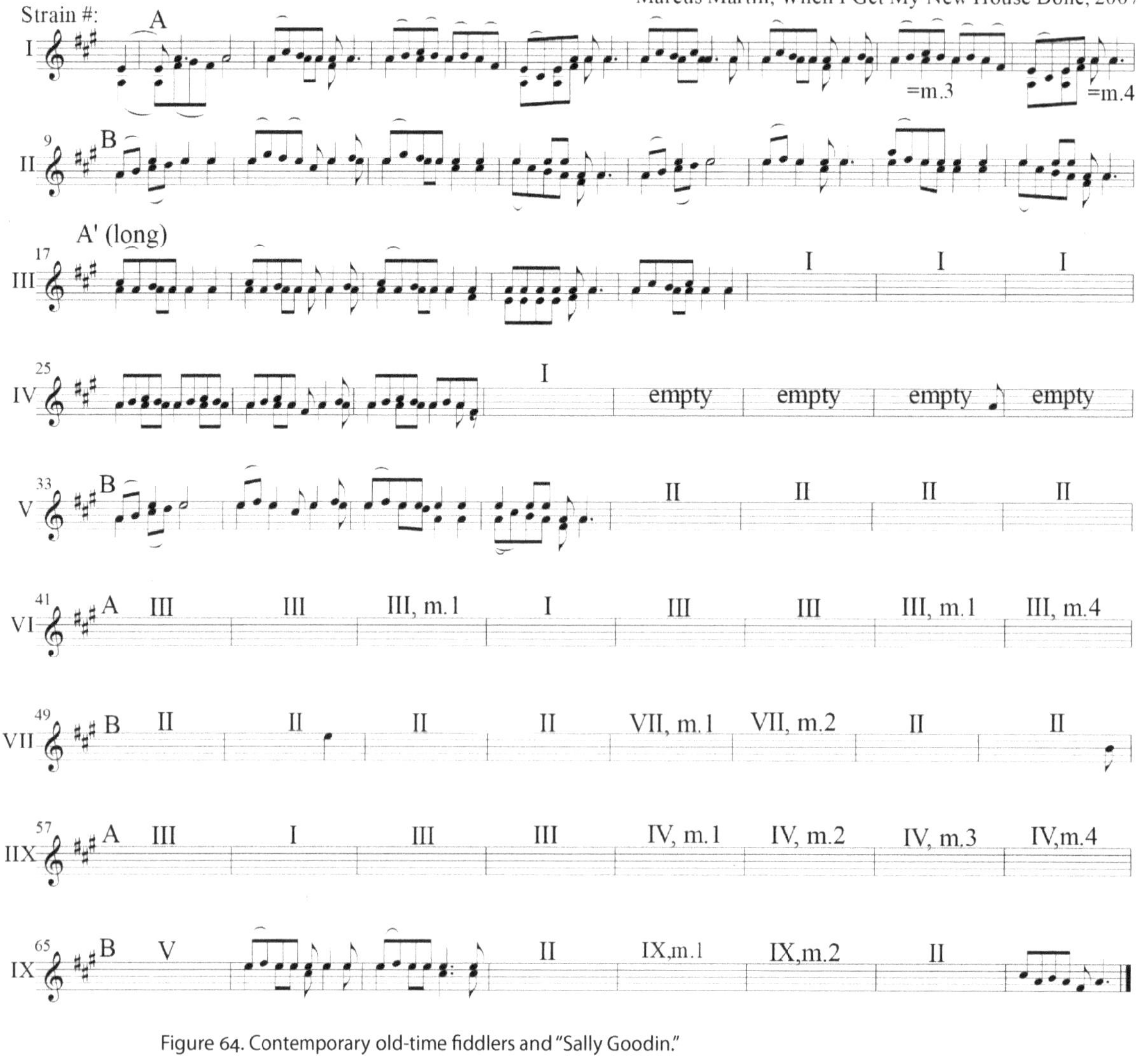

Figure 64. Contemporary old-time fiddlers and "Sally Goodin."

Fanitullen

Haakon Solaas, hardingfele (found on YouTube)
Sogn (W. Norway), date unknown

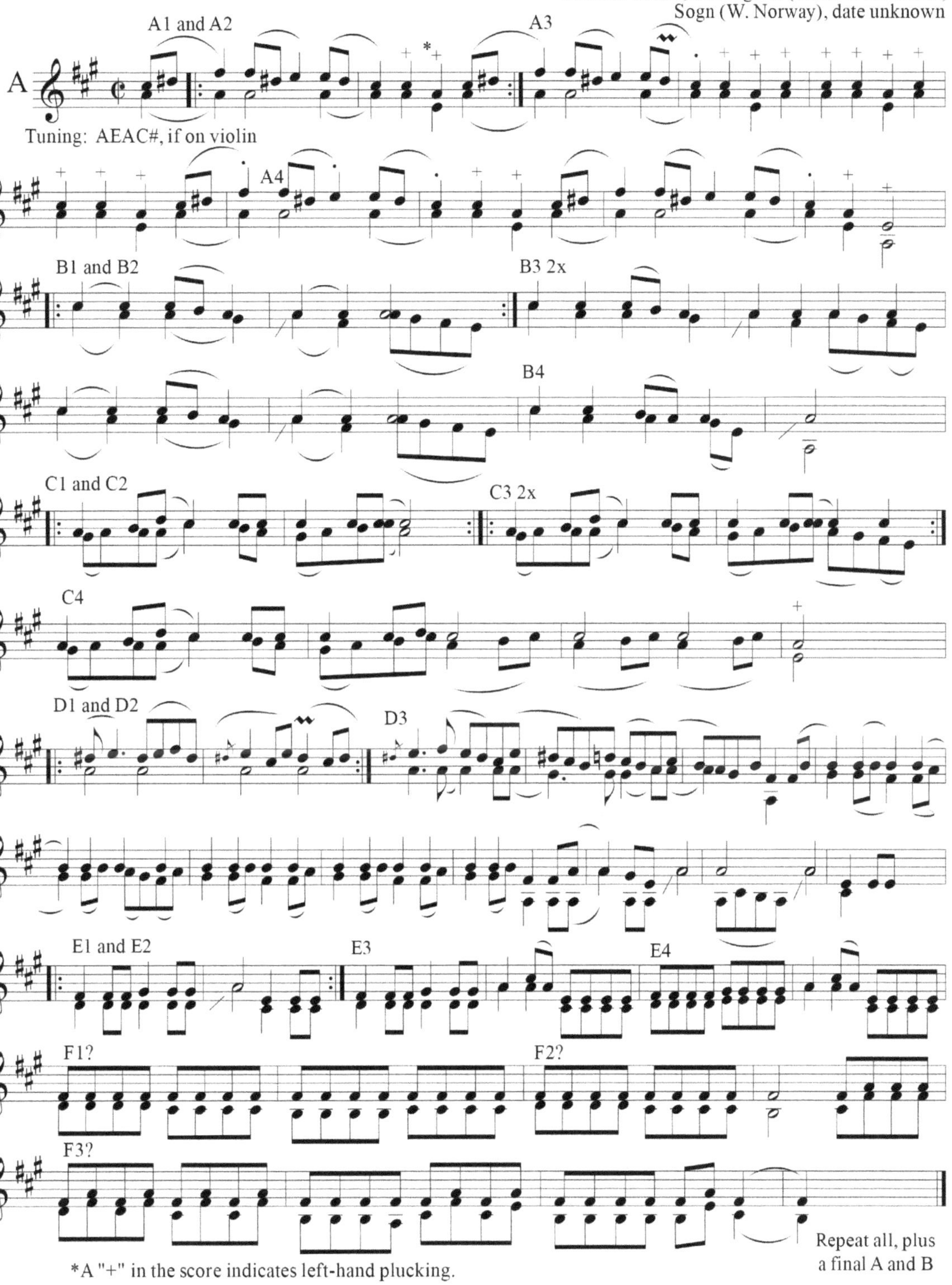
A1 and A2
A3
A
Tuning: AEAC#, if on violin
A4
B1 and B2
B3 2x
B
B4
C1 and C2
C3 2x
C
C4
D1 and D2
D3
D
E1 and E2
E3
E4
E
F1?
F2?
F
F3?
Repeat all, plus a final A and B
*A "+" in the score indicates left-hand plucking.

Figure 65. "Fanitullen": a Norwegian hardingfele hit illustrating the type of building blocks making up the "patches" in "Sally Goodin."

TUNE ANTHOLOGY

Grigsby's Hornpipe

Eck Robertson, 1963, Seeger

Tuning: AEAC#

Strains are transcribed in the order played; the whole package repeats. Is the strain beginning in measure 20 the real start of the B group of strains, or does the strain that starts in measure 25 creatively launch that section?

Figure 66. An alternative source for the procedures used to shape "Sally Goodin": "Grigsby's Hornpipe."

Say, Old Man, Can You Play a Fiddle?

Eck Robertson, 1959, Riddle

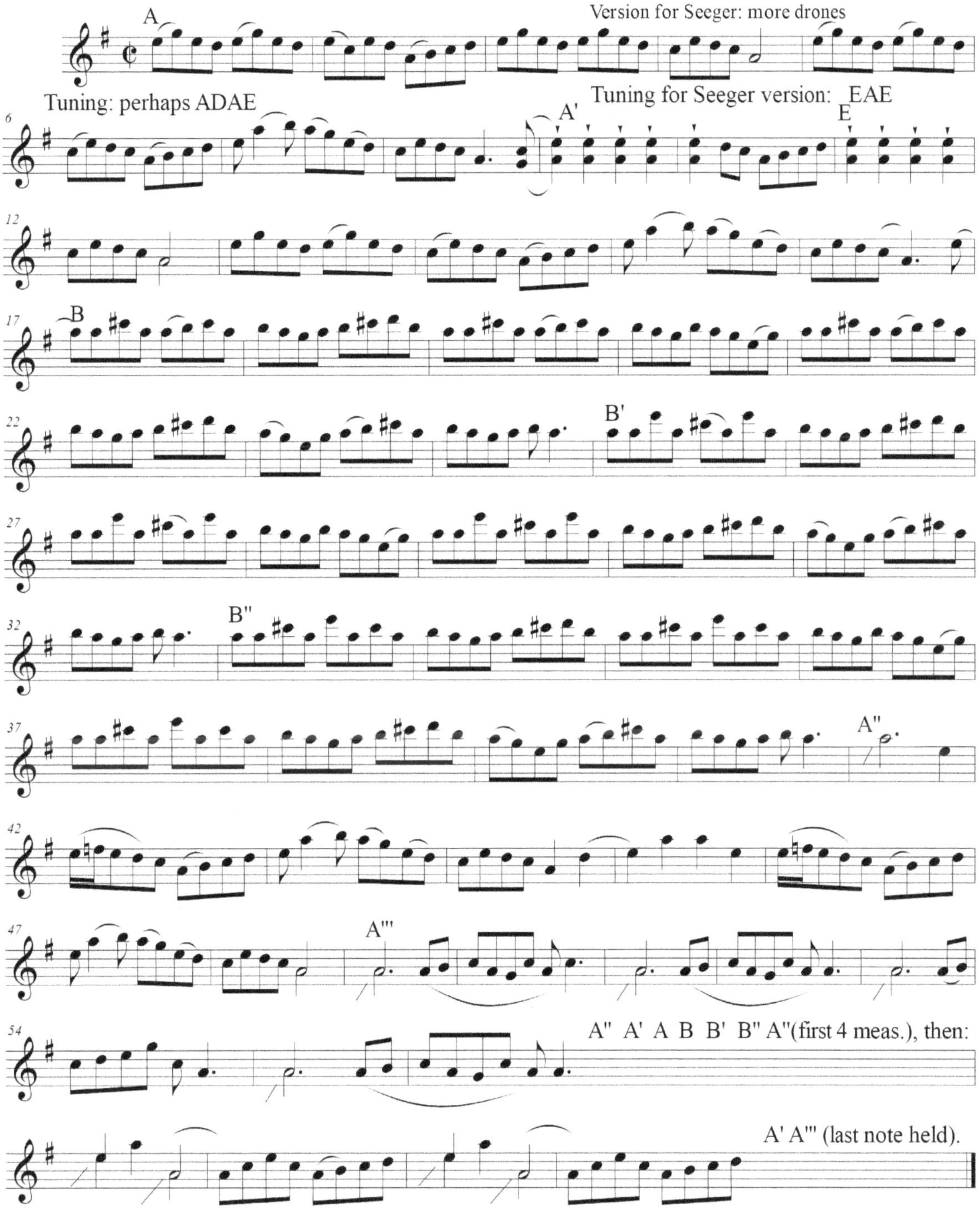
A
Version for Seeger: more drones
Tuning: perhaps ADAE
Tuning for Seeger version: EAE
A'
E
B
B'
B"
A"
A'''
A" A' A B B' B" A"(first 4 meas.), then:
A' A''' (last note held).

Total form: A A' B B' B" A" A''' A" A' A B B' B" A"(ending as shown) A' A'''.

Figure 67. Borrowing procedures from "Sally Goodin": Eck's "Say Old Man, Can You Play a Fiddle?"

Figure 68. Eck's two solutions to "improving" "Sally Johnson."

Figure 68. Eck's two solutions to "improving" "Sally Johnson."

Sally Johnson

Wes Westmoreland III, 2017 CD: *Salt River, Championship Fiddlin' by Wes Westmoreland,* cut B11

Figure 69. Wes Westmoreland's "Sally Johnson:" performance architecture.

Figure 69. Wes Westmoreland's "Sally Johnson:" performance architecture.

Sally Johnson, p. 3

Form: A As B! B'   As! A Cs C   As A As!! As!!   B B A A   Br Br A' A'   A'' A' Cs C   As A Bs B.

Figure 69. Wes Westmoreland's "Sally Johnson:" performance architecture.

Sally Johnson

Carl Hopkins, 2021, Goertzen

Figure 70. Romantic insider versus classical outsider: Carl Hopkins, Tristan Clarridge, and "Sally Johnson."

TUNE ANTHOLOGY

2 Sally Johnson

Form: B B's A As!   B+s Bs C8v C8v   Bs Bs C   As! As B! B

Sally Johnson

Tristan Clarridge, Weiser, 2021; from YouTube

Figure 70. Romantic insider versus classical outsider: Carl Hopkins, Tristan Clarridge, and "Sally Johnson."

TUNE ANTHOLOGY

Figure 70. Romantic insider versus classical outsider: Carl Hopkins, Tristan Clarridge, and "Sally Johnson."

TUNE ANTHOLOGY

Sally Johnson

Daniel Carwile, at "The Atherton [California] Session," 2014, Stephen Schaur.

Figure 71. Yet another part of the country heard from: Daniel Carwile and a Tennessee Valley "Sally Johnson."

Form: B Bs A As   B+ B C(s!) C(s!)   A' A' Bs!c Bc   Bs Bs A As! B+ B

Figure 71. Yet another part of the country heard from: Daniel Carwile and a Tennessee Valley "Sally Johnson."

TUNE ANTHOLOGY

Billy in the Low Grounds

Eck Robertson, Victor 19372, side A, 1922
(follows "Sally Johnson" without pause)

Figure 72a. A medley undone: "Billy in the Low Grounds" without "Sally Johnson."

Total form, 1922 recording after "Sally Johnson"):   A A   B B   As A A   B B   As A.

Form of performance recorded by Seeger in 1963:   A A   B B   As A A   B B   As A A   B B   As A.

Form of performance recorded by Conte in 1965:   A A   B B   As A   B B   As A A.

In the performance recorded by Conte, the second B strain is somewhat different:

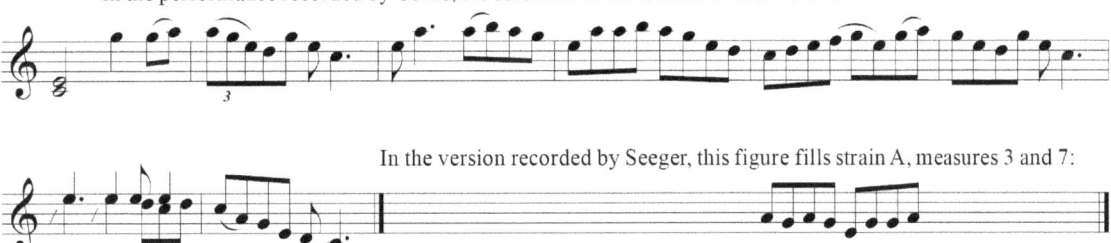

In the version recorded by Seeger, this figure fills strain A, measures 3 and 7:

Figure 72a. A medley undone: "Billy in the Low Grounds" without "Sally Johnson."

TUNE ANTHOLOGY

Apple Blossom

Eck Robertson, 1964, Seeger, in Los Angeles coffee house Golden Vanity, accompanied by New Lost City Ramblers

Recorded in 1922 and 1929, but never issued

Total Form: A A B B   A A B B   A8v A8v B B   A A B B A8v A8v.

Figure 72b. A tune finally recorded: "Apple Blossom."

Brilliancy Medley

Eck Robertson and family, Victor V40298, side A, 1929

D, D, E, then return to notation with:

Continues, creating total form of: A A B B C C D D E D D E F F' G G F' F' A A B B C C, ending with held half note.

Figure 73. A medley that stayed a medley: "Brilliancy Medley."

Leather Britches

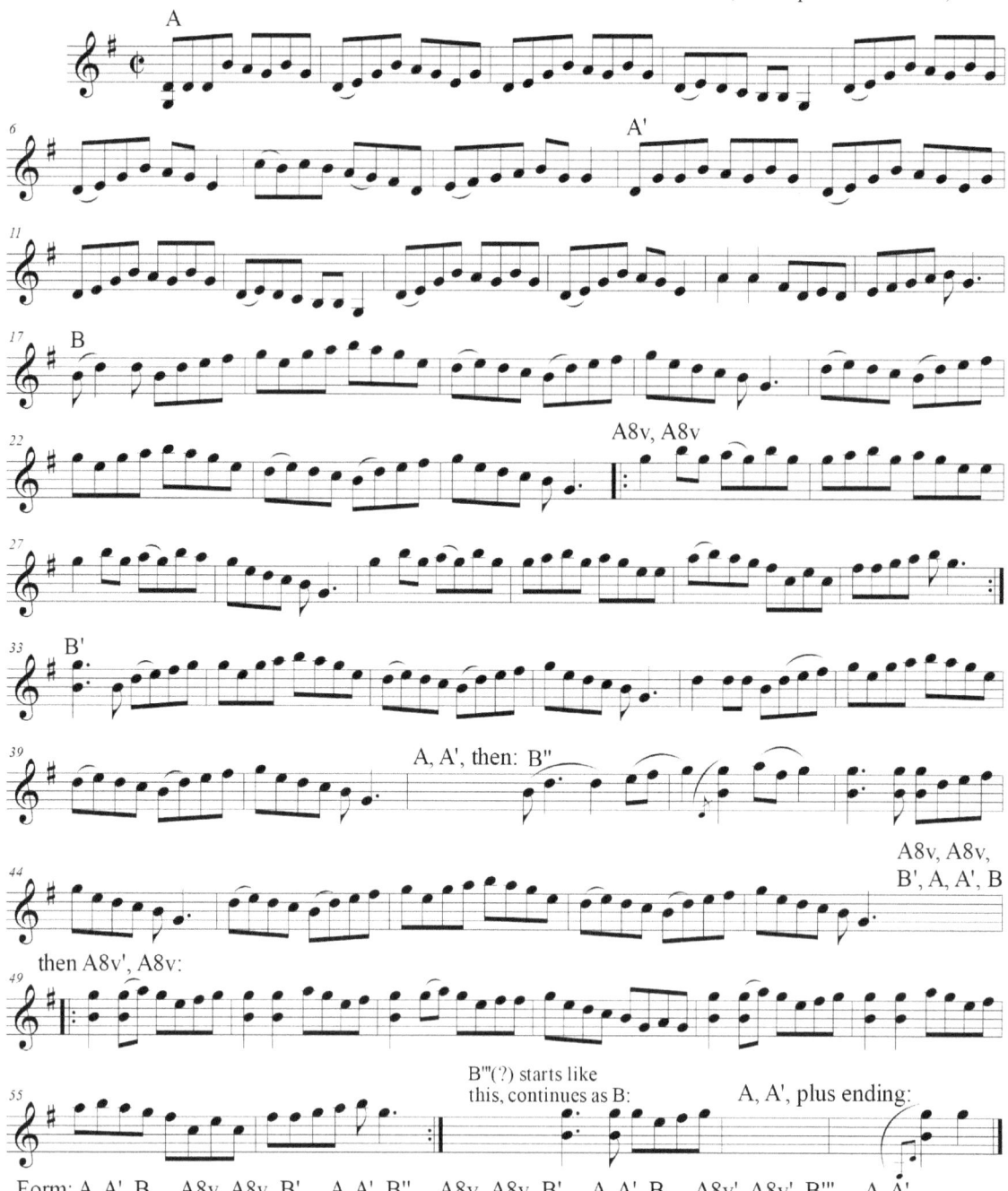

Figure 74. Old tunes that become new workhorses 1: "Leather Britches."

TUNE ANTHOLOGY

Old Lime Rock

Eck Robertson, 1959, Riddle

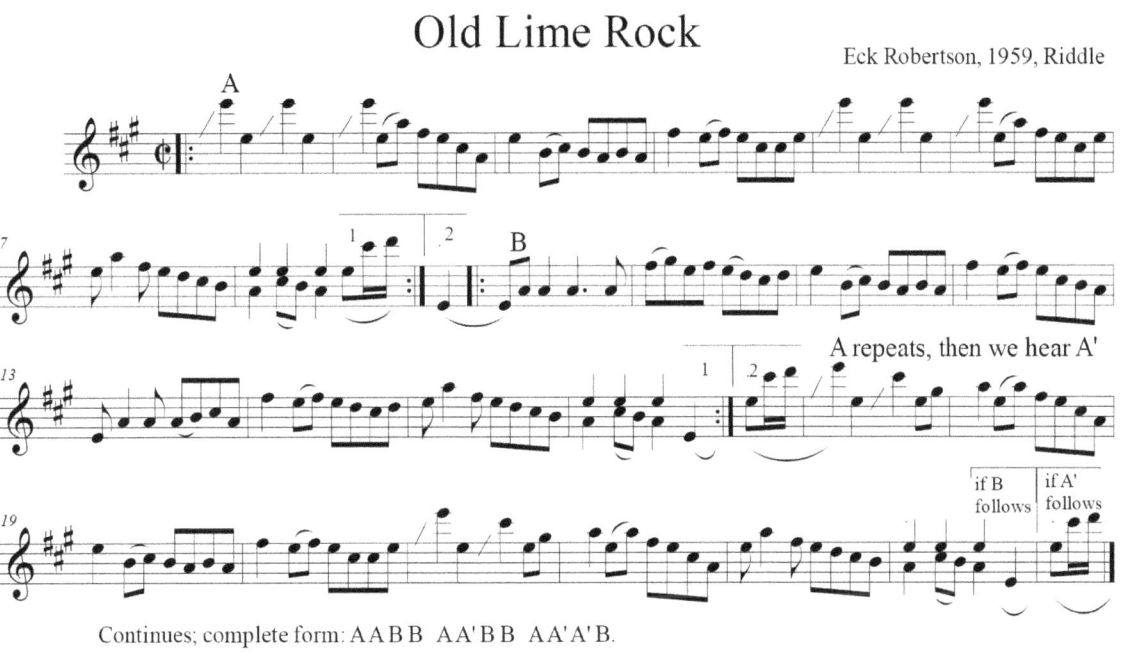

Continues; complete form: A A B B AA'B B AA'A'B.

Grey Eagle

Eck Robertson, 1959, Riddle

Continues, yielding this form: A A B B A A B8v B8v A' A' B B B8v B8v A B (last quarter note a held). In strain A' (not separately transcribed), measure 1 of A repeats immediately; A' is thus the same as A, but one measure longer.

Figure 75. Old tunes that become new workhorses 2: "Old Lime Rock" and "Grey Eagle."

Tom and Jerry

Eck Robertson, 1959, Riddle

Continues, creating the complete form: A A B B   A' C C'   A B B   A' C C'.

Figure 76. Old tunes that become new workhorses 3: "Tom and Jerry."

TUNE ANTHOLOGY

Wagner. Virginia Reel

W. C. Peters, Grey Eagle Cottilions [sic], 1846, p. 2

Miss Brown's Reel

Howe, Musician's Omnibus, 1862, p. 41

Figure 77. "Wagner" 1: in the nineteenth century.

Texas Wagoner

Figure 78. "Wagoner" 2: Eck's 1929 version of "Texas Wagoner."

TUNE ANTHOLOGY

Wagner's Hornpipe

Eck Robertson, 1959, Riddle

Figure 79. "Wagoner" 3: Is "Wagoner's Hornpipe" a new tune?

TUNE ANTHOLOGY

Done Gone

Eck Robertson, Victor 19372-B, 1922

Continues, so that the complete form is: A A B B   C C' A A   B B C C'.

*In the recordings of Eck playing this tune collected by Seeger, Conte's friend, and Riddle, this measure is omitted, so that the C strain is the more customary 8 measures long. A few bowings are unique in these versions, but the only other dramatic way that all three more recent performances are different from the 1922 recording is that the third measure of strain C is changed. Strain C substitutes the measure below at that point, while strain C' substitutes this fancier gesture:

Figure 80. Fiddler/composer Matt Brown: "Done Gone." Just enough surprising material?

TUNE ANTHOLOGY

Ragtime Annie

Eck Robertson, 1922, Victor 19149, side B

Continues; complete form, with each letter standing for a 16-measure strain: A A B B C   A B B   A B B C A.

Kansas City Rag

Eck Robertson, 1959, Riddle

Continues; complete form: A A B B A A B B A A, with last double at end held, then same double stop played again, staccato.

Figure 81. "Ragtime Annie." Compared to "Done Gone," a little too much surprising material? What should we think of Eck's "Kansas City Rag?"

Beaumont Rag

Samuel Peacock, in Smith's Garage Fiddle Band, Brunswick DAL 736, 10/26/28

Continues; total form: A A B B C C D D B B D D (ends with tag).

Figure 82. "Beaumont Rag" 1: Samuel Peacock, with Smith's Garage Fiddle Band.

Figure 83. "Beaumont Rag" 2: Eck's take, focusing on rhythms.

TUNE ANTHOLOGY

Beaumont Rag

Wes Westmoreland, 2015, Goertzen

Figure 84. "Beaumont Rag" 3: Wes Westmoreland's synthesis.

Form: A A B B C C A' D A".

TUNE ANTHOLOGY

Ten Cent Cotton

Eck Robertson, 1963, Seeger

Repeats exactly, yielding a total form of: A A B B A A B B.

Dusty Miller

Eck Robertson, 1963, Seeger

Continues, creating this total form: A A B A A B' B" A A B B'.

Figure 85. Last rags, rural themes 1: "Ten Cent Cotton" and a non-rag, "Dusty Miller."

There's a Brown-Skinned Girl Down the Road Somewhere

Eck Robertson and family, Victor V40145, Side B, 1929

Continues, creating this total form: A A B C C   A' A' B C C   A' A' B C C.

The C strain is positioned as the end of the B strain, but, due to its repetition, takes on an individual profile

This piece swings; that is, the first in each pair of eighth notes is longer than the second. This isn't very easy to hear due to the rapid speed of the performance.

Figure 86. Last rags, rural themes 2: "There's a Brown-Skinned Girl Down the Road Somewhere."

Over the Waves Waltz

Figure 87. "Over the Waves" 1: Eck studies a hit.

Over the Waves

Clark Kessinger. 1966. Clark Kessinger, Fiddler.
Folkways Records FA 2336, Side A, Cut 5.

Form: A B C A'.

Figure 88. "Over the Waves" 2: Clark Kessinger refines a hit.

Figure 89. Fiddler/composer Matt Brown 2, *and* Eck studying waltzes 2: "Brown Kelly Waltz."

All measures with six eighth notes should "swing," sounding as the quarter/eighth triplets in B.

Total form: A A B B C C A' A" A''' A'''.

Figure 90. A contemporary Texas waltz performance: "Kelly Waltz."

"Kelly's Waltz," first measures, played by Ridge Roberts in a jam at the 2022 Athens Texas contest, rec. Lyle Dixson.

"Kelly Waltz," first measures, Matt Hartz, Western Open Fiddle Championships, Judges' Concert, 2014, rec. Lyle Dixson.

TUNE ANTHOLOGY

Amarillo Waltz

Eck Robertson and family, Victor V40298, side B, 1929

One repeat of the A strain follows, so that the complete form is: A A8v B C A.

Figure 91. Eck writes a simple waltz: "Amarillo Waltz."

Stumptown Stomp in Grand Saline

Eck Robertson, 1963, Seeger

Continues; total form: A B B C C/2   B B C C/2   B B C (C/2 is the 4 measures constituting the second half of C).

Borger Wiggle

Eck Robertson, 1963, Seeger

Continues, yielding this complete form: A A B B A.

Figure 92. Eck's other compositions, honoring other cities.

TUNE ANTHOLOGY

The Island Unknown

Eck, Nettie, and Dueron Robertson
Victor V40145, sides A and B, 1929

Figure 93. A strange ballad: "The Island Unknown."

TUNE ANTHOLOGY

THE ISLAND UNKNOWN, COMPLETE LYRICS

1. Come all you kind friends, both fair, young and old: A story I'll tell, of a poor rambling soul.
He left his dear parents and strayed off from home. He's lost, I've been told, on the Island Unknown.

2. My history of life has never been read. A reckless hard-hearted life I have led.
A reckless hard-hearted life I have left. 'Til the hour of death came to me as it will.

3. It was early one morning, in the fair month of May, Unto my dear parents these words I did say:
Oh father and mother, please weep not for me. I've joined the Jolly Band to go across the wide sea.

4. My captain and comrades are all dressed in blue. Tomorrow we'll start with the Red, White and Blue.
Tomorrow our vessel—it now lies at shore. We'll start at sunrise, and let[?] the anchor no more.

5. I left my dear parents to weep and to mourn; My friends and relations, my own native home.
I left my true love with a sad broken heart. The time has now come for us to all part.

6. It was late in the evening on a clear purling stream, I left my true love in sorrow and pain.
I left my true love to weep and to sigh. I hope we'll all meet in the "Sweet Bye and Bye."

7. Three weeks had just passed since I left her on shore; The night was so dark as the high waves splashed o'er.
The lightning was flashing from the east to the west. I thought of my friends back home at their rest.

8. I thought of that night, on the clear purling stream; The girl I had left in sorrow and pain,
The girl I had left with a sad broken heart. The time has now come for us to all part.

9. A dark cloud had rolled, and the storm winds were high, & lightning flashed through the dark clouded sky.

The ship was all wrecked and scattered in fright. No one will ever know what happened that night.

10. I clung to a skiff and floated ashore. I found that no other had ever been there before.
I found that my country was a five miles by three. I found that no other'd ever been there but me.

11. One evening I rambled through the Island Unknown; I thought of my friends and relations at home.
I thought of the girl I'd left far behind. I thought that my body some day they might find.

12. I came to a place out on the sea sand, In a book from my pocket, with pencil in hand.
I wrote of my life and the country back home; I wrote a true history of the Island Unknown.

13. Upon some green grass there among some wild flowers, I studied my troubles all o'er that for hours.
I thought of my parents I'd left all alone. I thought that their prayers might bring me back home.

14. Farewell to the Stars and the Stripes up on high. The Death Hour has come, it's true I must die.
Down by a primrose I make my death bed; The one that composed this song is now dead

15. Farewell to America, I bid you adieu, Likewise to the flag, the Red, White and Blue.
Farewell to my friends and loved ones at home; Farewell is my prayer to the Island Unknown.

REFERENCES

Abbe, Donald, and Paul Howard Carlson. 2008. *Historic Lubbock County: An Illustrated History*. Historical Pub Network.

Abbe, Donald, Paul Howard Carlson, et al. 1989. *Lubbock and the South Plains: An Illustrated History*. Windsor Publishing.

Abbott, E. C. "Teddy Blue" and Helena Huntington Smith. 1955. *We Pointed Them North: Recollections of a Cowpuncher*. Revised edition. Norman: University of Oklahoma Press.

Agee, Jane Snyder. 2012. *Borger*. Mount Pleasant, SC: Arcadia Publishing.

American Vernacular Music Manuscripts ca. 1730–1910. Digital resource, accessed through American Antiquarian Society site: americanantiquarian.org.american-vernacular-music-manuscripts-ca-1730-1910.

Ancestry.com. 2002. *1930 United States Federal Census* [online database]. Enumeration District: 0034. Provo, UT, USA: Ancestry.com Operations, 2002. Original data: United States of America, Bureau of the Census. Fifteenth Census of the United States, 1930. Washington, DC: National Archives and Records Administration, 1930. T626, 2,667 rolls, 17.

Ancestry.com. 2004. *1900 United States Federal Census* [online database]. Enumeration District: 0139. Provo, UT, USA: Ancestry.com Operations. Original data: United States of America, Bureau of the Census. Twelfth Census of the United States, 1900. Washington, DC: National Archives and Records Administration, 1900. T623, 1854 rolls, 26.

Ancestry.com. 2006. *1910 United States Federal Census* [online database]. Enumeration District: 0154. Lehi, UT, USA: Ancestry.com Operations. Original data: Thirteenth Census of the United States, 1910 (NARA microfilm publication T624, 1,178 rolls). Records of the Bureau of the Census, Record Group 29. National Archives, Washington, DC, 6.

Ancestry.com. 2010. *1920 United States Federal Census* [online database]. Enumeration District: 0195. Provo, UT, USA: Ancestry.com Operations. Images reproduced by FamilySearch. Original data: Fourteenth Census of the United States, 1920 (NARA microfilm publication T625, 2076 rolls). Records of the Bureau of the Census, Record Group 29. National Archives, Washington, DC, 17.

Ancestry.com. 2012a. *1940 United States Federal Census* [online database]. Enumeration District: 33–1. Provo, UT, USA: Ancestry.com Operations, 2012. Original data: United States of America, Bureau of the Census. Sixteenth Census of the United States, 1940. Washington, DC: National Archives and Records Administration, 1940. T627, 4,643 rolls, 28 (Nettie).

Ancestry.com. 2012b. *1940 United States Federal Census* [online database]. Enumeration District: 188–15. Provo, UT, USA: Ancestry.com Operations, 2012. Original data: United States of America, Bureau of the Census. Sixteenth Census of the United States, 1940. Washington, DC: National Archives and Records Administration, 1940. T627, 4,643 rolls, 53 (Eck).

REFERENCES

Anonymous photograph, Grand Saline about 1910.

Arkansas Traveller's Song Book. [n.d.]. New York: Dick and Fitzgerald, Publishers.

Bayard, Samuel P. 1982. *Dance to the Fiddle, March to the Fife: Instrumental Folk Tunes in Pennsylvania.* University Park: Pennsylvania State University Press.

Black Hills Pioneer. November 4, 2013. "The Fighting Cowboys of Col. Melvin Grigsby." Rpt. South Dakota Historical Society Foundation (www.sdhsf.org).

Boyd, Gregory A. 2010. *Texas Land Survey Maps for Hunt County.* Arphax Publishing Company.

Buckley, J[ames] & Sons. 1855. *Buckley's Violin Tunes: A Collection of Beautiful Marches, Waltzes, Quadrilles, Polkas, Scottisches [sic], Operatic Melodies, Hornpipes, Reels, Jigs. Etc. Etc. and Many Other Melodies Never Before Published, Including Buckley's Celebrated Imitations of the Farm-Yard, and Brigg's Power of Music.* New York: Firth, Pond, and Co.

Carlson, Paul H., Donald Abbe, and Monte L. Monroe. 2008. *The Centennial History of Lubbock: Hub City of the Plains.* Virginia Beach, VA: Donning Company.

Cary, Preston. 2013. *Vernon.* Images of America. Charleston, SC: Arcadia Publishing.

Case, Mose. [1864?]. "The Arkansas Traveller." New York: S. T. Gordon & Son; also Buffalo: J. H. Blodgett.

[Case Mose]. [n.d.]. "The Arkansas Traveller." Below the title: "The Sheet Music of this Song can be had of H. J. Wehman, Song Publisher, No. 50 Chatham Street, New York." Broadside on deposit in the Kenneth S. Goldstein Collection, Center for Popular Music, MTSU.

Chamberlin, Don A. 1902 or soon after that. "Bob White's Ranger Company." In Geo. W. Tyler, compiler, *Proceedings of the Fourth Annual Reunion of the Old Settler's Association of Bell County, Held at Belton, Texas, September 27th, 1910, Together with Nearly All of the Papers Read at the Reunion.* n.l.: Old Settler's Association of Bell County, Texas. Rpt. Sacramento, CA: Andesite Press, 19–21.

Cohen, John. 1964. "Fiddlin' Eck Robertson." *Sing Out* 14, No. 2 (April–May): 55, 57, 59.

Cohen, John. 1972. "Fiddlin' Eck Robertson." *The Devil's Box* 17 (June 1), 14–17.

Cohen, Stan. 1997. *The Images of the Spanish-American War, April-August 1898.* London: Motorbooks Intl.

Populäre und traditionelle Lieder. Historisch-kritisches Liederlexikon des Deutschen Volksliedarchivs. Ongoing online as of 2022. *Volksliedarchiv.de.*

Curwood, James Oliver. 1921. *Flaming Forest: A Novel of the Canadian Northwest.* New York: Cosmopolitan Books Corporation.

Durang, John. 1966. *The Memoir of John Durang, American Actor, 1785–1816*, Alan S. Downer, ed. Pittsburgh, PA: University of Pittsburgh Press, for the Historical Society of York County and for the American Society for Theatre Research.

Ellestad, Laura. 2014. Notes to CD *Valdresspel i Amerika.* ta:lik TA127CD.

Fahey, John. 1995. "Eck Robertson." *Bluegrass Unlimited*, 32–35.

Fehrenbach, T. R. 2000. *Lone Star: A History of Texas and the Texans, from Prehistory to the Present.* Updated ed. Cambridge, MA: Da Capo Press.

[Gardner, Charles]. 2018. "Texas Old-Time Fiddlers Association Stories: The Origin of the Texas-Style of Traditional and Old-Time Fiddling." https://www.totfa.org/about/stories/texas_fiddle.htm.

Goertzen, Chris. 2012. "Texas Contest Fiddling: What Modern Variation Technique Tells Us." In Ian Russell and Chris Goertzen, *Routes and Roots: Fiddle and Dance Studies from Around the North Atlantic 4.* Aberdeen, UK: Elphinstone Institute, University of Aberdeen, 98–111.

Goertzen, Chris. 2017. *George P. Knauff's Virginia Reels and the History of American Fiddling.* Jackson: University Press of Mississippi.

Goertzen, Chris. 2020. *American Antebellum Fiddling.* Jackson: University Press of Mississippi.

Gow, Niel. [1792]. *A Third Collection of Strathspey Reels &c. for the Piano-Forte, Violin, and Violincello.* Edinburgh: author.

Hansford County Historical Commission. 1979. *Hansford County, Texas, 1876–1979.*

Harrison, W. Walworth. 1976. *History of Greenville and Hunt County, Texas.* Waco: Texian Press.

Haskell, Harry. 2007. *Boss-busters and Sin Hounds: Kansas City and its Star.* Columbia: University of Missouri Press.

Heller, Joseph. 1961. *Catch-22.* New York: Simon & Schuster.

Henderson, Mary. 1937. "The History of Borger, Texas." M.A. thesis, Texas Technological College.

Holder, August. 1892. "'Muss i denn, muss i denn zum Städtele naus.' Ein schwäbischer Beitrag zur Naturgeschichte der Volksliederdichtung." In: *Alemannia* 19, 144–48.

Hopkins, E. J. 1974. *E. J. Hopkins, Contest Fiddlin'.* LP. Stoneway Records STY 133.

Hopkins, Pandora. 1986. *Aural Thinking in Norway: Performance and Communication with the hardingfele.* New York: Human Sciences Press.

Howe, Elias, Compiler. 1844. *First Part of the Musician's Companion, Containing 18 Setts of Cotillions Arranged with Figures, and a Large Number of Popular Marches, Quick-Steps, Waltzes, Hornpipes, Contra Dances, Songs, &c, &c, Several of Which are in Three Parts— First, Second, & Bass, for the Flute, Violin, Clarionett, Bass-Viol, &c. Also, Several New and Popular Pieces in 6 and 8 Parts, for a Brass Band, viz. E♭ Bugle, ♭ Bugle, B♭ Post Horn, B♭ Cornopeon, Tenor Trombone, Bass Trombone, First Orphecleide, Second Orphecleide, &c. Containing in All Over 300 Pieces of Music, More Than 100 of Which Are Original.* Boston: Howe. Copy at the Library of Congress. Ditson reprint of 1850 (a faithful copy) available online.

Howe, Elias. 1862. *Musician's Omnibus, No. 1: Containing the Whole Camp Duty, Calls and Signals Used in the Army and Navy; Forty Sets of Quadrilles, (Including Waltz, Polka and Schottische), With Calls; and an Immense Collection of Polkas, Schottisches, Waltzes, Marches, Quicksteps, Hornpipes, Contra & Fancy Dances, Songs, &c. Containing Over 700 Pieces of Music. By Elias Howe.* Boston: Elias Howe. Numerous identical or nearly identical editions were printed in rapid order. The easiest to access on the internet, one from 1863, is in the Internet Archive: https://archive.org/details/musiciansomnibus00howe/page/n3/mode/2up.

Hunt County Historical Commission. 1983. *Blackland Memories: A Pictorial History of Greenville, Texas, 1850–1950.* Dallas: Taylor Publishing.

Hutchinson County Historical Commission. 1980. *History of Hutchinson County Texas 104 Years 1876–1980.* Dallas: Taylor Publishing. hutchinsoncountymuseum.org/stories.

Jaremko, Gordon. 2007. "Oilsands Gives a Little Texas Town its Future Back: Once-Roaring Refinery Town Was 'Dying' Before Alberta Bitumen Came Along." *Edmonton Journal*, April 26.

Johansson, Mats. 2017. "Non-isochronous Musical Meters: Towards a Multidimensional Model." *Ethnomusicology* 61/1 (winter): 31–51.

Jones, Sylvia. 1986. *Wilbarger County, Texas 1858–1986.* Wilbarger County Historical Commission.

Key, Della Tyler. 1972. *In the Cattle Country: History of Potter County 1887–1996.* 2nd ed. Wichita Falls, TX: Nortex Offset Publications.

Knauff, George P. 1839. *Virginia Reels.* 4 vols. Baltimore: Willig.

Kuntz, Andrew. Ongoing as of 2022. *Traditional Tune Archive*: https://tunearch.org.

Lawshae, Laurel. 2011. "The Mystery Fiddle of Bosque County, Texas." *Sound Post* (of Granite Falls, MN) 28/1 (January 1, 2011): 10–13.

Leroux, Gaston. c. 1911. *The Phantom of the Opera* (1910). New York; Indianapolis: Bobbs-Merrill.

Linsley, Judith Walker, Ellen Walker Rienstra, and Jo Ann Stiles. 2002. *Giant Under the Hill: A History of the Spindletop Oil Discovery at Beaumont, Texas, in 1901*. Austin: Texas State Historical Association.

Marshall, Howard Wight. 2022. *Keep It Old-Time: Fiddle Music in Missouri from the 1960s Folk Music Revival to the Present*. Columbia: University of Missouri Press.

Martin, Marcus. 2007. *When I Get My New House Done: Western North Carolina Fiddle Tunes and Songs*. CD produced by Wayne Martin, Beverly Patterson, and Steven Weiss. Biographical and tune notes by Wayne Martin. Notes on collectors and field recordings by Steven Weiss and Wayne Martin. Southern Folklife Collection SFC CD-100.

Nichols, A. A. 1935. "James Leander 'J. L.' Robertson." *Firm Foundation*, April 16, 8. Quoted in findagrave.com/memorial/111859303/james-leander-robertson.

Old Settler's Association of Bell County [TX]. 1902. *Proceedings of the Fourth Annual Reunion of the Old Settler's Association of Bell County, Held at Belton, Texas, September 27th, 1902, Together With Nearly All Of The Papers Read At The Reunion*. Bell County, TX: Old Settler's Association of Bell County, Texas. Rpt. Andesite Press (n.d.).

Old-Time Texas String Bands. 2001a. *Old-Time Texas String Bands, Volume I: Texas Farewell*. CO CD 3524. Charlottesville, VA: County Sales.

Old-Time Texas String Bands. 2001b. *Old-Time Texas String Bands, Volume II: Dallas Bound*. CO CD 3525. Charlottesville, VA: County Sales.

Owen, Blanton. 1991. Notes to *Eck Robertson: Famous Cowboy Fiddler*. County Records LP 202.

Owen, Blanton. 1992. "Eck Robertson." *The Old Time Herald* (Fall 1992): 20–25.

Parker, Dr. George. 1948. *Oil Field Medico*. Dallas: Banks, Upshaw and Company.

Pennington, Mrs. R. E. 1915. *The History of Brenham and Washington County*. Houston: Standard Printing and Lithographing Company.

"Population—Texas." United States Census 1910. https://www2.census.gov/prod2/decennial/documents/36894832v3ch6.pdf.

Pressler, Charles W. [1914]. "Hunt Co. General Land Office: June 1894. Compiled and Drawn by C. W. Pressler." Land ownership map, traced in October 1914 by O. O. Terrell. [Austin:] Texas General Land Office. *http://hdl.loc.gov/loc.gmd/g4033h.la001016*.

Raines, Howard. 2013. *The Old Texas Fiddle*. CD. Austin: performer.

Rathjen, Frederick W. 1998. *The Texas Panhandle Frontier* (1973). Rev. ed. Lubbock: Texas Tech University Press.

Robinson, John D. 1902 or soon after that. "Lovemaking in the Backwoods." In Tyler, Geo. W., compiler, *Proceedings of the Fourth Annual Reunion of the Old Settler's Association of Bell County, Held at Belton, Texas, September 27th, 1910, Together with Nearly All of the Papers Read at the Reunion*. Bell County, TX: Old Settler's Association of Bell County, Texas. Rpt. Sacramento, CA: Andesite Press, 27–30.

Ross, Weldon. 1937. "Memoirs of D. S. Ross, A Pioneer of the Black Prairie." Typescript. A class paper for "History 421" dated July 2, 1937, now on deposit at the Plains Museum in Canyon, Texas.

Russell, Charles H. 2006. *Undaunted: A Norwegian Woman in Frontier Texas*. College Station: Texas A&M University Press.

REFERENCES

Ryan, William B. 1883. *Ryan's Mammoth Collection*. Boston: Elias Howe.

Sears Roebuck & Co. 1897. *Sears Roebuck & Co. Catalogue*. Reprint New York: Skyhorse Publishing, 2007 and 2018.

Shaw, Amy M. 2020. *Ole Hendricks and His Tunebook: Folk Music and Community on the Frontier*. Madison: University of Wisconsin Press.

Shield, William, and John O'Keefe. 1808. *Poor Soldier: A Comic Opera in Two Acts, with all the Original Songs*. New York: D. Longworth. Many similar editions were issued before this one by various printers in London—the first in 1782.

Spielman, Earl V. 1972. "An Interview with Eck Robertson." *John Edwards Memorial Foundation Quarterly* 8/4 (winter): 179–88.

Syversen, Odd Magnar, and Derwood Johnson. 1982. *Norge i Texas: et bidrag tel norsk emigrasjon historie*. Stange, Norway: Stange Historie Lag.

Taylor, Carol, and Hunt County Historical Commission. 2010. *Greenville*. Mount Pleasant, SC: Arcadia Publishing Library Editions.

Thomasson, Benny. 2005. *Benny Thomasson, Legendary Texas Fiddler: Recordings from 1966–1969*. County Records CO-CD-2737.

Tyler, Geo. W., compiler. 1902 or soon after that. *Proceedings of the Fourth Annual Reunion of the Old Settler's Association of Bell County, Held at Belton, Texas, September 27th, 1910, Together with Nearly All of the Papers Read at the Reunion*. n.l.: Old Settler's Association of Bell County, Texas. Rpt. Sacramento, CA: Andesite Press.

United Confederate Veterans. 1920. *30th Annual Meeting of the United Confederate Veterans. Held At Houston, Texas on Wednesday, Thursday and Friday, October 6, 7, and 8, 1920*. New Orleans: Rogers Publishing Company.

United States Soil Conservation Service. 1981. "General Soil Map, Hunt County, Texas." Washington, DC: United States Soil Conservation Service. Consulted online: https://texashistory.unt.edu/ark:/67531/metapth130296/m1/1/.

Wells, Paul F. 2001. "Some Folks Call It 'Sally Johnson' But Us Folks Down South Call It 'Katy Hill': Questions of Fiddle Tune Identity." Read paper, American Folklore Society Annual Meeting.

Westmoreland, Howard Dee [Wes] III. 2017. *Salt River: Championship Fiddlin' by Wes Westmoreland*. CD. Austin: Tequila Mockingbird Studios.

White, John H. [n.d.; before 1938]. "Borger at Night, a pamphlet." [n.p.].

White, John T. 1980. "A Brief History of Hutchinson County, Texas." In Hutchinson County Historical Commission. 1980. *History of Hutchinson County Texas 104 Years 1876–1980*. Dallas: Taylor Publishing Company, 9–45.

Wilkison, Kyle G. 2008. *Yeomen, Sharecroppers, and Socialists: Plain Folk Protest in Texas, 1870–1914*. College Station: Texas A&M University Press.

Wolfe, Charles. 1997. *The Devil's Box: Masters of Southern Fiddling*. Nashville: Country Music Foundation Press and Vanderbilt University Press.

INDEX

Page numbers in **bold** indicate melodies cited in music notation.

Abbott, Edward (E. C., "Teddy Blue"): "Teddy Blue," 113; *We Pointed Them North*, 151
Abrahams, Roger, 9, 73, 75, 110
African American music performances, 34, 36, 110–11, 158
Agee, Jane Snyder, 59
"Alexander's Ragtime Band," 79, 81–82
"Alf Taylor's Fox Chase," 75, 85, 111, **187**
All Panhandle Old Fiddlers Contest, 50
Allen, A. W., 54
Allen, Elvis, 17–19
Allied Expeditionary Air Force, 66
Altus, Oklahoma, ix, 31–32, 34, 57, 128
Amarillo, Texas, 32; Municipal Auditorium, 91
Amarillo Blue Boys, 62
Amarillo Brass Band, 47
Amarillo Daily News, 33, 43, 50–51, 53, 57, 63, 67–70, 72–73, 91
Amarillo Sunday News Globe, 52
"Amarillo Waltz," x, 17, 63–64, 75, 77–79, 81–82, 147–49, **238**
Amati, Nicola, 43
American Vernacular Music Manuscripts, 1730–1910, 116
Amos, Therman J., 60
Andrew, Jason, 117, 192–93
Appel, George, 60
"Apple Blossom," 75, 87, 143, **216**
Arkansas, 3, 5–6, 16–17, 60
"Arkansas Traveller," vii, x, 47, 54, 59, 64, 80, 84, 90–101, 104, 111, 120, 131, 139, 156–57, **161–65**; associated skit, 91–95
Armes, Ethel, *The Story of Iron and Coal in Alabama*, 113–14

"Around the World on a Dime," 64
Ashley, Louis, 119
Athens Texas Fiddle Contest, 237
Atherton [California] Session, The, 212
Atlanta Constitution, 40

Baggett, Eula, 27
Baggett, William, 27
Baker, Trustin, 107–8
Baldwin Piano Company, 31
banjo, 11, 14, 19–20, 22, 24, 34, 39, 53, 63–64
"Banjo-Pickin' Bill," 41
Barker, Babe, 53–54
Barnes, George F., 39
Barnes, John W., 39, 41
"Barnyard Blues," 64
"Battle of Prague, The," 112
"Battle of Trenton, The," 111–12
Bayard, Samuel P., 111
Beach, P. M., 53–54
"Beach of Balley, Balley," 78
Beaumont, Texas, 146–47
"Beaumont Rag," 49, 75, 77, 79–82, 84, 131, 144, 146–47, **226–29**; analysis, 147
"Beer Barrel Polka," 82
Bell, U. H., 54
Benny Thomasson, Legendary Texas Fiddler, Recordings from 1966–69, 183
Berline, Byron, 72, 120
"Big Sis," 84
"Bill Cheatum," 70, 85
"Billy in the Low Grounds" / "Billy in the Low Ground," x, 18, 47, 59, 74–75, 83–84, 131, 138, 142–43, 145, 156–57, 204, **214–15**
"Black Cat's Foot," 84
Black Hills Pioneer, 125

INDEX

"Black Jack Grove," 84
"Black Mountain Rag," 70
"Black Satin," 84
Blackburn-Shaw Quartet, 69
"Black-Eyed Susie," 84
blackface minstrelsy, 22, 91–108, 177, 180–81; power reversal ritual, 93
Blackwell, "Shorty," 41
Blue Devils of Denver, 62
"Blue Eyes," 78
Bluegrass music, 137
"Bonaparte's Retreat," 76, 84, 111–12, 156, **182–83**
Bonner, Mose/M. J., 39, 41
"Bonnie Blue Flag," 84
Borger, A. P. "Ace," 59–60
Borger, Texas, 32, 57–67, 147, 158; town both rough and civilized, 59–62
Borger at Night, 61
Borger Daily Herald, 57, 59, 61–62
Borger Townsite Company, 59
"Borger Wiggle" / "Borger Bounce," 17, 75, 79, 81–82, 84, 149, **239**
Bosque County, Texas, 130
Bowman, Richard, 122, 200
"Braes of Auchtertyre, The," 155
"Brannigan's Pup," 84
Brenham, Texas, 21–22, 83–89, 102
"Brickyard Joe," 119
"Brilliancy Medley," x, 74–75, 81, 84, 131, 138, 157, **217**
"Brindle Steer," 84
Brown, Anson, 54
Brown, Cal, 69–70, 72
Brown, Matt, 144–46, 148, 150, 157, 224, 234
"Brown Kelly Waltz" / "Kelly Waltz," x, 64, 78, 80–82, 84, 95, 131, 147–49, 157, **234–37**
"Brown-Skin Girl." *See* "There's a Brown-Skin Girl Down the Road"
Bryan Texas Eagle, 21
Buckley, James, 109
"Buckley's Farmyard, or Farmer's Medley," 109–10, 180–81
Buckley's Violin Tunes (James Buckley), 164, 180–81
"Buffalo Girls," 84
Buffalo Soldiers, 26
Bull, Ole, 128
"Bull Frog's Eye," 84
"Bully of the Town," 79

Burden, Omega, 71
"Butterfly Hornpipe," 70
"Buttermilk and Cider," 119
Byers, "Uncle" Bill, 41

"Cacklin' Chickens," 83
"Cacklin' Hen" / "Barnyard Blues," 64, 74, 77, 83–84, 89, 95, 109, 156, **180–81**
"Cake All Dough," 85
"Call of the Wild Goose." *See* "Lost Goose"
Campbell, Alexander, 7
Campbell, Katherine, vii
"Campbells Are Coming," 85
Carlotta, 61. See also *Phantom of the Opera, The*
Caroll, Jeanne, 69
Carson, Fiddling John, 39–41, 46, 120, 128
Carwile, Amy, 142
Carwile, Daniel, 121–23, 141–42
Cary, Preston, vii, 28
Case, Mose, 92–93, 96, 161
Castlebury, Mattie, 61
"Catfish and Minnow," 85
"Cattle in the Cane Break" / "Cattle in the Cane." *See* "Hell Among the Yearlings"
censuses: of 1890, 5; of 1900, 3–4, 16, 32; of 1910, 25; of 1920, 29–30; of 1930, 58, 60; of 1940, 66
Center for Popular Music, Middle Tennessee State University, vii, 76
"Chadwick," 74, 85, 115, 156, **188**
Chancellor, James ("Texas Shorty"), 72–73, 105
Chapman, Jim, 54
"Charlie is a Ladies Man," 119
"Chicken in the Bread Tray," 85
"Chicken Reel," 85
"Cinda, Fare You Well," 85
Clarendon, Texas, 31–32, 57
"Clarinet Tickler," 85
Clark Kessinger, Fiddler, 233
Clarridge, Tashina, 141
Clarridge, Tristan, 141, 209–11
"Clear the Track," 85
Cloverport Breckenridge News, 119
Cohen, John, 73, 75, 126
"College Hornpipe," 70, 74–75, 80, 85, 102–3, 112, 157, **168**
Comanche Frank (Lewis Franklin), 41, 45
Comanche Indians, 25–26; Red River Wars, 25–26

"Coming Around the Mountain," 85
Confederate and cowboy images, 48; joint-themed reunions, 47–48 Confederate Choir, 46
Confederate Reunions, ix, 39, 45–47, 128
"Connie on the Ground," 85
Conte, Pat, 74, 102, 116–17, 167, 169–71, 175, 189, 191, 215, 224, 232
"Cotton-Eyed Joe," 54, 85
Country Music Hall of Fame and Museum, vii, 31, 76–77
cowboy culture and image, 48, 50, 125, 129–30, 151–53, 158
"Cowboys Yodel," 82
Cranfill, J. B. (James Britton Buchanan Boone Cranfill), x, 106, 115, 188
Crawford, Thomas G., 53–54
"Cubaniola Glide," 80, 85
"Cubianola Rag," 77, 85
Cumming, William, 96, 161
Curtis, Sonny, 70
Curwood, James Oliver, *The Flaming Forest*, 38

Dahlberg, Edward, 147
Dallas, Texas, 32, 57
Dallas Theological Seminary, 57
"Dark Town Strutter's Ball," 79, 81–82, 85
Deal, "Long Tom," 41
Der Freischütz (Von Weber), 148
"Devilish Mary," 85
Devil's Box: Masters of Southern Fiddling, The, 151
"Devils' Dream" / "Big Devil Medley," 70, 72, 74, 80, 85, 102, 138, 157, **169**
Dice, Dixie, 69
Dice, Harry V., 60
Dick Morton's Orchestra, 69
"Dill Pickles Rag," 79, 81–82, 85
"Dipsy Doodle," 82
"Dixie," 46–47, 85
Dixie Fiddlers, 49, 62
Dixson, Lyle, 237
"[Do You] Want to Go to Meetin' Uncle Joe?," 81
dog-trot cabin, 2, 11–13
"Dominion Hornpipe," 74, 78, 85, 100, 102, 156, **170**
"Done Gone," x, 64, 70, 74, 76, 79–80, 85, 95, 106, 137, 142–45, 157, **224**, 225
"Dopey the Puppet," 69

"Down Yonder," 79, 83, 85
"Downfall of Paris, The," 119. *See also* "Mississippi Sawyer"
"Drifting and Dreaming," 81
"Drums and Fifes," 111
"Drunkard's Hiccups," 54, 85
"Dry and Dusty," 85
Duling, Rodney, 69
Dunn, William "Schnozz," 69
Dunning, P. H., 54
Durang, John, *The Memoir of John Durang, American Actor 1785–1816*, 115–16, 190
"Durang's Hornpipe," 74, 85, 102–3, 115–17, 131, 142, **190–93**
"Dusty Miller," 75, 81, 85, 131, **230**

E. J. Hopkins, Contest Fiddlin', 173
"Eagle's Whistle, The," 111
Eastview Memorial Cemetery, 158
"Echo in the Valley," 78
Eckles, William, 70–71
Edmond, Oklahoma *Enterprise*, 38
Edmond, Oklahoma Gem, 38–43
Eggert, Luke, 131
"Eighth of January," 85
El Paso Daily Herald, 21
Elmore, Marty, 131
Emmett, Bob, 53
"Engagement Quadrille," 100–101, 164–65
Evensen, Lena, 128–29
Evensen, Ole, 43, 45, 57, 128–30, 152

Famous Cowboy Fiddler, 75, 109, 151, 178
"Fanitullen," 201
"Farewell, Whiskey," 85
Fehrenbach, T. R., *Lone Star*, 151
Fergerson, Thomas, 129
fiddle: Amati, 44–45, 128; Black Forest, 43, 45; Cordavora, 43–45, 128; expensive, 38–43, 128; gourd, 9–11; Jacob Stainer, 10, 43; Sears & Roebuck, 10, 43; Stradivarius, 40, 42–45, 128; versus violin, 36, 42–43, 58
fiddle contests: audiences, 21, 34–35, 48, 52; comedic elements, 34; competition brackets, 71–72; general flavor, 20–21, 34, 48; generations, 21, 41, 48, 52, 72; jamming, 131–32; judging, 41, 48–49, 52–53, 131; lists of judges, 54, 72; nostalgia, 21, 34; prizes, 21, 48, 51, 53, 69–70, 72; publicity, 20, 34; radio broadcast, 51;

rules, 52; stage banter, ix; tickets, 34, 52; travel to, 71; with beard-growing contest, 69; women fiddlers, 69–70, 72
fiddle tunes: analysis, xi, 117, 121–24, 132–33, 140–42, 145–46, 149, 200–202, 224, 237; blackface minstrel associations, x, 20–22, 34, 106; forms, 117, 121–24, 132–36, 140–42, 145–47, 149, 155, 195, 200–220, 222–27, 232–33, 235, 238–39; general character, 96, 155; genteel usage, 101, 163–65; medleys, x, 47, 53–54, 74–75, 80–81, 84–86, 100–102, 109–10, 138, 142, 157, 159, 214–15, 217; modes and tunings, 34, 37, 96–97, 103–6, 117, 120–21, 135, 174–75, 177, 182–86, 203; repertoires, x, 27, 70, 131, 158; titles, 156; transcribing, xii, 159; tunings other than GDAE, 34, 37, 47, 75, 112–13, 121, 127, 135, 156, 158, 179, 182–87, 194, 201–3; waltzes, 147–49, 232–38
fiddling: contest fiddle style, 117–18, 155–57; of contest fiddle sub-styles, 132, 141–42; dances, ix, 9, 11, 22–23, 34, 46, 50, 68, 79, 116; definitions, 47; ensemble, plus piano, 47; ensembles, fiddle duet, 47, 96–97, 106, 115; ensembles, for contests, 52; ensembles, old-time, x, 19, 24; family activity, 11; harmonics, 108–9, 156, 179; house-raisings, 11, 19–20; imitating human voice, 38, 134–35; imitating miscellaneous sounds outside of music, 105–13, 145, 179–83, 187; old-time, 50, 97, 121–22, 150, 200; play parties, 11; rhythms, 96, 231, 235; technique, x, 148–50; techniques on hardingfele, 126–28; trick, 24, 34, 37, 52, 54, 58, 64, 106–8, 134, 148, 157, 179–81, 186; variation or arrangement techniques, 23, 97, 99–100, 118–20, 123–24, 133–43, 145; versus art violin performance, 42–3, 54, 58
Fiddler's Companion, The (Kuntz), 120, 148
Fiddlers Frolics. *See* Texas State Championship Fiddlers Frolics
"Fine Times at Our House," 85
First Christian Church, Borger, 65
"Fisher's Hornpipe," 54, 70, 74, 80, 85, 102–3, 112, 131, **166–67**
Flaming Forest, The (Curwood), 38
"Flower Song, The," 85
Floyd County Fair Parade, 69
Folkways Records, 233

Food, Drug and Insecticide Administration, 35
Ford, Henry, 49
"Forked Deer," 54, 74–75, 85, 131, **170**
Foster, Stephen, 164
"Fox Chase." *See* "Alf Taylor's Fox Chase"
Fox News, 43
Franklin, Larry, 117
Franklin, Lewis ("Lefty"), 39, 41, 43–47, 53–54, 128–29; crime and incarceration, 46, 62, 70
Franklin, Louis, 70, 72, 117
Franklin, Major, ix, 70–71
"Freischütz," 148
Freischütz, Der (Von Weber), 148
Fritch, Texas, 159
Fry, Segel, 73
Fulton, W. D., 54
"Fuss in the Family," 85

"G and E Rag," 79, 83
"Gal on the Log," 85
Galveston Daily News, 114
"Gammel Gauken" ("Old Cuckoo"), 109, **179**
Gatesville Texas Fiddle Contest, 131
gender-based channeling of professions, 27
"General Logan's Reel," 85
"Georgia Blues," 85
Gertrude's Western Band, 68
"Get Up in the Cool," 75–76, 85, 113–15, 135, 156, **185**
"Getting Upstairs," 86
Gilliland, Henry, ix, 34, 39, 41, 47, 57, 91, 96, 101, 128, 156, 161, 176–77
"Give the Fiddlers a Dram," 86
"God Be With You Till We Meet Again," 46
Goertzen, Valerie, vii, ix, 2, 5, 7, 12, 28
"Gold Mine in the Sky," 83
Golden Vanity (coffee house), 75, 216
"Goodnight Waltz," 78, 82, 86
Gouce, Charles, 54
Gow family of Scottish fiddlers, 103–4
Grand Ole Opry, 74
Grand Master Fiddler Championship, 141
Grand Saline, Texas, 17–19, 32; music teachers, 18; neighborhood of Stumptown, 17–18
"Great Big Taters in Sandy Land," x, 106, 178
Green, Archie, 73
Green, Steve, vii, 21, 113–15
"Green Brier," 86

"Green Corn," 59
Greenville, Texas, 18–19, 22
Grey, Zane, 152
"Grey Eagle," 74–75, 80, 86, 119, 131, **219**
"Grey Eagle Cottilions," 221
Grigsby, Melvin, 125–26
Grigsby's Cowboys, 125–26
"Grigsby's Hornpipe," 75, 86, 125, 135–36, **202**
Guthrie, Woody, 120

H. M. S. *Pinafore*, 61
Hale Center, Texas, 69–72
Hallam, Lewis, 116
Hallettsville, Texas, ix
halling dance and music, 126–28
Hamlin, Texas, 5–6, 32
Hardanger fiddle. *See* hardingfele
hardingfele, 44–45, 126–30, 201; tunings, 127
Harper, "Shorty," 41
Harris, J. K. P., 39
Harris, Polk, 150, 157
Hartz, Matt, 237
Harwood, Carl, 72
Hash, Robert C., 67
Haskell, Harry, 147
"Haste to the Wedding," 86
Hastings, H. E., 54
"Have You Ever Been Lonely," 78
"Hawk Got a Chicken," 75–76, 86, 106, 156, **178**
"Hell Among the Yearlings," 54, 70, 74–76, 85–86, 131, **171**
"Hell in Georgia," 86
Helton, Babe, 53–54
Henderson, Mary, *History of Borger, Texas*, 60
Herwig, Richard "Two-Gun Dick," 60
Hewitt, James, 111
History of Borger, Texas (Henderson), 60–61
Hoffmeister/Hoffmaster, Mr., 116, 190
"Hog-Eyed Man," 86
Holmes, John A., 60
"Home on the Range," 78–79, 81, 83, 86
Hooker, "Brother" Walker, 125
Hooker, P. H., 54
Hooker, Pat, 125
"Hop High Ladies," 86
Hopkins, Carl, 131–34, 139, 141, 157, 195–97, 209–11
Hopkins, E. J., 105, 131, 173
Hopkins, Pandora, 126–27

Hopkins, Tonya Rast, 132
Hopkins County Museum and Heritage Park, vii, 2, 12–13
hornpipes, 103
Houston, Bryant, 72
Houston Daily Post, 21, 48
"How Firm a Foundation," 46
Howard, Abner Perry, 38–47, 49, 62–63, 128–30
Howe, Elias, 116, 156, 166–69, 176, 190, 221; *The Musician's Companion*, 166–67; *The Musician's Omnibus*, 168, 169, 176, 190, 221
Hunt County, Texas, 2, 32, 130; character of farmland, 5, 8 15; cultivation of cotton, 16–17, 25; demography, 16; education, 16; half-tenant farming, 4–6, 9–10, 15–17, 25; history, 9, 11; professions, 16
Hunter, R. I., 54
Hunter, William R., 60
Hutchinson County Historical Museum, vii, 59

"I Saw Your Face in the Moon," 78
"I Want to Go to Meeting, but Got No Shoes," 86
"If I Had a Girl Like You," 86
"I'm an Old Cow Hand," 78
"In the Shade of the Old Apple Tree," 79
"In the Sweet Bye and Bye," 119
"In the Valley of the Moon," 78
"Indian Whoop," 110. *See also* "Lost Indian"
"Irish Washerwoman," 54, 74, 86, 102–3, 105, 111–12, 156, **174**, 175
Irvin, Frances, 69
"Island of Capri, The," 79, 83
"Island Unknown, The," x, 86, 149, **240–42**
"It Makes No Difference Now," 83
"It's a Sin to Tell a Lie," 78, 82–83
Iucho, Wilhelm/William, 97, 99–100, 163

Jacek, Daniel, 97, 162
Jackson, E. W., 54
James, Jesse, 147
Jazz Pirates Girl Band, 62
Jefferson Texas Jimplejute, 21
"Jenny Nettle," 54, 86
"Jenny on the Railroad," 86
"Jenny Put the Kettle On," 86
"John's Got a New House," 86
Johnson, Josh, 189

Johnson County, Missouri, 133
Johnston, "Big Earl," 41
Julia Dean Evans' A Capella Choir, 69
"Just Because," 79, 82, 86

Kahn, Ed, 73
"Kansas City Rag," 74, 79, 81–82, 86, 147, **225**
Kansas Wheat Show, 46
"Katy Hill," 137, 247
"Keller's Waltz," 148
Kelly, J. O., 53–54
"Kelly Waltz." *See* "Brown Kelly Waltz"
Keowee Courier Newspaper Archives, 119
Kessinger, Clark, 148, 233
"Kid the Fiddler," 41
"Killie Krankie," 86
King, Lucky, 54
"Kitty is the Gal for Me," 86
Kleber, Henry, 100, 164–65
Knauff, George P., 110
Knowles, W. B., 54
Kotzwara, Franticek, 112
Krack, Jake, 187
Kuntz, Andrew: *The Fiddler's Companion*, 91, 120, 148; and *Traditional Tune Archive*, 91

"Lady's Fancy," 85
lantern slides, 151
"Last Roundup, The," 78
"Lead, Kindly Light," 46
"Leather Britches," 70, 72, 74–76, 86, 112, 156, **218**
Leroux, Gaston, *The Phantom of the Opera*, 61
"Let Me Call You Sweetheart," 79
"Lime Rock." *See* "Old Lime Rock"
"Listen to the Mockingbird," 69, 107
"Little Brown Jug," 86
"Little More Cider," 86
"Little Ser Echo," 81
Littleton, Martin W., 91
"Liza Jane," 86
Lone Star (Fehrenbach), 151
"Lone Star Trail, The," 54, 86
"Lost Goose" / "Call of the Wild Goose" / "Wild Goose Crossing the Ocean," 74–75, 86–87, 108–9, 156, **179**
"Lost Indian," 74–75, 80, 86, 110, 131, 156, **179**
"Love Letters in the Sand," 79, 83
"Loveless Love," 78

Loyd, O. H., 50–54
Lubbock, Texas, 5, 25–27, 32; changing emphases in agriculture, 26
Lubbock Avalanche Journal, 67–73
Lubbock Morning Avalanche, 67–72, 107
Lucille McKay farm, 2
Ludiker, Dennis, 131

"Makes No Difference Now," 82, 86
"Maple on the Hill," 78
Marcus Martin: When I Get My New House Done (Martin), 200
Marshall, Helen, Lois, and Jean, 69
Marshall, J. T., 53–54
Martin, Marcus, *Marcus Martin: When I Get My New House Done*, 200
"Massa is in the Cold, Cold, Ground," 86
Massy, W. C., 54
McGraw, Frank, 72
McMurtry, Larry, 152
McPherson, Joe, 54
Mears, A. J. "Jack," 69–70, 72
medicine shows, 24
"Medley Hornpipe," 53–54, 86
Mel Tillis' Country Western Band (Brandon, Missouri), 139
Memoir of John Durang, American Actor 1785–1816, The (Durang), 116
Merrick, Anna, 54
"Methodist Preacher," 86
"Mexicana Rose," 78, 81–83, 86
Miami Record-Herald, 114
Michael, Tom, 70
Milbank, George, 93
Miller, John R., 59
"Miss Brown's Reel," **221**
"Miss McLeod's Reel," 86
"Mississippi Sawyer," 87, 119
Mitchell, Tom, 70
Mitchell House, Amarillo, 66
Mohawk Aces, 61–62
"Money Musk," 87
More/More's Theater, Vernon, 28, 33–34
Morris, Rachel, vii
"Mosquito Parade," 49
Murry, M., 54
Musician's Companion, The (Howe), 166–67
Musician's Omnibus, The (Howe), 168, 169, 176, 190, 221
Muus, Rudolph, 152
"My Blue Heaven," 87

"My Cabin of Dreams," 78
"My Darling Hold Me Closer Still," 78
"My Experience on the Ranch," x, 64, 78, 80–81, 87, 151
"My Frog Ain't No Bullfrog," 79, 82, 87
"My Little Girl," 79, 82–83
"My Wild Irish Rose," 78

Nagy, Szabo, 9–10, 13, 23, 66, 75, 110, 147, 187, 227
"Nancy Rowland," 87
"Natchez Under the Hill," 87, 102
National Old-Time Fiddlers' Contest and Festival, 141
"Negro's Dream, The," 82
New Deal support of seamstresses, 67
New Lost City Ramblers, 73, 75–76, 147, 218
Newport Folk Festival, 76, 218
NewspaperArchive.com, 21
Nib Noble's Orchestra, 69
"N____ in the Woodpile," 87
"Nightingale Song," 87
"Nobody's Business," 87
"Nobody's Darling But Mine," 78, 81, 83
Norway, 42–43, 45, 126
Norwegian fiddle types, 126
nostalgia, 34–36, 48, 68, 153–55

Odde, Kristen, 179
"Off to Georgia," 87
"Oh Johnny," 82, 87
Oklahoma City Orpheum Theater, 58
Oklahoma Vagabonds, 62
"Old Apple Tree, The," 79
"Old Cuckoo." See "Gammel Gauken" ("Old Cuckoo")
"Old Dan Tucker," 87
"Old Faithful," 77–81, 83, 87
Old Fiddlers Association, 39
"Old Grey Goose," 87
"Old Hen Cackle," 87
"Old Lime Rock," 74, 86–87, 131, 148, **219**
"Old Molly Hare," 87
"Old Muse and Pups," 87
"Old Sallie Gooden." See "Sally Goodin" / "Sallie Gooden"
"Old Straw Bonnet," 87
Old Time Herald, 24
Old Time Texas String Bands, 150
"Old Uncle Ned," 87
"Old Zip Coon," 115, 176–77

Olustee, Oklahoma, 129, 152
"One Rose, The," 78, 82, 87
"One-Eyed Riley," 87
"Orange Blossom Special," 70, 75, 107–8
"Over the Waves" / "Over the Waves Waltz," 70, 77, 87, 148, **232–33**
Owen, Blanton, 5, 24
Owenby, Caleb, 58, 158
Owenby, Odessa (Robertson), 58, 158

"Paddy on the Turnpike," 70
Panhandle, Texas, 32, 62, 66–67
Panhandle-Plains Historical Museum, vii, 68
Pantex Ordnance Plant, 67
Pantex Villages, Amarillo, 67
Parides, 79
Parker, Julie, vii
Peacock, Samuel, 49, 150, 226
Peters, W. C., 221
Peterson, McKenna, 107–8
Pettigrew, Paul, 60
Pfeiffer, S. L., 158
Phantom of the Opera, The (Leroux), 61
Poor Soldier, The (Shield and O'Keefe), 115
"Pop Goes the Weasel," 64, 77–78, 80–81, 83, 87, 107
"Popeye" cartoons, 102
Presley, C. P., 54
Pressley, J. A., 43
"Pretty Polly Ann," 54, 87
Propps, Louis J., 54
pump organ, 57
Pure Food and Style Show, Vernon, 35
Pyron, Bob, 49

quadrille, 100–101

"Rackensack Jig," 100–101. See also "Arkansas Traveller"
Radio Station WOS, 49
"Ragtime Annie," x, 49, 70, 79, 87, 131, 146–48, 157, **225**
"Rain," 82
Raines, Howard, 150
"Rancho Grande," 79, 82, 87
"Rareback Davy," 87
Ray, John S., 54
Red Cross, 34–35
"Red Wing," 109
Reece, Deborah, vii
Reményi, Ede, 93–95

INDEX

Republic Supplies Company, Borger, 65
Rex Theater, Stinnett, 63
"Rhubarb," 74–75, 87, 115, 152, **189**
"Ricker's Hornpipe," 87
Riddle, Harold Vernon, 73–75, 102, 109, 115, 139, 145, 149, 168, 172, 179, 181, 188–89, 203–5, 219–20, 223–25
Riggs, Pat, 10, 13, 23, 66, 75, 110, 147, 187, 227
Riley, Bartow, 70
Riley, Edward, *Riley's Flute Melodies*, 116, 190
Riley's Flute Melodies (Riley), 190
"Ringtail Coon," 87
Rinzler, Ralph, 73
"River, Stay Away From My Door," 79
Roberts, Ridge, 237
Robertson, Alexander Campbell ("Eck"): banjo (5-string and tenor), 11, 13–14, 19–23, 53, 62; building gourd fiddle, 9–11, 28, 58–59; comedy, x, 29–30, 95, 106–7, 134; competing, 44; cowboy outfit and ranch associations, ix–xi, 24, 38, 47–48, 151; family band, x, 56, 63–66, 91, 95; first recording, ix–x, 47–48; gravestone, 158; in New York, ix; lantern slides, 24; learning to fiddle, 9, 24; newspaper ads, 29, 34, 38; piano tuner and salesman, ix, 29, 57, 62–63, 67, 152–53; pictured, 56, 64, 68, 76; playing at confederate reunions, 45–48; playing for dances, x, 10, 13–14, 23, 68; playing for movies, 24, 38, 151, 153; playing in an "orchestra," 57, 62, 66–69, 83, 154–55; playing in theaters, 24, 28, 33–34, 154; relocations, 27, 31–32, 51; repertoires and repertoire lists, 3, 54–55, 59, 63, 77–90; revision technique, 104, 145; respect and influence of "the old masters," 36, 104, 122, 130, 143, 155, 157; sources for biography, 3; style (as distinct from modern contest style), 72, 104, 156–57; truck farmer, 25; virtuosity, 37, 40, 56, 58, 64, 69, 77, 97, 102–5, 109, 112, 118, 121–24, 143, 147–48, 155–57; winning prizes at fiddle contests, 69–73; "World Champion Fiddler," 29, 38, 158
Robertson, Audrey, 64–65
Robertson, Daphne, x, 63–66
Robertson, Dueron, x, 53, 63–66, 95, 148
Robertson, Jack, 65
Robertson, James Leander (J. L.), 4–5, 25, 67; fiddler, 10–11, 14; religious calling and profession, 7, 13–14, 25
Robertson, John Q. ("Quince"), 10–11, 17, 20, 125
Robertson, Lafayette V. (Vird), 25, 31, 57
Robertson, Marguerite, 64–65, 95
Robertson, Mary Jane Reed, 4–5, 7, 13, 25
Robertson, Nettie, x, 17, 24, 29, 63–67, 95, 151
Robertson families: fiddlers, 11; mobility, 5–7, 14–15
"Rocky Road to Dublin," 87
Roden, Hugh, 54, 64
Rodgers, William, 64
Rosas, Juventino, 148
"Rose Tree," 115
"Rosebud Waltz," 87
"Rubber Dolly," 82–83, 87
"Rubies," 79, 83
Rubinoff, David, 43
"Run N____, Run" / "Run Boy, Run," x, 87, 115
Russell, W. G., 119
"Rye Straw," 87
"Rye Whiskey," 75, 89, 87, 156, **186**

S. T. Gordon and Son, 97–98
"Saddle Old Spike," 87
"Sailor's Hornpipe," 102
"Sally Goodin" / "Sallie Gooden," x–xi, 33–35, 37, 39, 44, 47, 54, 59, 64, 70–72, 74–75, 77, 80–81, 87, 91, 103, 118–27, 130–37, 141, 158, **194–200**, 201–3; form, 121; lyrics and legend, 120; mode, 120–21
"Sally Johnson," x, 70, 74–75, 79–80, 87, 131, 137–39, 141–42, 144, 157, **204–15,** 247
Salt River, 206
"San Antonio Rose," 78, 83, 88
"Sandy Land," 88
"Satisfied," 79, 82, 88
"Say Old Man" / "Say Old Man, Can You Play a Fiddle?," 74–77, 80, 88, 113, 131, 135–36, **203**
Schaur, Stephen, 212
Scholes, Stephen, 154
"Schottische in F," 88
Schwarz, Tracy, 73, 109
Scottish fiddling and fiddle collections, 100
Sing Out!, 73, 75
Singer, "Laughing Ben," 41

Seeger, Mike, 73, 75, 109, 125, 134–35, 139, 143–45, 147, 170, 171, 177–78, 182, 184–86, 202–3, 215–16, 224, 230, 239; Robertson quoted from interview with, 7, 13–14, 18–19, 31–32, 39, 60, 65–66, 102, 107, 109, 112–13, 115, 147, 152–53, 155
Shield, William, and John O'Keefe, *Poor Soldier*, 115
"Shoo Fly," 88
"Sidewalks of New York," 88
Sleep Disturbers, The, 67–68, 83, 154–55
"Sleepy Time Down South," 79, 83
Smith, Harry, 73
Smith's Garage Fiddle Band, 49, 150, 226
"Snowbird in the Ashbank," 74–75, 105–6, 157, **172–73**
"Soapsuds Over the Fence," 88
"Sobre las Osas," 148
Solaas, Haakon, 127, 201
"Soldier's Joy," 74–75, 88, 102–3, 131, 157, **171**
Solomon, Mike, 72
Solomon, Norman, 70–72
Solomon, Rick, 72
Solomon, Vernon, 70, 72
"Some of These Days," 82
"Somebody Loves You," 78
South Dakota Historical Society Foundation, 125
"South of the Border," 80, 82, 88
Spielman, Earl V., 77, 121, 125, 155, 246
"Springtime in the Rockies," 88
"Stay All Night, Then Stay a Little Longer," 54, 88
Stinnett, Texas, 58, 64, 158
Stoneking, Fred, 133
Stoneking, Lee, 133
Story of Coal and Iron in Alabama, The (Armes), 113–14
Strathspey, 96
Stricker, Warren, vii
"Stump Tail Deer," 88
"Stumptown Stomp" / "Stumptown Stomp in Grand Saline," 17, 75, 88, 149, **239**
"Sugar in the Coffee," 88
"Sugar in the Gourd," 88
"Suwannee River," 88
"Sweet Jenny Reel," 88
"Sweet Little Headache," 81
"Sweetheart of Sigmachi," 78

"Tailor in the Loft," 88
Tanner, Gid, 41
Taylor, Bob, 51
Taylor, Governor Alf, 45, 47, 51, 110
Taylor County News, 113
"Tears Waltz," 82, 88
Teddy Blue (Abbott), 113
"Ten Cent Cotton," 88
"Tennessee Mountain Fox Chase," 111, **187**
Tennessee Valley Old Time Fiddlers' Convention, 141–2
"Tenting Tonight," 46
Texas character, 26, 151–53
Texas Digital Newspaper Program, 21
Texas Panhandle, ranching, 26
"Texas Quickstep," 81, 83
Texas Rangers, 60–61
Texas State Championship Fiddlers Frolics, ix, 107, 131–33, 139, 148, 154, 162
Texas State Real Estate Convention, 48
"Texas Wagoner." *See* "Wagoner" / "Texas Wagoner" / "Wagner"
"Theme Song" (Robertson's radio show), 88
Theobaldi, Ole, 128
"There's a Brown-Skin Girl Down the Road" / "Brown Skin Girl," x, 81, 83, 88, 131, **231**
"There's a Gold Mine in the Sky," 79, 81, 88
"There's an Empty Cot in the Bunkhouse," 78, 81, 88
Thomasson, Benny, ix, 70–72, 102, 183
"Three Little Fishes," 82
"Tie Me To Your Apron Strings," 79
"Tight Like That," 88
"Tinner's Hornpipe," 88
Tokio Club, Borger, 61–62
"Tom and Jerry," 54, 74, 88, 131, **220**
Traditional Tune Archive (Kuntz), 91
Tri-State Fair, 46, 50–54, 63–64
Trout, Milt, 54
"Turkey in the Straw," x, 88, 115
"Two-Eyed Jane," 88

"Uncle Joe," 83. *See also* "[Do You] Want to Go to Meetin' Uncle Joe?"
United Confederate Veterans, 46
University of California, Santa Barbara, 76
"Unnamed Tune in D," 76

vanlig fele ("normal fiddle"), 126
vaudeville, 95
Venth, Carl, 43
Vernon, Texas, ix, 28–34
Vernon Daily Record, 29, 49

INDEX

Vernon Fiddlers, 38–39, 43, 45, 49, 55, 62, 70, 128
Vernon Record, 30, 33–34, 39, 43, 46–49, 128
Vernon Weekly Record, 118
Victor Catalog, 47, 76, 128
Victor Talking Machine Company and Victor records, ix, 47–48, 91, 118, 130, 137–38, 143, 148–49, 176, 188, 194–95, 204, 214, 217, 222, 224–25, 231, 234, 238, 240
violin. *See* fiddle
"Virginia Reel," 46, 74–75, 77, 80, 88
Von Weber, Carl Maria, *Der Freischütz*, 148

"Wagoner" / "Texas Wagoner" / "Wagner," x, 70, 74–75, 77, 88, **221–22**
"Wagoner's Hornpipe," 74, 88, 131, **223**
"Walk Along, Jawbone," 88
"Walk Along, John," 88
"Walk the Georgia Road," 88
Walling, W. E., 53–54
"Walls of Jericho," 88
"Waltz in F," 88
"Waltz You Saved for Me, The," 77–78, 82, 88
"Want to Go To Meeting, Uncle Joe." *See* "[Do You] Want to Go to Meetin' Uncle Joe?"
We Pointed Them North (Abbott), 151
"Wedding Bells Waltz," 88
Weilding, Julius, 54
Weiser, Idaho, 141
Weisgerber, Alita Stoneking, 131–33, 149, 198–99
Weisgerber, Tom, 133–34, 149, 236–37
Wells, Paul F., vii
West, Johnny, 69
Western Cowpunchers Association BBQ and Convention, 68
western dime novel, 152–53
Western Open Fiddle Championships, 237
Western Trail, 32
Westlawn Memorial Park, 158
Westmoreland, Howard Dee (Wes), III, 131, 139–40, 206–8, 228–29; as fiddle contest emcee, ix
"What's the Reason I'm Not Pleasing You?," 79
Whelchel, H. E., 53–54
"When I Grow Too Old to Dream," 78, 82, 88

"When Irish Eyes Are Smiling," 78
"When It's Lamp Lighting Time in the Valley, 78, 81
"When the Bloom is on the Sage," 78
"When the Moon Comes Over the Mountain," 78
"When the White Azaleas Are Blooming," 81
"When You and I Were Young, Maggie," 77, 79–80, 88
"Where are You Going, My Pretty Gal," 54, 89
"Whispering," 79, 81–82, 88
White, John H., 61
White, John T., 59
White Way, The (in Borger), 61
Wichita Daily Times, 21
Wilbarger County Historical Museum, vii
"Wild Goose Crossing the Ocean." *See* "Lost Goose"
Wilkison, Kyle G., *Yeomen, Sharecroppers, and Socialists*, 15
Williams, Bill, 41
Williams, Hank, 120
Wills Point, Texas, 18–19
"Wind That Shakes the Barley," 89
Wise County Messenger, 21
Wolfe, Charles, 151
Worcester [MA] Skating Rink, 93–94
World Fiddle Championship, Crockett, Texas, 70

"Yankee Doodle," 111
Yeomen, Sharecroppers, and Socialists (Wilkison), 15
"You Can't Stop Me From Dreaming," 78, 81
"Young Gal, So Deceiving," 89

Zellner, Bob, 70

ABOUT THE AUTHOR

Chris Goertzen is professor emeritus of music history and world music at the University of Southern Mississippi. His books include *Fiddling for Norway: Revival and Identity*; *Southern Fiddlers and Fiddle Contests*; *Made in Mexico: Tradition, Tourism, and Political Ferment in Oaxaca*; *George P. Knauff's "Virginia Reels" and the History of American Fiddling*; *American Antebellum Fiddling*; and *Rugs, Guitars, and Fiddling: Intensification and the Rich Modern Lives of Traditional Arts*, the latter five published by University Press of Mississippi.

www.ingramcontent.com/pod-product-compliance
Lightning Source LLC
Chambersburg PA
CBHW061141230426
43663CB00028B/2992